MORPHOLOGY-DRIVEN SYNTAX

LINGUISTIK AKTUELL

This series provides a platform for studies in the syntax, semantics, and pragmatics of the Germanic languages and their historical developments.
The focus of the series is represented by its German title *Linguistik Aktuell* (Linguistics Today).
Texts in the series are in English.

Series Editor

Werner Abraham
Germanistisch Instituut
Rijksuniversiteit Groningen
Oude Kijk in 't Jatstraat 26
9712 EK Groningen
The Netherlands
E-mail: Abraham@let.rug.nl

Advisory Editorial Board

Volume 15

Bernhard Wolfgang Rohrbacher

Morphology-Driven Syntax. A theory of V to I raising and pro-drop.

MORPHOLOGY-DRIVEN SYNTAX

A THEORY OF V TO I RAISING AND PRO-DROP

BERNHARD WOLFGANG ROHRBACHER

Northwestern University

JOHN BENJAMINS PUBLISHING COMPANY

AMSTERDAM / PHILADELPHIA

TM The paper used in this publication meets the minimum requirements of
American National Standard for Information Sciences — Permanence of Paper
for Printed Library Materials, ANSI Z39.48-1984.

Library of Congress Cataloging-in-Publication Data

Rohrbacher, Bernhard Wolfgang.
   Morphology-driven syntax : a theory of V to I raising and pro-drop / Bernhard Wolfgang Rohrbacher.
      p.   cm. -- (Linguistik aktuell / Linguistics today, ISSN 0166-0829; v. 15)
   A revised and expanded version of the author's 1994 University of Massachusetss at Amherst Ph.D. dissertation. The Germanic VO languages and the full paradigm : A theory of V to I raising.
   Includes bibliographical references and index.
   1. Grammar, Comparative and general. 2. Generative grammar. I. Title. II. Series: Linguistik aktuell ; Bd. 15.
P151.R73   1999
415--dc21   99-19817
ISBN 90 272 2736 5 (EUR) / 1 55619 234 7 (US) (Hb; alk. paper)   CIP

John Benjamins Publishing Co. · P.O.Box 75577 · 1070 AN AMSTERDAM · The Netherlands
John Benjamins North America · P.O.Box 27519 · Philadelphia PA 19118-0519 · USA

Table of Contents

Acknowledgments vii

CHAPTER 1
Introduction 1

CHAPTER 2
Verb Movement in the Germanic Languages 11
2.1 Introduction 11
2.2 Verb Second in the Germanic Languages 11
2.3 Verb Movement to Comp 20
2.4 Verb Movement to Infl 29
    2.4.1 V to I Raising in the Germanic OV Languages 29
    2.4.2 V to I Raising in the Germanic VO Languages 42
        2.4.2.1 English 42
        2.4.2.2 Mainland Scandinavian 56
        2.4.2.3 Faroese 67
        2.4.2.4 Icelandic 69
        2.4.2.5 Yiddish 80
2.5 Conclusion 82

CHAPTER 3
Agreement Morphology in the Syntax and the Lexicon 93
3.1 Introduction 93
3.2 Previous Accounts for V to I Raising 94
    3.2.1 Negation (Ouhalla 1990, 1991; Benmamoun 1991) 94
    3.2.2 Case (Trosterud 1989) 101
    3.2.3 Number Agreement (Roberts 1993; Falk 1993) 106
3.3 Person Agreement 113

3.4 The Representation of Inflectional Affixes 128
3.5 Residual V to I Raising in Faroese 141

CHAPTER 4
Diachronic Germanic Syntax and the Full Paradigm 155
4.1 Introduction 155
4.2 On the Loss of V to I Raising in Some Germanic VO Languages ... 156
    4.2.1 English 156
    4.2.2 Mainland Scandinavian 171
4.3 Auxiliaries in the History of English and Mainland Scandinavian 178
    4.3.1 The Modern Contrast: English Aux^Neg versus Mainland
        Scandinavian Neg^Aux 178
    4.3.2 Historical Reanalysis in English and the Lack thereof in
        Mainland Scandinavian 184

CHAPTER 5
Beyond Verb Movement in the Germanic VO Languages 205
5.1 Introduction 205
5.2 V to I Raising in Romance 206
    5.2.1 Italian 206
    5.2.2 French 213
    5.2.3 European and Brazilian Portuguese 221
    5.2.4 Object Clitics in Romance: Evidence for Verb Movement? 234
5.3 Pro-Drop 242
5.4 NP Object Shift and Transitive Expletive Constructions 261

CHAPTER 6
Conclusions 275

Bibliography 277

Subject Index 291

Acknowledgments

This book is a revised and extended version of my 1994 University of Massachusetts at Amherst Ph.D. dissertation "The Germanic VO Languages and the Full Paradigm: A Theory of V to I Raising". I no longer assume that "weak" agreement projects an empty-headed projection; rather, I now assume that it does not project at all (cf. Section 3.4). The new assumption is in the spirit of "Bare Phrase Structure" (Chomsky 1995) and allows me to adopt the theory of transitive expletive constructions and full-NP object shift developed in Bobaljik (1995) (cf. Section 5.4). Other extensions of the original manuscript include a more detailed discussion of word order in German in light of recent proposals by Haider (1993) and Kayne (1994) (cf. Section 2.4.1) and a different approach to *pro*-drop in Yiddish based on new findings by Prince (1994) (cf. Section 5.3).

I would like to reproduce in full the acknowledgments from the dissertation on which this book is based:

> Many people, linguists and others, contributed to this dissertation. They did so in various ways, although I alone am responsible for the shortcomings in my work.
>
> First and foremost, gratitude is due to the members of my committee, namely (in alphabetical order) Hagit Borer, James Cathey, Angelika Kratzer and Peggy Speas. Both their criticism and their encouragement kept me going.
>
> Comments from (among others) Elena Benedicto, Jóhannes Gísli Jónsson, Halldór Ármann Sigurdsson, Sten Vikner, Akira Watanabe and audiences at FLSM '92, WECOL '92, CONSOLE '92, Tübingen University and LSA '93 improved my work.
>
> Günther Grewendorf was my first linguistics teacher at the Goethe Universität at Frankfurt. It is because of him that I became a linguist. Then and now, Gereon Müller and Wolfgang Sternefeld were and are my teachers, colleagues and friends.
>
> The unique atmosphere at the U Mass Amherst Linguistics Department was essential for my studies. It is created by faculty, students, secretarial staff and

visitors. Instead of (rather arbitrarily) mentioning some but not others by name, I would like to thank them all.

Most of all, I thank Mechthild Nagel.

This dissertation is dedicated to my parents, Heinrich Rohrbacher and Eva Rohrbacher née Stüler.

Since these lines were written, many other people have influenced my thoughts on the issues discussed then in my dissertation and now in this book. Below is an attempt to thank some of them.

Richard Kayne, Christer Platzack and two anonymous reviewers for John Benjamins thoroughly read the entire manuscript and gave me invaluable comments. Other particularly helpful comments came from Michel DeGraff, Tony Kroch and Beatrice Santorini. Parts of this book were presented to and benefited from audiences at the University of Pennsylvania, the 13th West Coast Conference on Formal Linguistics, the Workshop on the L1– and L2–Acquisition of Clause Internal Rules at the University of Berne, Georgetown University, Princeton University, the University of Reykjavik, Brown University, the University of Essex, the 21st Annual Boston University Conference on Language Development, Northwestern University, the City University of New York, Vanderbilt University, the University of Wisconsin at Madison, and the Syntax Workshop at Ybbs a.d. Donau. Finally, I would like to thank Werner Abraham and Kees Vaes at John Benjamins for help with the publication of this book. Nobody explicitly or implicitly mentioned above should be held accountable for any part of this book.

CHAPTER 1

Introduction

One rather striking difference between e.g. Icelandic on the one hand and e.g. Swedish (and the remaining Scandinavian languages) on the other hand is that in certain embedded clauses, the verb must precede negation in Icelandic (cf. (1a) based on Holmberg and Platzack 1991, ex. (7c)) but the reverse order is required in Swedish (cf. (1b) based on Holmberg and Platzack 1991, ex. (7d)).

(1) a. Jón harmar að María **keypti** *ekki* bókina.
         J. regrets that M.   bought not book-the
         'John regrets that Mary didn't read the book.'   (Icelandic)
     b. Jag beklager att Eva *inte* **köpte** boken.
         I   regret   that E. not bought book-the
         'I regret that Eve didn't buy the book.'   (Swedish)

According to the syntactic framework adopted in here, i.e. Principles and Parameters Theory (cf. Chomsky 1981, 1986a, 1989, 1992, 1995), the sequential contrast in (1) reflects a structural difference between Icelandic and Swedish: the finite verb moves to the inflectional head Infl ('V to I raising') in Icelandic (cf. (2a), the structure of (1a)) but stays in situ ('V in situ') in Swedish (cf. (2b), the structure of (1b)).[1]

(2)   a.

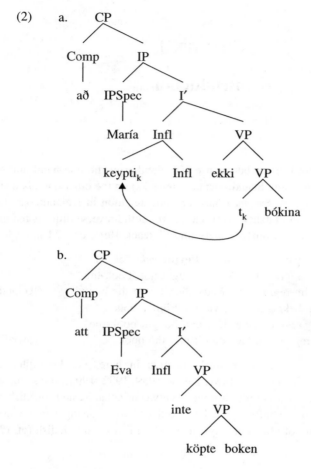

The central problem investigated in this book is why the verb must move to Infl in some languages and why it must stay in situ in others. This question is part and parcel of a more general question, namely how children acquire a particular grammar on the basis of limited evidence and within a relatively short period of time (an instance of 'Plato's Problem', cf. Chomsky 1986b). The answer given to Plato's Problem within Principles and Parameters Theory is that the child is born with a U[niversal] G[rammar] consisting of a set of cross-linguistically invariant principles and a number of parameters that are later set language-specifically on the basis of readily available data. Invariant principles and language-specific parameter settings interact to yield a large but limited number of highly complex grammars. The idea behind this model is to solve Plato's Problem by minimizing the amount of learning (now equated with parameter setting) needed in order for the child to acquire a language. Obviously, learning cannot be eliminated altogether or there would be only a single human language. But the range of linguistic facts that are both language-specific and a priori unlikely to be derivable from other linguistic facts is rather limited. Most examples that come to mind concern the (lexical) properties of the terminal elements in trees like (2a, b). Thus a child acquiring English has to learn that the object represented in (3) is called *rooster* and that there is only a single form of the indefinite masculine singular determiner, independent of the abstract Case of the noun (cf. (4a)). In contrast, a child acquiring German has to learn that the object represented in (3) is called *Hahn* and that there are many different forms of the indefinite masculine singular determiner, depending on the abstract Case of the noun (cf. (4b)).

(3)

(4)	a.	English	b.	German
		INDEF.MASC.SG		INDEF.MASC.SG
	NOM	a rooster		ein Hahn
	ACC	a rooster		einen Hahn
	GEN	a rooster's		eines Hahnes
	DAT	a rooster		einem Hahn

Ideally, we would like to be able to say that only properties of this type have to be learned, i.e. that syntactic parameters are set solely on the basis of lexical properties like the ones illustrated in (3) and (4) which have to be learned anyway. Chomsky (1989) follows Borer (1984) in espousing an even more radical view and proposes that only a subset of these lexical properties are used as input for the setting of parameters:

'It has been suggested that parameters of UG do not relate to the computational system, but only to the lexicon... If substantive elements (verbs, nouns, etc.) are drawn from an invariant universal vocabulary, then only functional elements will be parametrized. The narrower assumption seems plausible...'

(Chomsky 1989 [1995]:131)

Let us assume that this is indeed the case. As a consequence, syntactic phenomena such as V to I raising cannot be governed by the lexical properties of the substantive elements involved (e.g. the verb), but must instead depend solely on the lexical properties of the functional elements involved (e.g. Infl). It is often assumed that the properties in question are abstract rather than concrete. Thus Chomsky (1992) proposes that in V to I raising languages, Infl contains a strong V-feature (attracting the verb already in overt syntax) whereas in V in situ languages, Infl contains a weak V-feature (attracting the verb only in covert syntax), yet the distinction between strong and weak V-features is perhaps phonetically silent. Here lurks the danger of circularity: functional features 'explain' syntactic phenomena while at the same time these syntactic phenomena are often the only evidence for the relevant functional features, given that the latter can be entirely abstract. This problem would be less severe if each functional feature were associated with a whole variety of syntactic phenomena. In this case, exposure to one of these syntactic phenomena would be enough to determine the nature of the corresponding functional feature and once this has been done, all the other syntactic consequences of this feature will follow automatically. But more often than not, the ratio between a feature and its syntactic consequences is much less favorable, and sometimes it is one to one. The following case might seem extreme, but examples of a similar kind are actually not all that uncommon in the literature.

In complex tenses, object clitics appear in front of the finite auxiliary in Italian (cf. (5a) = Bianchi & Figueiredo Silva 1993, ex. (3b)) but in front of the main verb participle in Brazilian Portuguese (cf. (5b) = Bianchi & Figueiredo Silva 1993, ex. (4b). See Section 5.2.4 for a discussion of clitic placement in the Romance languages.).

(5)   a.   Gianni **mi** *aveva* proprio deluso.
              G.   me had   really   deceived   (Italian)
         b.   O   José *tinha* realmente **me** decepcionado.
              the J.   had   really   me deceived
              'John had really deceived me.'   (Brazilian Portuguese)

Bianchi and Figueiredo Silva (1993) argue that the auxiliary and the participle have been moved from Tense and V to AgrS and AgrO, respectively, and that the clitic has adjoined to AgrS in Italian and to AgrO in Brazilian Portuguese, as shown in (6) and (7).

(6)

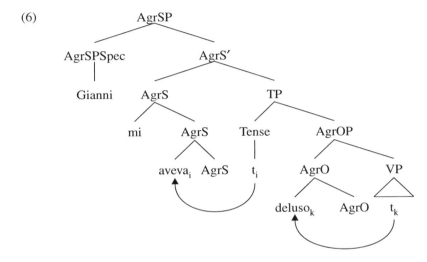

(7)

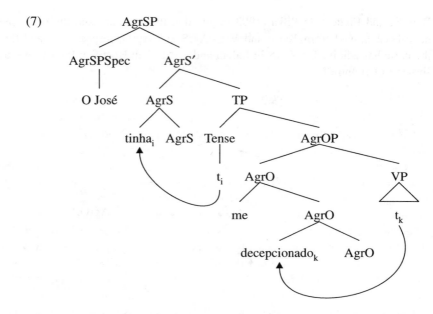

According to Bianchi and Fuigueiredo Silva, object clitics adjoin to AgrS in Italian but to AgrO in Brazilian Portuguese because

> "...clitic pronouns have to be left-adjoined to a functional head endowed with the person specification. ...in Italian, the Agreement-Object system contains the heads Number and Gender, but not Person. [The Agreement-Subject system contains all three heads.] ...As for Brazilian Portuguese, we propose that the Agreement-Object system includes the heads of Gender, Number and Person... Even if there is no morphological evidence [for this difference], the syntactic evidence is sufficient..."   (Bianchi and Fuigueiredo Silva 1993: 10–12)

Yet the only syntactic evidence supporting the claim that AgrO contains person features in Brazilian Portuguese (which shows no object agreement whatsoever in complex tenses) but not Italian (which shows object agreement in number and gender in complex tenses when the object is preposed) comes from the object clitic placement facts in (5), i.e. the very phenomenon that the different location of person agreement in Brazilian Portuguese and Italian is supposed to explain. The proposal is hence circular, amounting to a description rather than an explanation of the data. It is my contention that all syntactic theories based on the abstract (i.e. phonetically silent) content of functional categories run similar risks.

In this book, I will therefore take a different route. The central claim of "Morphology-Driven Syntax" is that all syntactic parameters are set exclusively on the basis of the concrete (i.e. phonetically perceptible) content of functional categories. Before we briefly return to a general discussion of this central claim, let us see what Morphology-Driven Syntax means for V to I raising, the particular phenomenon that this book is designed to explain. According to the theory to be developed below, the presence or absence of overt distinctive marking of the subject-verb agreement features [1ST] and [2ND] person is responsible for the presence or absence of V to I raising. Whether features like the person features [1ST], [2ND] or the Case features [NOM], [ACC], [GEN] and [DAT] are distinctively marked can be determined only by looking at the entire paradigm in which they appear. The first entry in each of the English and German indefinite masculine singular paradigms in (4) does not by itself reveal whether [NOM] is distinctively marked. Only when the first entry is compared to the three other entries in each of these paradigms does it become clear that [NOM] is distinctively marked in German but not in English. If distinctive feature marking triggers V to I raising as argued here, we must have linguistic access not only to individual forms, but also to whole paradigms of forms. This means that the notion 'paradigm' is linguistically relevant and psychologically real, a conclusion that intuitively seems correct but that has not been reflected in much recent linguistic theory, as pointed out by Spencer (1991):

> "There is a feeling among many linguists that the notion of paradigm must be important, perhaps even in some sense primary. But it has proved extremely difficult to characterize the idea adequately, let alone give it a formal definition, and in most contemporary theories of morphology, the notion of 'paradigm' doesn't play any role."   (Spencer 1991:12)

Why should the distinctive marking of the subject-verb agreement features [1ST] and [2ND] trigger V to I raising? I argue that when a paradigm of Infl-affixes distinctively marks these features, the paradigm is referential since the affixes it is comprised of can unambiguously identify the subject of the clause as referring to the speaker(s), the hearer(s) or other(s). Like other referential elements, referential Infl-affixes are listed in the lexicon. Inserted under Infl at D-structure, they must be affixed to (or bound by) a verbal host at S-structure and hence trigger V to I raising. When an inflectional paradigm does not distinctively mark [1ST] or [2ND], it is non-referential since its affixes cannot unambiguously determine the referential value of the subject. Such a paradigm is therefore not listed in the lexicon, and its affixes are not active in the syntax. Instead, they are only later generated directly on the verb by PF spell-out rules.

We expect this difference between D-structure-introduced, syntactically active inflectional affixes under Infl on the one hand and PF-introduced, syntactically inactive inflectional affixes on the verb on the other hand to be reflected in other parts of the grammar, too. Recent research suggests that this is indeed the case.

Speas (1994) argues that a Principle of Economy of Projection requires each phrase to receive independent content from either its specifier or its head. As a consequence, the specifier of the highest inflectional projection can remain empty (and null subjects are hence possible) in languages with distinctive marking of the person features where the highest inflectional head is filled by an agreement affix drawn from the lexicon. Conversely, the specifier of the highest inflectional projection must be filled (and null subjects are hence impossible) in languages without distinctive marking of the person features where the highest inflectional head remains empty because the agreement affixes are generated directly on the verb.

Bobaljik (1995) argues that transitive expletive subject constructions and full NP object shift depend on the availability of SpecAgrSP and SpecAgrOP as landing sites for the subject and the object. Bobaljik's proposal can be straightforwardly integrated into the current approach by assuming that only languages with distinctive marking of the person features have SpecAgrSP, an assumption that is independently required by the "Bare Phrase Structure" theory of Chomsky (1995). Thus a single parameter whose setting involves the salient language-specific properties of a functional head ("inflectional paradigm does (not) distinctively mark the person features [1ST] and [2ND]") interacts with different universal principles ("Affixes must be bound at S-structure", "Projections must receive independent content from either their specifier or their head", "Arguments must appear in licensed positions") to have far-reaching syntactic consequences in superficially independent parts of the grammar (V to I raising, null subjects, transitive expletive subject constructions, full NP object shift). This is of course a desired result, given Plato's Problem and the solution to it suggested by Principles and Parameters Theory.

This book is organized as follows. Chapter 1 lays out the verb movement data from the Germanic languages. To exclude interference from unrelated phenomena such as verb movement to Comp and underlying adjacency of verb and Infl, we are forced to concentrate on certain embedded clauses in those Germanic languages where the verb precedes the direct object in underlying structure ('VO-languages'). A closer look at the Germanic VO languages reveals that Yiddish and Icelandic have V to I raising while English, the Mainland Scandinavian languages and Faroese have V in situ. In Chapter 3, I first discuss a number of previous proposals that attempt to explain the distribution of V to I raising and find that all of them encounter serious empirical problems. Descriptively, what sets the V to I raising languages Yiddish and Icelandic apart from the V in situ languages English, Mainland Scandinavian and Faroese is that only the former have unique inflectional affixes for both first and second person in either the singular or plural of at least one tense. I then go on to propose that (minimal) distinctive marking of the referential Infl-features [1ST] and [2ND] triggers V to I raising along the rough lines sketched above. Chapter 4 looks into the diachronic implications of this theory. Historically, all Germanic languages once had 'rich' agreement system that distinctively marked the person features [1ST] and [2ND]. The theory proposed here predicts that these older variants had V to I raising and that this process was lost in English and Mainland Scandinavian as a consequence of the loss of distinctive feature marking. Both predictions are borne out by the evidence. In addition, I propose a diachronic explanation for certain differences between the English and Mainland Scandinavian auxiliary systems that again capitalizes on the importance of distinctive feature marking for V to I raising. Chapter 5 widens the discussion to topics outside the narrow confines of V to I raising in the Germanic VO languages. Data from the Romance languages are adduced to show that distinctive feature marking plays a pivotal role in V to I raising outside the Germanic languages, too. The analyses of empty subjects, expletive transitive subject constructions and full NP object shift are unified with the analysis of V to I raising as discussed earlier. Chapter 6 concludes this book by pointing out issues of Morphology-Driven Syntax that will have to be addressed by future work.

Notes

1. The structures in (2) assume a single inflectional head (cf. Chomsky 1986a). Some of the structures that are yet to come will assume that subject-verb agreement, tense and object-verb agreement as well as negation all head their own projections (cf. Chomsky 1989). According to the latter proposal, the contrast in (1) reflects the fact that while finite verbs must raise to the highest inflectional head (i.e. AgrS) in Icelandic, they cannot raise to this highest inflectional head but could in principle raise to an intermediate inflectional head (i.e. AgrO or Tense) in Swedish (cf. (i)). (In Section 2.4.2.2, I will show that the Swedish verb in fact does not raise

past AgrO if it raises at all.) Although it might then be more accurate to speak of 'verb movement to the highest inflectional head' instead of 'V to I raising' and 'verb movement to at most an intermediate inflectional head' instead of 'V in situ', I will continue to use the shorter and hence less cumbersome terms. Similarly, I will use the smaller and hence more manageable IP-tree whenever it is not necessary to refer to any of the individual inflectional projections as such.

(i)

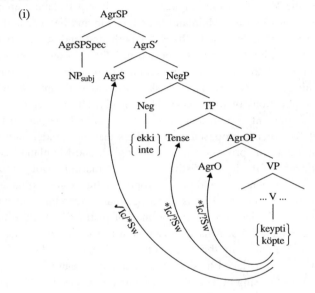

CHAPTER 2

Verb Movement in the Germanic Languages

2.1 Introduction

This chapter summarizes the distribution of V to I raising in the Germanic languages and the next chapter will attempt to explain this distribution. All Germanic languages have at least some verb movement (cf. Section 2.2). But in matrix clauses and in the asserted sentential complements of certain ('bridge-') verbs, this movement is to Comp rather than to Infl (cf. Section 2.3). Moreover, in OV languages like German or Dutch, V to I raising can never be detected because it is always string-vacuous (cf. Section 2.4.1). In VO languages like English, Yiddish or the Scandinavian languages on the other hand, the post- or pre-verbal position of sentential negation and adverbs in embedded clauses that are not the asserted complements of bridge verbs indicates whether V to I raising has applied or not. According to this test, Yiddish and Icelandic have V to I raising whereas English, Mainland Scandinavian and Faroese have V in situ (cf. Section 2.4.2).

2.2 Verb Second in the Germanic Languages

It is well known that all Germanic languages except English obey a general Verb Second or V2 constraint: In matrix declaratives (as well as in direct complement questions) in Yiddish, Icelandic, Faroese, Mainland Scandinavian, German and Dutch, the finite verb obligatory surfaces in 'second position', i.e. immediately after a clause-initial phrasal unit such as the subject (cf. (1)) or a topicalized XP (cf. (2)). Other word orders such as Verb First (cf. (3a)), Verb Third (cf. (3b)) or Verb Last (cf. (3c)) are by and large excluded from matrix declaratives.[1]

(1)   a.   Max *shikt* nit avek dem brif.
            M. sends not away the letter
            'Max doesn't mail the letter.'
                              (Yiddish, based on Diesing 1990, ex. (3a))
       b.   Jón *keypti* ekki bókina.
            J. bought not book-the
            'John didn't buy the book.'
                              (Icelandic, Holmberg 1986, ex. 4(121a))
       c.   Janus *nevndi*   ongantið mammu.
            J.   mentions never   mother
            'John never mentions mother.'
                              (Faroese, Lockwood 1964:156)
       d.   Peter *drikker* ofte kaffe om morgenen.
            P.   drinks often coffee in morning-the
            'Peter often drinks coffee in the morning.'
                              (Danish, Vikner 1995a, ex. 3(33c))
       e.   Johan *köpte* inte boken.
            J.   bought not book-the.
            'John didn't read the book.'
                              (Swedish, Holmberg 1986, ex. 4(122a))
       f.   Johann *kjørte* heldigvis bil.
            J.   drove luckily   car
            'Luckily, John drove a car.'
                              (Norwegian, Åfarli 1991, ex. (16))
       g.   Hans *vergißt* immer seine Hausaufgaben.
            H.   forgets always his   homework
            'John always forgets his homework.'   (German)
       h.   Jan *leest* waarschijnlijk dat boek
            J. reads probably   that book
            'John probably reads that book.'
                              (Dutch, Peter Ackema, p.c.)

(2)   a.   Dos bukh *shik* ikh avek.
            the book send I   away
            'I mail the book.'   (Yiddish, Diesing 1990, ex. (1c))

b. Þennan mann *hélt*   ég að   farið hefð verið með á sjúkrahús.
    this   man thought I that gone had been with to hospital
    'This man I thought had been taken to the hospital.'
             (Icelandic, Rögnvaldsson & Thráinsson 1990, ex. (52c))

c. Frá Bíggjarmönnum *fekk* hann at vita, hversu vorðið var.
    from Bøur-men   got he   to know how   become had
    'It was from the men of Bøur that he got to know how things
    stood.'   (Faroese, Lockwood (1964:154))

d. Denne film   *har* børnene   set.
    this   movie have children-the seen
    'This movie the children have seen.'
                        (Danish, Vikner 1995a, ex. 3(11c))

e. Igår   *köpte* Lena en ny bok.
    yesterday bought L. a new book
    'Yesterday Lena bought a new book.'
                        (Swedish, Holmberg 1986, ex. 4(59b))

.f. Dette spørsmålet *skjønte*   Jens ikke.
    this question   understood J.   not
    'This question John didn't understand.'
                        (Norwegian, based on ex. from Taraldsen 1986)

g. Seine Hausaufgaben *macht* Hans immer in der Badewanne.
    his   homework   makes H. always in the bathtub
    'His homework John always does in the tub.'   (German)

h. Dat boek *leest* Jan waarschijnlijk.
    That book reads J. probably
    'That book John probably reads.'
                        (Dutch, Peter Ackema, p.c.)

(3) a. **Har børnene   set   denne film.
    have children-the seen this   movie
    'The children have seen this movie.'   (Danish)

b. *Studenterna inte *läste* boken.
    students-the not read book-the
    'The students didn't read the book.'   (Swedish)

c. *Hans immer seine Hausaufgaben *vergißt*.
    H.   always his   homework   forgets
    'John always forgets his homework.'   (German)

English is unique among the Germanic languages in not obeying a general V2 constraint. In subject-initial matrix clauses containing an adverb and in topic-initial sentences, Verb Third (compare (4a) and (5a) with (3b)) rather than Verb Second (compare (4b) with (1) and (5b) with (2)) are normal.[2]

(4)   a.   Mary never *liked* trashy movies.
       b.   *Mary *liked* never trashy movies.

(5)   a.   Artsy movies Mary *liked*.
       b.   *Artsy movies *liked* Mary.

In direct complement questions, a finite main verb results in ungrammaticality, regardless of the word order (cf. (6a) with Verb Third and (6b) with Verb Second). In these questions, a finite auxiliary in V2–position is required (cf. (6c)). English is therefore often considered to be a residual Verb Second language (cf. the discussion in Rizzi 1990b, 1991).

(6)   a   *What kind of movies Mary *liked*?
       b.   *What kind of movies *liked* Mary?
       c.   What kind of movies *did* Mary like?

Verb Second is also possible in embedded clauses, but here a number of important differences separate Yiddish and Icelandic on the one side from Faroese and Mainland Scandinavian (and, at least on the surface, German and Dutch) on the other side. In asserted subject-initial complements of bridge verbs,[3] Verb-Second is obligatory in Yiddish and Icelandic (compare (7b) with (8a)) and optional in Faroese, Mainland Scandinavian, German and Dutch (compare (7c, g) with (8b, c)).[4] The optionality of V2 in Faroese, Mainland Scandinavian, German and Dutch subject-initial bridge verb complements stands in marked contrast to the obligatoriness of V2 in subject-initial matrix declaratives in these languages.

(7)   a.   Ikh gloyb   az   Max *shikt* nit avek dem briv.
             I   believe that M.   sends not away the   letter
             'I believe that Max doesn't mail the letter.'
                                      (Yiddish, based on Diesing 1990, ex. (3b))
       b.   Ég taldi   að   María *læsi* ekki bókina.
             I   believed that M.   read not book-the'
             'I believed that Mary didn't read the book.'
                                      (Icelandic, Hornstein 1990)

    c.   Tróndur segði, at   dreingirnir *vóru* als   ikki ósamdir.
        T.   said that boys-the   were at-all not disagreed
        'Trond said that the boys didn't disagree at all.'
                                (Faroese, Vikner 1995, ex. 5(40a))

    d.   Vi ved   at   Peter *drikker* ofte kaffe om morgenen.
        we know that P.   drinks often coffee in   morning-the
        'We know that Peter often drinks coffee in the morning.'
                               (Danish, Vikner 1995a, ex. 3(33g))

    e.   Jag vet   att Eva *kommer* alltid i   tid.
        I   know that E.   comes   always on time
        'I know that Eve always comes on time.'
                     (Swedish, based on Holmberg 1986, ex. 4(79b))

    f.   ??Vi vet   at   Jens *skjønte*   ikke dette spørsmålet.
        we know that J.   understood not this   question
        'We know that John didn't understand this question.'
                           (Norwegian, Taraldsen 1986)

    g.   Ich glaube (*daß) Hans *hat* seine Steuern noch nicht bezahlt.
        I   believe (that) John has his   taxes   yet   not   paid.
        'I believe John hasn't paid his taxes yet.'   (German)

    h.   Jan zei (*dat) hij *zou*   naar huis gaan.
        J.   said (that) he would to   home go
        'John said he would go home.'   (Dutch, Peter Ackema, p.c.)

(8)   a.   *Ég taldi   að María ekki *læsi* bókina.
        I   believed that M.   not   read book-the'
        'I believed that Mary didn't read the book.'
                            (Icelandic, Hornstein 1990)

    b.   Tróndur segði, at   dreingirnir als   ikki *vóru* ósamdir.
        T.   said that boys-the   at-all not were disagreed
        'Trond said that the boys didn't disagree at all.'
                          (Faroese, Vikner 1995a, ex. 5(40b))

    c.   Ich glaube *(daß) Hans seine Steuern noch nicht bezahlt *hat*.
        I   believe (that) H.   his   taxes   yet not   paid   has
        'I believe John hasn't paid his taxes yet.'   (German)

In asserted topic-initial complements of bridge verbs, Verb-Second is obligatory in Yiddish, Icelandic, Faroese and Mainland Scandinavian alike (compare (9a, f) with (10a, b)). In German, asserted topic-initial complements of bridge verbs require V2 when the complementizer is absent (cf. (9g)) and non-V2 when the complementizer is present (cf. (10c)). The situation is thus similar to that in German asserted subject-initial complements of bridge verbs (cf. (7g, 8c). For some reason, embedded topicalization is altogether impossible in Dutch (compare (9h) with (10d))

(9) a. Ikh gloyb az   oyfn   veg *vet* dos yingl zen a kats.
         I   believe that on-the way will the boy   see a cat
         'I believe that on the path the boy will see a cat.'
                                    (Yiddish, Santorini 1989, ex. 3(25b))

     b. Ég veit að   þessum hring *lovaði*   Olafur   Maríu.
         I   know that this   ring   promised O.(NOM) M.(DAT)
         'I know that Olaf promised this ring to Mary.'
                                    (Icelandic, Vikner 1995a, ex. 4(131a))

     c. Tróndur segði, at   í gjár   *vóru* dreingirnir als   ikki
         T.   said that yesterday were boys-the   at-all not
         ósamdir.
         were disagreed
         'Trond said that yesterday the boys didn't disagree at all.'
                                    (Faroese, Vikner 1995, ex. 5(40c))

     d. Vi ved   at   om   morgenen *drikker* Peter ofte   kaffe.
         we know that in-the morning   drinks P.   often coffee
         'We know that in the morning Peter often drinks coffee.'
                                    (Danish, Vikner 1995a, ex. 3(33h))

     e. Jag vet   att Eva *kan* man lita på.
         I   know that E.   can one rely on
         'I know that one can rely on Eve.'
                                    (Swedish, Holmberg 1986, ex. 4(82a))

     f. Vi tenkte at   penger *ville* han ikke ha.
         We thought that money would he   not have
         'We thought that money he wouldn't have.'
                                    (Norwegian, Taraldsen 1986)

     g. Ich glaube (*daß) seine Steuern *hat* Hans noch nicht bezahlt.
         I   believe (that) his   taxes   has H.   yet   not paid
         'I believe his taxes, John hasn't paid yet.'   (German)

     h. *Jan zei (dat) naar huis *zou*   hij gaan.
         J.   said (that) to   home would he go
         'John said he would go home.'
                                    (Dutch, Peter Ackema, p.c.)

(10)   a.   *Ikh gloyb   az   oyfn   veg doz yingl *vet* zen a kats.
               I   believe that on-the way the boy   will see a cat
                                      (Yiddish, Santorini 1989, ex. 3(26))

        b.   *Vi tenkte   at   penger han ikke *ville*   ha.
              We thought that money he not would have
              'We thought that money he wouldn't have.'
                                     (Norwegian, Taraldsen 1986)

        c.   Ich glaube *(daß) seine Steuern Hans noch nicht bezahlt *hat*.
              I   believe (that) his   taxes   H.   yet not paid   has
              'I believe his taxes, John hasn't paid yet.'   (German)

        d.   *Jan sei (dat) naar huis hij *zou*   gaan.
              J.   said (that) to   home he would go
              'John said that he would go home.'
                                  (Dutch, Peter Ackema, p.c.)

In embedded clauses that are not the asserted complements of bridge verbs, Verb Second is again obligatory in Yiddish and Icelandic (compare (11b) with (12a) and (13a) with (14a)) but it is impossible in Faroese, Mainland Scandinavian, German and Dutch (compare (11e) with (12b) and (13c) with (14b)). With the exception of German, the latter set of languages does not allow topicalization in non-bridge verb complements at all.[5]

(11)   a.   Avrom bedoyert az Max *shikt* nit avek dem briv.
             A.   regrets   that M.   send not away the   letter
             'Abraham regrets that Max doesn't mail the letter.'
                         (Yiddish, based on Diesing 1990, ex. (3b))

        b.   Það var gott að Jón *keypti* ekki bókina.
             it   was good that J. bought not book-the
             'It was good that John didn't buy the book.'
                      (Icelandic, Holmberg 1986, ex. 6(172c))

        c.   Har vóru nógv fólk, eg ikki *kendi*.
             here were many people I not knew
             'There were many people I didn't know.'
                          (Faroese, Lockwood 1964:156)

        d.   Jeg tror ikke at   Peter ofte *spiser* tomater.
             I   think not that P.   often eats   tomatoes
             'I don't think that Peter often eats tomatoes.'
                          (Danish, Vikner 1995a, ex. 3(7b))

e. Jag beklagar att jag aldrig *träffade* henne.
    I regret that I never met her
            (Swedish, based on Holmberg 1986, ex. 4(19d))

f. Vi tenkte ikke at han aldri *ville* ha penger.
    we thought not that he never would have money
    'We didn't think that he would never have money.'
            (Norwegian, based on ex. from Taraldsen 1986)

g. Ich bezweifle daß Hans bis drei zählen *kann*.
    I doubt that H. to three count can
    'I doubt that John can count to three.'   (German)

h. Ik betreurde dat Jan dit boek niet *las*.
    I regretted that J. this book not read
    'I regretted that J didn't read this book.'
            (Dutch, Peter Ackema, p.c.)

(12) a. *Það var gott að Jón ekki *keypti* bókina.
    it was good that J. not bought book-the
    'It was good that John didn't buy the book.'
            (Icelandic, based on Holmberg 1986, ex. 6(172c))

b. *Jag beklagar att jag *träffade* aldrig henne.
    I regret that I met never her
    'I regret that I never met her.'
            (Swedish, based on Holmberg 1986, ex. 4(19c))

(13) a. Es iz a shod vos hayntike tsaytn *kenen* azoy fil mentshn
    it is a shame that today's times can so many people
    afile nit leyenen.
    even not read
    'It is a shame that nowadays so many people can't even
    read.'   (Yiddish, Diesing 1990, ex. (5b))

b. Jón harmar að þessa bók *skuli* ég hafa lesið.
    J. regrets that this book should I have read
    'John regrets that this book, I should have read.'
            (Icelandic, Vikner 1995a, 4(20a))

c. Ich glaube nicht *(daß) auf dem Weg eine Katze *sitzt*.
    I believe not that on the path a cat sits
    'I don't believe that a cat is sitting on the path.'   (German)

(14)   a.   *Es iz a shod   vos hayntike tsaytn azoy fil   mentshn *kenen*
            it is a shame that today's   times so   many people   can
            afile nit leyenen.
            even not read
            'It is a shame that nowadays so many people can't even
            read.'   (Yiddish, based on Diesing 1990, ex. (5b))

       b.   *Ich glaube nicht (daß) auf dem Weg *sitzt* eine Katze.
            I   believe not   that on the path sits a   cat
            'I don't believe that a cat is sitting on the path.'   (German)

The distribution of embedded residual Verb Second in English closely resembles
that of embedded Verb Second in Faroese and Mainland Scandinavian. Take the
case of residual Verb Second in clauses with an 'affective' topic followed by a
finite auxiliary (cf. ex. (iii) in note 2). This word order is possible in the asserted
complements of bridge verbs (cf. (15a)), but it is impossible in all other embedded clauses (cf. (15b) and the discussion in Authier 1992).[6]

(15)   a.   Mary swears that under no circumstances *would* she watch
            artsy movies.

       b.   *Mary's claim that under no circumstances *would* she watch
            artsy movies has often been disputed.

The distribution of declarative Verb Second in the Germanic VO languages is
summarized in tables 2.1 and 2.2.

Table 2.1: *Verb-Second in matrix declaratives*

	SUBJ-First		TOP-First	
	V2	Other	V2	Other
Yiddish	✓	*	✓	*
Icelandic	✓	*	✓	*
Faroese	✓	*	✓	*
Mld. Sc.	✓	*	✓	*
German	✓	*	✓	*
Dutch	✓	*	✓	*
English	*	✓	*/✓	✓/*

Table 2.2: *Verb-Second in embedded declaratives*

	Bridge-Verb Complements				Other Embedded Clauses			
	SUBJ-First		TOP-First		SUBJ-First		TOP-First	
	V2	Other	V2	Other	V2	Other	V2	Other
Yiddish	✓	*	✓	*	✓	*	✓	*
Icelandic	✓	*	✓	*	✓	*	✓	*
Faroese	✓	✓	✓	*	*	✓	*	*
Mld. Sc.	✓	✓	✓	*	*	✓	*	*
German	✓	✓	✓	✓	*	✓	*	✓
Dutch	✓	✓	*	*	*	✓	*	*
English	*	✓	*/✓	✓/*	*	✓	*	*

Table 2.2 shows that Verb Second is much more general in Yiddish and Icelandic, where it is obligatory in all embedded clauses, than in Faroese, Mainland Scandinavian, German and Dutch, where it is optional in asserted subject-initial sentential complements of bridge verbs and impossible in embedded clauses that are not the asserted complements of bridge verbs. Below I will argue that this is so because Verb Second involves in fact two distinct syntactic processes: Verb movement to Comp, which occurs in all of these languages (cf. Section 2.3), and Verb movement to Infl, which occurs only in Yiddish and Icelandic (and maybe in German and Dutch, where it cannot be detected due to the underlying adjacency of the verb and Infl), but not in Faroese, Mainland Scandinavian or English (cf. Section 2.4.).

2.3 Verb Movement to Comp

Matrix Verb Second clauses are standardly analyzed as the product of verb movement to Comp and XP movement to SpecCP, an analysis that goes back to a paper by den Besten (cf. den Besten 1983, which was in fact written in 1977).[7] Holmberg and Platzack (1991) propose that the V to C movement is triggered by a tense operator [+F] in Comp which needs to be lexicalized in order to assign nominative Case to the subject (or its trace) in SpecIP (see Santorini 1994 for a similar proposal). A variety of other explanations have been argued for in the literature,[8] but not much hinges on the choice between them as far as the main topic of this book, V to I raising, is concerned. For the sake of concreteness, I will adopt Holmberg and Platzack's proposal, essentially ignoring the reasons for the XP movement to SpecCP. The relevant part of matrix Verb Second clauses then has the abbreviated S-structure in (16).

(16)

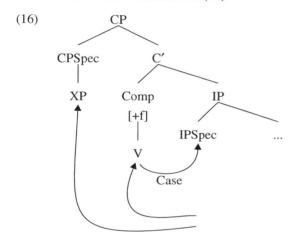

This analysis can be extended to Verb Second in the sentential complements of asserted bridge verbs. In regular finite embedded clauses, Comp is lexicalized by an overt complementizer (e.g. Icelandic *að* in (17a)), hence it can assign nominative Case to the subject in SpecIP without the help of V to C movement. Asserted bridge verbs have the option of embedding two CPs ('CP-Recursion') as shown in (17b). In this case, the tense operator [+F] is situated in the lower, underlyingly empty Comp and must be lexicalized via matrix-style V to C movement. Following Iatridou and Kroch (1992), I will assume that the lexically filled Comp of the higher CP is semantically empty and that it can be therefore deleted at LF, thus allowing the matrix verb to govern and select a second CP. What one would want to say is that bridge verbs are exactly those verbs that embed a CP headed by a semantically empty Comp, but the matter is far from trivial and I will not address it here.

(17)   a.

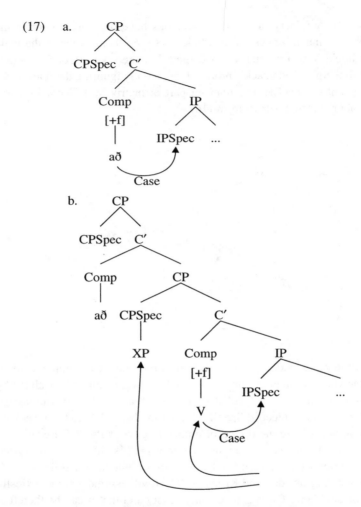

The Head Movement Constraint of Travis (1984) effectively states that heads do not move across other heads. It is therefore usually assumed that the verb never moves directly to Comp as shown in (18)) but instead always adjoins first to Infl and then moves (with the rest of Infl) to Comp as shown in (19).

(18)

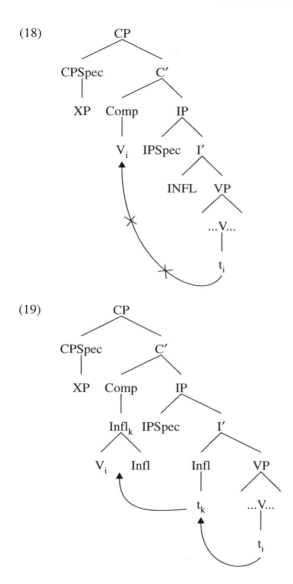

(19)

The Head Movement Constraint, if it is indeed empirically correct, should not have to be stipulated but should rather follow from general locality restrictions within the theory. In pre-Minimalist terms, Head Movement Constraint violations such as (18) are ungrammatical because they violates the Empty Category Principle (ECP): The verb in Comp cannot properly govern its trace in VP across the IP-barrier. Consider the following definition of the term 'barrier' taken from Baker (1988).

(20)   Barrierhood:
        Let D be the smallest maximal projection containing A.
        Then C is a BARRIER between A and B iff C is a maximal projection that contains B and excludes A and either
        a.   C is not [IP, VP or θ-marked], or
        b.   the head of C is distinct from the head of D and selects some XP equal to or containing B.   (Baker 1988:56)

(21)   Distinctness:
        X is **distinct** from Y only if no part of Y is a member of a (movement) chain containing X.   (Baker 1988:64)[9]

According to these definitions, Infl ("the head of C") and Comp ("the head of D") are distinct in (18) and IP ("C") constitutes a barrier between the verb in Comp ("A") and its trace in VP ("B") across which proper government is impossible. In (19) on the other hand, the trace of Infl (i.e. t_k) and Comp are not distinct since a part of Comp (namely $Infl_k$) is a member of a movement chain containing t_k. IP does therefore not constitute a barrier between the verb in Comp and its trace in VP and proper government of t_i by V_i is possible. Alternatively, one could simply say that since t_k is the trace of the V_i+Infl complex, it is able to govern t_i.

The structure in (18) can however be salvaged if after direct verb movement to Comp has taken place, Infl adjoins to the verb in Comp. This is in fact the proposal made by Deprez (1990) for French Complex Inversion. (Johnson 1992a made a similar proposal for Italian participles.) The resulting structure is shown in (22).

(22)

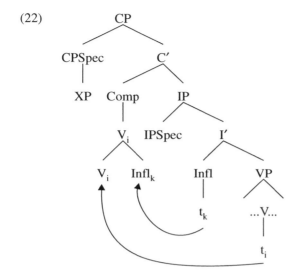

In (22), t_k, the trace of Infl, is again non-distinct from Comp because $Infl_k$, a part of Comp, is a member of a movement chain containing t_k. Accordingly, IP does not constitute a barrier between the verb in Comp and its trace in VP and V_i can again properly govern t_i. Note that the derivations in (19) and (22) arguably involve the same number of steps and that economy principles therefore do not prefer one over the other.[10]

In Minimalist terms, Head Movement Constraint Violations such as (18) are ungrammatical because they violate Shortest Move: The verb has made a move (to Comp) which was not the shortest possible move (to Infl). The original formulation of Shortest Move by Chomsky (1992) does not cover head movement but the following reformulation by Manzini (1994) does.

(23)   Minimal Domain:
        The minimal domain (X) of a head X consists of all and only the elements that are immediately contained by, and do not contain, a projection of X.   (Manzini 1994: 482)

(24)   Adjacency:
        (X) and (Y) are adjacent iff there is no (Z) such that some member of (Z) contains (X) and does not contain (Y), or vice versa.
                                                                (Manzini 1994: 483)

(25)   Locality [i.e. Shortest Move]:
        For all i, let A_i be in (X_i). Given a dependency $(A_1, ..., A_n)$, for all
        i, (X_i) and (X_{i+1}) are adjacent.   (Manzini 1994: 483)

According to these definitions, the minimal domain of Comp and the minimal domain of V in (18) are non-adjacent because there is a minimal domain (namely the minimal domain of Infl) such that one of its members (namely VP) contains the minimal domain of V but does not contain the minimal domain of Comp. As a consequence, the dependency between the verb (i.e. A_i) which is in the minimal domain of Comp and its trace (i.e. A_{i+1}) which is in the minimal domain of V violates Shortest Move as defined in (25). In (19) on the other hand, the minimal domain of Infl and the minimal domain of V are adjacent. Consequently, the dependency between the verb which is in the minimal domain of Infl and its trace which is in the minimal domain of V satisfies Shortest Move.

Direct verb movement to Comp can however again be salvaged if we add one independently motivated assumption. Consider the Minimalist LF-structure in (26) where subject and object have moved to SpecAgrSP and SpecAgrOP, respectively, to have their Case checked. As matters stand, the dependency between the subject in the minimal domain of AgrS and its trace in the minimal domain of V violates Shortest Move because the two minimal domains are not adjacent: There is a minimal domain of a head (namely that of AgrO) such that one of its members (namely VP) contains the minimal domain of V but does not contain the minimal domain of AgrS.

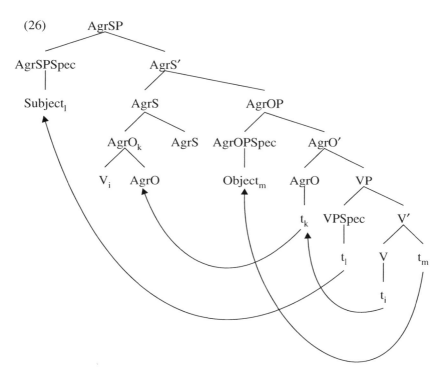

The structure in (26) satisfies Shortest Move as desired if we assume that movement of a head X to a head Y renders the two heads non-distinct in the sense of Baker (1988) and turns YP into a projection of X. Under this assumption, the subject in the SpecAgrSP of (26) is now in the minimal domain of AgrO by virtue of being immediately contained by AgrSP, a projection of AgrO after movement of the latter to AgrS. The trace of the subject is in the minimal domain of V as before and since the two minimal domains are adjacent, the dependency between the subject and its trace in (26) satisfies Shortest Move.

Direct movement of the verb to Comp can now be salvaged by prior movement of Infl to Comp. The resulting structure is shown in (27).

(27)

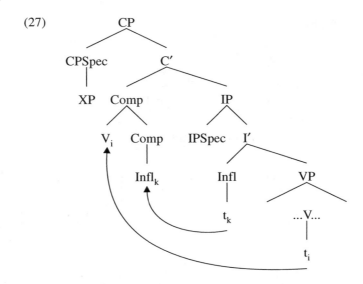

Under the independently motivated assumption that movement of a head X to a head Y turns YP into a projection of X, the verb in the Comp of (27) is now in the minimal domain of Infl by virtue of being immediately contained by the higher Comp node, a projection of Infl after adjunction of the latter to the lower Comp node. The trace of the verb is in the minimal domain of V as before and since the two minimal domains are adjacent, the dependency between the verb and its trace in (27) satisfies Shortest Move.

I conclude that neither in pre-Minimalist theory nor in Minimalist theory does the Head Movement Constraint follow from general locality restrictions and there are therefore no theoretical reasons that would force us to assume that verb movement to Comp requires verb movement to Infl. To my knowledge, empirical reasons for this assumption are absent, too. We therefore have to disregard examples of verb movement to Comp (such as Verb Second matrix clauses and Verb Second embedded clauses that are asserted complements of bridge verbs) for the purpose of our study of the triggering conditions for V to I raising. With respect to all Germanic languages except English, this means that the syntactic behavior of embedded clauses that are not the complements of asserted bridge verbs plays a crucial role in determining whether a language has or does not have V to I raising.

2.4 Verb Movement to Infl

2.4.1   *V to I Raising in the Germanic OV Languages*

The traditional view holds that German and Dutch are underlyingly an SOV language (cf. Bach 1962) and that the inflectional projections are also right-headed (cf. Grewendorf 1988:150). Moreover, sentential negation and adverbs are adjoined to the left of VP so that they do not intervene between the base-positions of the highest verb and Infl. Due to this fact, the position of sentential negation and adverbs cannot be used to determine whether the verb raises to Infl or stays in situ in German and Dutch embedded clauses that are not the asserted complements of bridge verbs and that therefore lack verb movement to Comp. To see this, consider the example in (28) and its structure in (29). In (28) the position of the non-finite verb *essen* "eat" to the right of the negation marker *nicht* "not" shows that *nicht* must be adjoined to the left of the VP. The clause final position of the finite verb *will* "wants" is therefore compatible with both V to I raising and V in situ, as indicated by the question mark next to the move-ment path in (29).

(28)   Die Eltern   bedauern daß Kaspar seine Suppe nicht essen will.
        the parents regret   that K.   his   soup not eat   wants
        'The parents regret that Caspar doesn't want to eat his soup.'

                                                            (German)

(29)

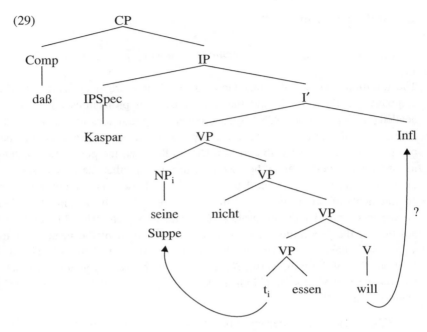

Without the position of sentential negation and adverbs as a diagnostic, there remain no convincing arguments for or against V to I Raising in German or Dutch. Below, I will discuss two arguments against V to I Raising in German that at first glance appear to be valid but upon closer scrutiny turn out to be flawed.[11]

German has a set of separable verb-prefixes that are left behind by V2–style verb movement to Comp and a set of inseparable verb-prefixes that are not. Höhle (1991) observes that when a separable prefix is embedded under an inseparable prefix, V2 is impossible with verbs bearing such a prefix cluster, regardless of whether the prefixes are both carried along (cf. (30a)) or both left behind (cf. (30b)). Since V2 is obligatory in matrix clauses, the verbs in question cannot be used as the highest matrix verb.

(30)   a.   *Das Frankfurter Theater uraufführte Faßbinders Stück.
              the F.   theater premiered F.'s   play
        b.   *Das Frankfurter Theater führte   Faßbinders Stück urauf.
              the F.   theater premiered F.'s   play PART
              'The theater in Frankfort premiered Faßbinder's play.'

Whereas the first variant is ungrammatical because *auf-* must be left behind by verb movement to Comp, the second variant is ungrammatical because *ur-* cannot be left behind by verb movement to Comp. Höhle assumes that (30b) violates a prohibition against structural separation of the inseparable prefix from the verb stem. In that case, it should be impossible to use the verbs in question as the highest verb not only in matrix clauses, but also in embedded clauses, if German has V to I Raising. The sentence in (31) for example should have either the structure in (32) which should be ungrammatical because verb movement has not left behind *auf-* (like (30a)) or the structure in (33) which should be ungrammatical because verb movement has structurally separated *ur-* from the verb stem (like (30b)).

(31) Die Zeitung   berichtet daß das Frankfurter Theater Faßbinders
      the newspaper reports   that the F.   theater F.'s
      Stück uraufführte.
      play   premiered
      "The newspaper reports that the theater in Frankfort premiered
      Faßbinder's play."

(32)

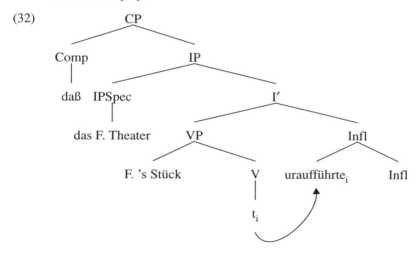

(33)

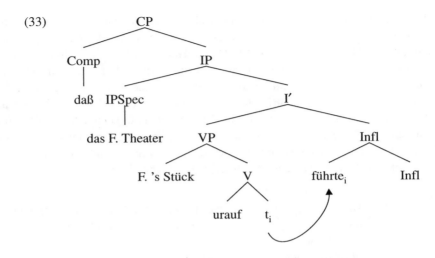

From the fact that (31) is grammatical, Höhle concludes that German does not have V to I Raising and that (31) has neither the structure in (32) nor the structure in (33) but rather a structure in which the verb remains in situ and in which the issue of the separation of the prefixes from the verb stem by verb movement does not arise. This conclusion however rests entirely on Höhle's earlier assumption that that (30b) violates a prohibition against *structural* separation of the inseparable prefix from the verb stem. Let us instead assume that (30b) violates a prohibition against *linear* separation of the inseparable prefix from the verb stem. In that case, (33) is a grammatical structure for (31) since string-vacuous V to I Raising (unlike non-string-vacuous verb movement to Comp) does not linearly separate the inseparable prefix from the verb stem. What I am proposing is that the relevant constraint involves wellformedness in phonetic form rather than wellformedness in syntax. Insofar as this proposal is reasonable, the contrast in (30–31) is compatible with the hypothesis that German has V to I Raising.

Haider (1993) presents an argument against V to I Raising in German that is based on the distribution of extraposed relative clauses. According to Haider, the fact that VP-topicalization in matrix clauses carries along extraposed clauses (cf. (34) = Haider 1993, ex. 3(17a)) shows that the latter are right-adjoined to VP. If German had rightward V to I Raising, then we would expect VP-right-adjoined extraposed clauses to precede the highest verb (cf. (35a) = Haider 1993, ex. 3(18a)) rather than follow it (cf. (35b) = Haider 1993, ex. 3(18c)) in complementizer-introduced-embedded clauses without movement of the highest verb to Comp. The fact that the opposite word order is the attested one appears to show that German does not have V to I Raising. The structure of (35) is given in (36).

(34)   Einem Kind beistehen das nach Hilfe ruft wird doch wohl
        a   child help   that for   help calls will PART PART
        jeder.
        everybody
        'Everybody would help a child that is calling for help.'

(35)   a. *Man kann nur hoffen, daß doch wohl jeder   einem
            one   can   only hope   that PART PART everybody a
            Kind beistehen das nach Hilfe ruft wird.
            child help   that for   help calls would
      b. Man kann nur hoffen, daß doch wohl jeder   einem
            one   can   only hope   that PART PART everybody a
            Kind beistehen wird das nach Hilfe ruft.
            child help   will that for   help calls
            'One can only hope that everybody would help a child that is calling for help.'

(36)

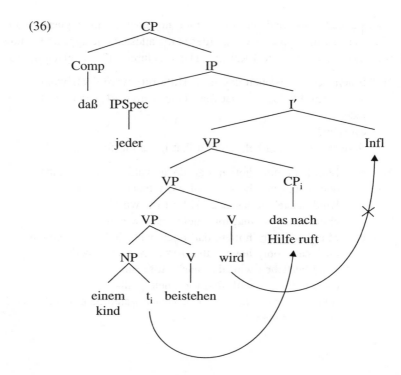

Notice that in order for this explanation to go through, it has to be stipulated that extraposed clauses are right-adjoined not just to any VP, but rather to the highest available VP: If the extraposed clause could be adjoined to the lower VP in (36), the ungrammatical word order in (35a) would be the result, regardless of whether the highest verb has moved to Infl or not. The extraposed clause must however be adjoined to the lower VP in (34), where this VP has been topicalized.[12] Why extraposition can right-adjoin clauses to the lower VP when the latter has been topicalized but not when it has been left in situ remains unclear.

Assume instead that extraposed clauses are right-adjoined to IP rather than VP. The contrast in (35) follows without any further stipulation, regardless of whether the highest verb moves to Infl or not. VP-topicalization results in the ungrammatical word order in (37): The IP-right-adjoined extraposed clause does not c-command (and hence does not properly govern) its trace within the topicalized VP in SpecCP, in violation of the ECP.[13] The construction can however be saved if the extraposed clause leaves its position on the periphery of

IP and right-adjoins to SpecCP, a position from which it c-commands and hence properly governs both traces as required. The resulting word order is that in (34); its structure is that in (38). Since it cannot be determined whether V to I Raising has taken place, I have chosen not to depict it — solely for reasons of space and without prejudging the matter.

(37) *Einem Kind beistehen wird doch wohl jeder   das nach Hilfe
       a   child help   will PART PART everybody that for   help
       ruft.
       calls
       'Everybody would help a child that is calling for help.'

(38)

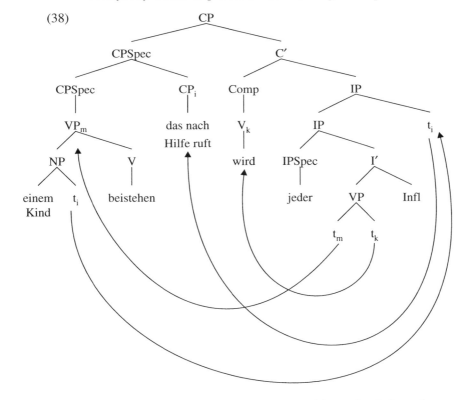

The IP-adjunction-based approach to the extraposition of relative clauses provides a reasonable (and, in light of the comments in the paragraph directly below (36), perhaps less stipulative) alternative to the VP-adjunction-based, approach to the same phenomenon. Since the IP-based approach does not force the conclusion that German lacks V to I Raising, relative clause extraposition cannot be used to argue for or against V to I Raising in German.

The picture that emerges from this discussion is that in the Germanic OV languages, we cannot tell whether V to I raising applies: Verb Second in matrix clauses and sentential complements of asserted bridge verbs is compatible with direct V to C and as well as V to I to C and Verb Last in embedded clauses is compatible with V in situ or V to I. This conclusion however depends on the standard assumption that German, Dutch and their various dialects are in fact OV languages with a right-headed IP. Since this assumption has been recently challenged, I want to spend a little more time on the issue.

Early suggestions that German and Dutch have a left-headed IP can be found in Travis (1984), von Stechow & Sternefeld (1988) and Zwart (1991). Kayne (1994) proposes that universally, all phrases are left-headed. This proposal (which was adopted in Chomsky 1995 and has since then been very popular) ascribes to German and Dutch not only a left-headed IP, but also a left-headed VP, thus turning both languages into VO languages. Certain formulations in an unpublished draft of Kayne (1994) that circulated since 1993 gave rise to a misunderstanding in the field according to which the universal left-headedness of phrases follows from the independently motivated centerpiece of the theory, i.e. the Linear Correspondence Axiom. Although the published version makes it quite clear that the left-headedness of phrases has in fact to be stipulated, the misunderstanding persists. But the difference is a crucial one: If left-headedness follows from the general design of the theory, then the recalcitrant data from German and Dutch (as well as other languages that have traditionally been assumed to be OV languages) can simply be assumed to find a solution at some later point. If on the other hand left-headedness has to be stipulated, then a solution for the same data is urgently needed because they are among the major consequences of this stipulation. I will therefore briefly summarize the theoretical relation between the Linear Correspondence Axiom before I turn to the empirical side of the question. With respect to the latter, I will conclude that a satisfactory left-headed analysis of basic word order in German (and perhaps Dutch, although this is less obvious, cf. Zwart 1997) is nowhere in sight and the traditional right-headed analysis is to be preferred, at least for the time being.

The essential definitions that are original to Kayne's theory are listed in (39–41); for c-command, the definition in note 13 can be used.

(39) *Asymmetric C-Command*
X asymmetrically c-commands Y iff X c-commands Y and Y does not c-command X.

(40) *Dominance Images*
   a. $d(X)$ = the set of terminals that the non-terminal category X dominates.
   b. $d\langle X,Y\rangle$ = the Cartesian product of $d(X)$ and $d(Y)$ = the set of all ordered pairs$\{\langle a, b\rangle\}$ such that a is a member of $d(X)$ and b is a member of $d(Y)$.
   c. $d(A)$ = the union of all $d\langle X,Y\rangle$ for $\langle X,Y\rangle \in A$.

(41) *Linear Correspondence Axiom* (Formal Version)
Let P be a phrase marker, T the set of P's terminals and A the maximal set of ordered pairs $\{\langle X,Y\rangle\}$ such that X and Y are non-terminals in P and X asymmetrically c-commands Y. Then $d(A)$ is a linear ordering of T.

It is important not to confuse the mathematical expression "linear ordering" with the syntactic expression "linear (word) order". A binary relation L defines a linear ordering iff it is total (i.e. $x\in S \wedge y\in S \Rightarrow xLy \vee yLx$) and antisymmetric (i.e. $\neg (xLy \wedge yLx)$) as well as transitive ($xLy \wedge yLz \Rightarrow xLz$). With this understanding of linear ordering in mind, the Linear Correspondence Axiom can be roughly paraphrased as follows:[14]

(42) *Linear Correspondence Axiom* (Informal Version)
For every two terminal nodes in a tree, exactly one terminal is dominated by a non-terminal that asymmetrically c-commands a non-terminal dominating the other terminal.

As is evident from a glance at (43), all four basic word orders that are logically possible given the usual assumptions about argument structure and phrase structure can be generated by trees that satisfy either version of the Linear Correspondence Axiom. n_1, n_2 and v are the terminals (i.e. words) of the subject, the object and the verb, respectively. (43a) represents underlying SVO, (43b) represents underlying OVS, (43c) represents underlying SOV, and (43d) represents underlying VOS. Formally, each of these trees satisfies the Linear Correspondence Axiom because they all share the set of pairs of non-terminals ordered by asymmetric c-command in (44a) and the dominance image of this set in (44b) which is a linear ordering of the set of terminals of each tree, as required.[15,16]

(43)   a.

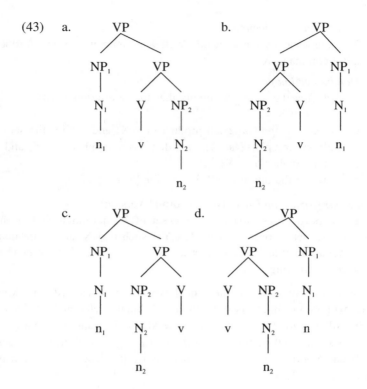

(44)   a. $A = \{\langle NP_1, VP\rangle, \langle NP_1, V\rangle, \langle NP_1, NP_2\rangle, \langle NP_1, N_2\rangle, \langle V, N_2\rangle\}$
        b. $d(A) = \{\langle n_1, v\rangle, \langle v, n_2\rangle, \langle n_1, n_2\rangle\}$

This brief discussion has shown that left-headedness does not follow directly
from the Linear Correspondence Axiom. It follows only indirectly if it is
stipulated (as is explicitly the case in Kayne (1994) but not in the earlier draft)
that asymmetric c-command translates always into linear precedence. This
stipulation excludes the OVS structure in (43b) because all its asymmetric c-
command relations translate into the opposite of precedence, the SOV structure
in (43c) because V asymmetrically c-commands yet follows N_2, and the VOS
structure in (43d) because NP_1 asymmetrically c-commands yet follows VP, V,
NP_2 and N_2, leaving only the SVO structure in (43a) in which all c-command
relations translate into precedence. Since the stipulation that asymmetric c-
command translates always into precedence serves the sole purpose of excluding
right-headed phrases (and phrases with the specifier on the right), it is of

paramount importance to show that the theory can adequately deal with the switch from right-headed to left-headed VP and IP it necessitates for German and Dutch. I now turn to this issue.

The degree of success that left-headed approaches to word order in German and Dutch are able to achieve depends on whether V to I raising or V in situ is assumed for these languages. If V to I raising is assumed, the word order in (28) can be derived in a left-headed fashion only if it is assumed that in German, a) as already pointed out by Kayne (1994), if the standard view is correct and adjunction to I' is impossible, the subject is located not in SpecIP but in a higher, yet to be identified specifier (or perhaps adjoined to IP), b) negation and sentential adverbs are attached above the moved verb, i.e. higher than in Yiddish and Icelandic, c) all objects must move out of VP, again in contrast to Yiddish and Icelandic, and d) the lower VP moves to the specifier of or adjoins to IP or a higher, yet to be identified projection. An analysis along these lines is shown in (45).

(45)

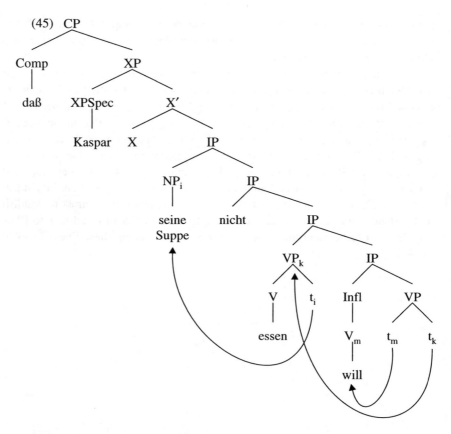

In order to be able to account for the contrast in (46), a left-headed V to I approach to word order in German must also assume that e) separable verb prefixes are left behind by verb movement to Comp but not by verb movement to Infl.

(46)   a.   Das Frankfurter Theater führte Faßbinders Stück auf.
            the F.   theater staged F.'s   play PART
            'The theater in Frankfort staged Faßbinder's play.'

b. Die Zeitung   berichtete, daß das Frankfurter Theater
    the newspaper reported   that the F.   theater
    Faßbinders Stück aufführte.
    F.'s   play   staged
    'The newspaper reported that the theater in Frankfort staged
    Faßbinder's play.'

None of the assumptions in a) through e) are plausible, and a left-headed V to I
approach to word order in German must therefore be rejected.

    If V in situ is assumed, a left-headed derivation of (28) does not have to
assume a), b) and e) but still needs to assume c) and d), as shown in (47).

(47)

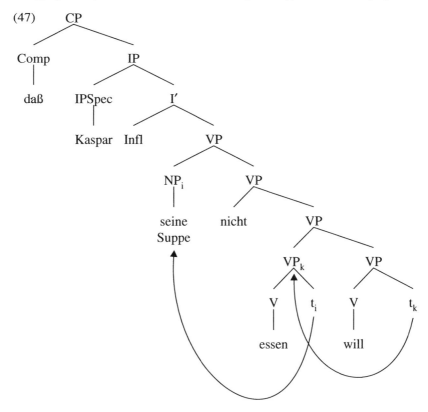

Especially the assumption that the lower VP (moves to the specifier of or) adjoins to the higher VP (or some higher projection) again lacks all plausibility. Notice that the movement is obligatory, but it is entirely unclear what its trigger could be.[17] A left-headed V in situ approach to word order in German should therefore be rejected as well.

I conclude that German, Dutch and their dialects are OV languages whose sentences are always ambiguous between V to I Raising and V in situ. Due to this ambiguity, the Germanic OV languages will not play a major role in the rest of this book and I will instead focus on the Germanic VO languages where, as we will see immediately, there is overt evidence for or against V to I raising.

2.4.2   V to I Raising in the Germanic VO Languages

2.4.2.1 English

For the Germanic VO languages, it is reasonable to assume that Infl is left-headed, and that this is indeed the case can be seen at least in English by the clause-medial position of the dummy auxiliary *did* in (48a).[18] This example also shows that the negation marker intervenes between Infl and the VP and the same is true with respect to sentential adverbs. The ungrammaticality of (48b) and (49b) with the main verb preceding the negation marker and the sentential adverb is then often taken as an indication that main verbs must stay in situ in English as argued first in Emonds (1976) and later in Pollock (1989). This is illustrated in the representation in (50).

(48)   a.   Sue did not see the movie.
        b.   *Sue saw not the movie.

(49)   a.   Sue frequently saw the movie.
        b.   *Sue saw frequently the movie.

(50)

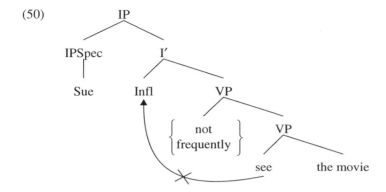

Pesetsky (1989) however notes that main verbs that take a prepositional phrase instead of a noun phrase as their complement do have the ability to optionally precede certain sentential adverbs (cf. (51a, b)), although they still cannot precede the negation marker (cf. (51c)). Pesetsky argues that the V^Adv order in (51a) is not due to adjunction of the adverb to the right of the VP plus PP-extraposition (cf. (61) below), but that it arises instead via adjunction of the adverb to the left of the VP plus verb movement to an intermediate (but not the highest) functional head. Pesetsky explains the ungrammaticality of (49b) via the assumption that the main verb cannot assign Case from this intermediate functional head. Consequently, NP-taking verbs, whose complements are dependent on them for Case, cannot move to this head (cf. (49b)) whereas PP-taking verbs, whose (logical) complements receive Case from the preposition, are free to do so (cf. (51a)). Branigan and Collins (1993) identify the landing site of such 'short' verb movement as AgrO and assign (51a) the S-structure in (52).[19]

> (51) a. Sue looked carefully at him.
>   b. Sue carefully looked at him.
>   c. *Sue looked not at him.

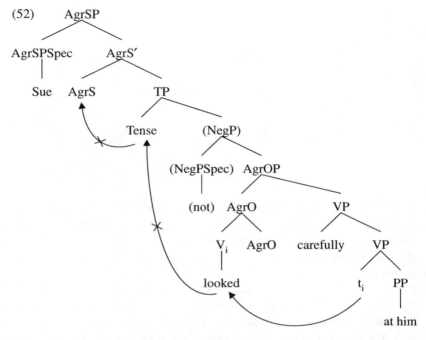

Johnson (1991, 1992a, b) claims that English main verbs move not only to AgrO, but also to Tense, i.e. one head further up in the tree. He observes that object NPs may optionally precede separable verb particles (cf. (53a, b)) and that object pronouns must do so obligatorily (cf. (54a, b)). Johnson draws a parallel between the construction in (53a,54a) and Scandinavian object shift (see the discussion in sections 2.4.2.2, 2.4.2.4 and 5.4) and argues that both involve movement of the object out of VP and into the specifier of AgrOP. If this is correct, the main verb must have moved past AgrO since it precedes the shifted object. (53c) and (54c) on the other hand show that it has not moved all the way up to AgrS. Johnson assumes that it has moved to Tense and assigns (54a) the S-structure in (55).

(53) a.   Betsy blew the bridge up.
      b.   Betsy blew up the bridge.
      c.   *Betsy not blew the bridge up.

(54)   a.   Betsy blew it up.
        b.   *Betsy blew up it.
        c.   *Besty not blew it up.

(55) AgrSP

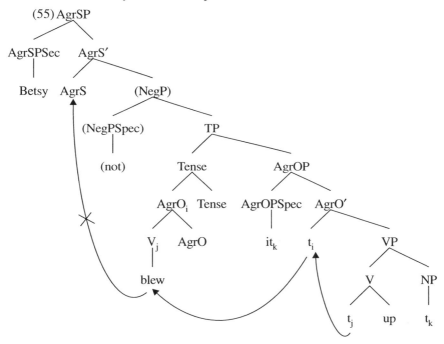

I want to discuss three pieces of evidence against main verb movement in English before I briefly return to the particle construction exemplified in (53a,54a) to suggest that this construction does not involve verb movement. The first piece of evidence involves floating quantifiers (cf. Sportiche 1988). When a quantified subject is moved from its D-structure position in SpecVP to its S-structure position in SpecAgrSP, the quantifier can be carried along to this specifier (cf. (56a)), but it can also be stranded either in SpecVP (cf. (56b) and its structure in (57a)) or in SpecTP (cf. (56c) and its structure in (57b)).

(56)   a.   All the children have probably seen the movie.
        b.   The children have probably all seen the movie.
        c.   The children have all probably seen the movie.

(57) a.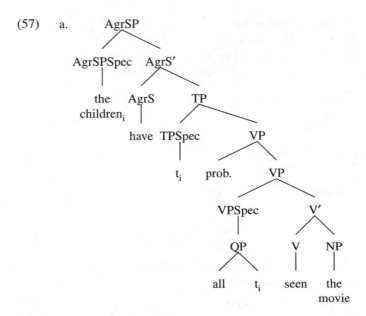

b.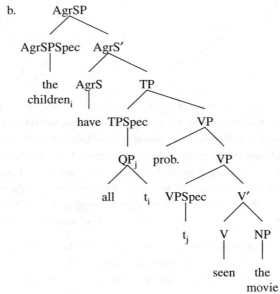

If English main verbs moved out of VP as proposed by Pesetsky, Branigan and Collins and Johnson, we would expect them to be able to occur to the left of quantifiers stranded in SpecVP. This is however not the case: Example (58) with the main verb to the left of *all* is markedly worse than example (56b) with the main verb to the right of *all*. Yet if main verbs moved out of VP, the grammatical structure in (59) should be available for (58). The ungrammaticality of (58) strongly suggests that English main verbs stay in situ inside VP.

(58)   *The children looked (probably) all at John.

(59)

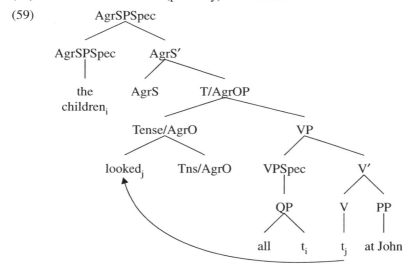

The second and third piece of evidence against main verb movement in English involve the placement and scope of adverbs. If (51a) repeated below as (60a) involves V in situ instead of V to AgrO/Tense, then the adverb following the verb must have been generated on the right edge of the VP, an option that is clearly available in light of the surface order in (60b). In addition, the clause final PP must have been extraposed. The S-structure of (60a) is given in (61).[20]

(60)   a.   Sue looked carefully at him.
        b.   Sue looked at him carefully.

(61)

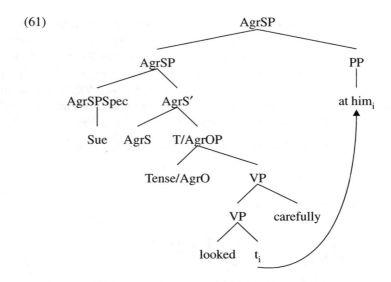

Independent evidence for this analysis comes from adverbs like those in (62) which as usual may appear on the left edge of the VP (compare (63a) with (51b)) but have the special property of being barred from the right edge of the VP (compare (63b) with (60b) and see the discussion in Jackendoff 1972 and Emonds 1976). The verb movement analysis in (52) predicts that the order V^Adv^PP is grammatical with adverbs of this type, since it can be straightfor-wardly derived from (63a) via V to AgrO/Tense. The V in situ analysis in (61) on the other hand predicts that this order is ungrammatical with these adverbs, since the latter do not allow adjunction to the right of VP. The ungrammaticality of (63c) shows that the V in situ analysis but not the V to AgrO/Tense analysis makes the right prediction and thus corroborates our conclusion reached above in connection with Quantifier Floating that English main verbs do not move.

(62)   barely, hardly, merely, nearly, really, scarcely, simply, utterly, virtually

(63)   a.   John scarcely glanced at the students.
           b. *John glanced at the students scarcely.
           c. *John glanced scarcely at the students.

Pesetsky (1989: fn. 20) acknowledges that the ungrammaticality of (63c) is problematic for his account but notes that this word order improves when the verb is focused (cf. (64a)). However, the order in (63b) also improves under verb focus (cf. (64b)). It thus seems that verb focus simply makes the right VP-edge marginally available even for the class of adverbs listed in (62), in which case the relative acceptability of (64a) does not bear on the question under consideration and the ungrammaticality of (63c) continues to strongly favor the V in situ approach over the V to AgrO/Tense approach.

(64)   It was easy to get their attention...
        a.   ?John SHOUTED simply to them, and they came.
        b.   ?John SHOUTED to them simply, and they came.

The V to AgrO/Tense analysis in (52) and the V in situ analysis in (61) make different predictions with respect to the c-command relations between multiple post-verbal adverbs. In the sequence V^Adv$_1$^Adv$_2$^PP, either adverb can c-command the other according to the V to AgrO/Tense analysis (where not only (65b) but also (65a) is available). According to the V in situ analysis (where only (65b) is available), the second adverb unambiguously c-commands the first.

(65)   a.

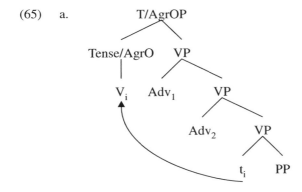

b.

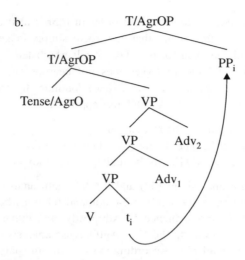

Consider now the relative scope of multiple adverbs. If scope is based on c-command, then both the V to AgrO/Tense and the V in situ analysis predict that *intentionally* has scope over *twice* in (66a) which can only have the structure in (65a) minus verb movement and that *twice* has scope over *intentionally* in (66b) which can only have the structure in (65b) minus PP-extraposition. In other words, (66a) should refer to one intentional event of knocking twice whereas (66b) should refer to two events of intentional knocking. But when the adverbs are sandwiched between the verb and the PP as in (66c), the two theories make different predictions. According to the V to AgrO/Tense analysis, both wide and narrow scope of either adverb should be possible, depending on whether (65a) or (65b) is chosen. According to the V in situ analysis, only wide scope of *twice* over *intentionally* should be possible, since only (65b) is available.

(66) a. John intentionally twice knocked on the door.
      b. John knocked on the door intentionally twice.
      c. John knocked intentionally twice on the door.

Pesetsky reports that the facts are as predicted by the V to AgrO/Tense analysis. I however think that it makes little sense to discuss the interpretations of (66a–c) without paying attention to prosody.[21] There are two more or less natural intonational patterns for the adverbs in (66): An asymmetric intonation with considerably more emphasis on the second adverb (*intentionally twíce*) and a symmetric intonation with almost equal emphasis on both adverbs (*inténtionally twíce*).

(66a, b) are most natural with the asymmetric intonation while (66c) is most natural with the symmetric intonation. What is crucial is that (66a, b) become ambiguous when the symmetric intonation is chosen and that (66c) becomes unambiguous (with wide scope of *twice* over *intentionally*) when the asymmetric intonation is chosen. If we disregard the question which intonation is most natural for which sentence (a question that I assume is irrelevant with respect to the problem at hand), then it turns out that (66c) is entirely parallel to (66b): Both of these sentences require wide scope of the second adverb over the first with the asymmetric intonation, and both are ambiguous with the symmetric intonation. (66a) is the odd man out, requiring wide scope of the first adverb over the second with the asymmetric intonation. If semantic scope depends on syntactic structure as assumed by Pesetsky, then this pattern suggests that (66c) is structurally similar to (66b) and dissimilar from (66a). In this case, the adverbs in (66c) must be stacked to the right of VP (as in (66b)) and not to the left of VP (as in (66a)). This is as predicted under the V in situ analysis, according to which the post-verbal position of adverbs indicates that they are adjoined to the right of VP, but it is incompatible with the V to AgrO/Tense analysis, according to which post-verbal adverbs can be the result of their adjunction to the left of VP plus verb movement to an inflectional head. The contrast in (66) thus turns out to be evidence for the V in situ analysis and against the V to AgrO/Tense analysis.

Above, I assumed that the successive adjunction (i.e. stacking) of two or more adverbs to the right or left of VP gives rise to the asymmetric intonation. But what is the syntactic structure that gives rise to the symmetric intonation? I propose that in this case, either the first adverb is adjoined to the second as in (67) or the second adverb is adjoined to the first as in (68). According to the definition of c-command in note 13, *intentionally* c-commands and has therefore scope over *twice* in (67) but not vice versa. In (68), the opposite holds: *twice* c-commands and has therefore scope over *intentionally* but not vice versa.

(67)

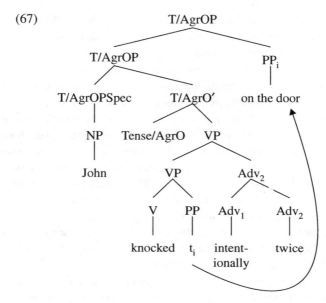

(68)

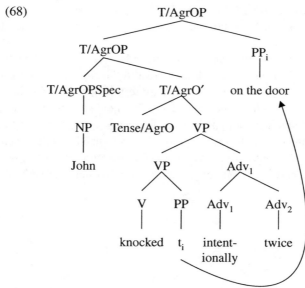

I have argued above that evidence involving Quantifier Floating, adverb place-ment and adverb scope suggests that main verbs do not move out of VP in English. If this conclusion is correct, the Particle Construction examples in (53a) and (54a) cannot involve main verb movement and (55) cannot be the correct structure of (54a). Fortunately, another structure is available that does not involve main verb movement. The Particle Construction examples in (53) and (54) share important syntactic and semantic properties with the adjective-headed Small Clause examples in (69) and (70). Bolinger (1971:68) notes that "at least some conjunctions between particles and adjectives are perfectly normal" (cf. (71)), a fact that suggests that particles and adjectival heads of Small Clauses have the same syntactic status.

(69)   a.   Betsy blew the bridge sky-high.
        b.   *Betsy blew sky-high the bridge.

(70)   a.   Betsy blew it sky-high.
        b.   *Betsy blew sky-high it.

(71)   He held the gun out and ready.

It is hence tempting to analyze (53, 54) and (69, 70) along the same lines, i.e. to extend the Small Clause analysis to Particle Constructions. Such a proposal was first formalized in Kayne (1984), who assigns the structure in (72) to the examples in (53a, 54a) and (69a, 70a).

(72)

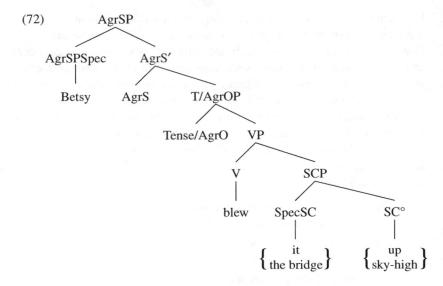

As shown, this analysis does not have to make use of verb movement. Rather, what had been previously regarded as the object of the verb is now understood to be the subject of the Small Clause headed by the particle or the adjective, respectively. Accordingly, the examples in (53a, 54a) and (69a, 70a) do not involve Object Shift but show the subject of the Small Clause in its underlying position and the examples in (53b, 54b) and (69b, 70b) do not directly reflect D-structure, but have the Small Clause subject extraposed to the right. Such rightward movement of noun phrases is otherwise restricted to 'heavy' elements (Heavy NP-Shift). But Kayne points out that syntactic heaviness cannot be defined in absolute terms. Instead, it must be defined relative to the element with which inversion occurs, i.e. the head of the Small Clause. When the Small Clause is headed by a 'light' particle, even a 'middleweight' full NP but not a 'light' pronoun counts as 'heavy' relative to this particle, and Heavy NP-Shift is hence possible in (53b) but not in (54b). When the Small Clause is headed by a 'middleweight' adjective, neither an 'middleweight' full NP nor a 'light' pronoun counts as 'heavy' relative to this adjective, and Heavy NP-Shift is hence impossible in both (69b) and (70b). (73) shows the derivation of (53b), the only grammatical member of the set of four examples involving Heavy NP-Shift around a particle or adjective discussed in this paragraph.[22]

(73)

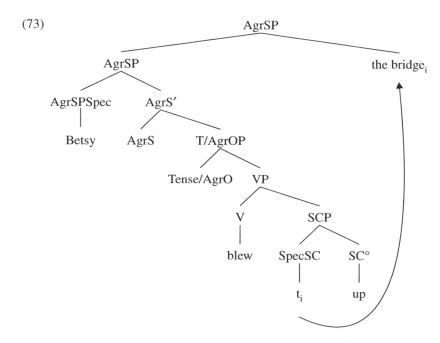

I do not have the space to discuss the details of this account, but it seems to constitute a viable alternative to the V to Tense analysis in (55) and has the advantage of being compatible with the V in situ analysis advocated in this section. But even if Pesetsky, Branigan and Collins and Johnson are on the right track and English main verbs move out of VP and to the intermediate inflectional heads AgrO (cf. (52)) or Tense (cf. (55)), it remains a fact that English main verbs never move past negation to AgrS, the highest inflectional head. Thus it is clear that English does not have V to I raising of main verbs in the sense of Chapter 1 of this book (see in particular note 1 of Chapter 1).

Unlike English main verbs, English dummy auxiliaries (cf. (48a)), temporal auxiliaries (cf. (74a)) and modal auxiliaries (cf. (74b)) do occur to the left of negation.

(74) a. Sue has not seen "Terminator II".
      b. You must not watch New Age movies.

I will however argue in Chapter 4 that English auxiliaries are not first generated in V and then moved to AgrS. Instead, they are generated in intermediate

inflectional heads such as MOOD or ASP(ect) above (and hence to the left of)
negation and do not move at all. In conclusion, I have argued in this section that
English, the first Germanic VO language we have investigated, does not have V
to I raising. I will now turn to the Scandinavian languages.

2.4.2.2 *Mainland Scandinavian*
In Mainland Scandinavian embedded clauses that are not the asserted complements of bridge verbs, the highest verb obligatorily follows sentential negation
and adverbs, cf. the Swedish examples in (11e) and (12b) repeated below in (75).
This immediately suggests that Mainland Scandinavian does not have V to I
raising (cf. (76a)), which is in fact the standard interpretation of these data (see
e.g. Holmberg and Platzack 1991 or Vikner 1995a). In earlier work, Holmberg
(1986) and Platzack (1986a) had argued that Mainland Scandinavian does have
V to I raising and that the pre-verbal position of negation and adverbs is a result
of their adjunction to I′ instead of VP (cf. (76b)).

(75)   a.   Jag beklagar att jag *aldrig* **träffade** henne.
            I regret   that I never met   her
       b.   *Jag beklagar att jag **träffade** *aldrig* henne.
            I regret   that I met   never her
            'I regret that I never met her.'
                        (Swedish, based on Holmberg 1986, ex. 4(19d,c))

(76)   a.

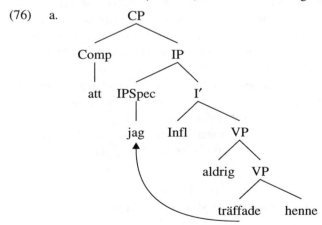

b.

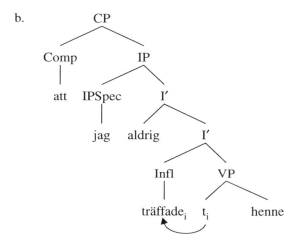

Several reasons lead me to reject the structure in (76b) and the analysis in Holmberg (1986) and Platzack (1986a). First, it is usually assumed that structure preservation does not allow adjunction of X^0 or XP (e.g. an adverb) to X′ (e.g. I′). Second, we will see in Section 2.4.2.4 that Icelandic adverbs cannot be adjoined as high as I′ since they appear post-verbally even where verb movement to Comp is impossible and V to I raising is the only option. Holmberg's and Platzack's account reduces this important word order difference between Icelandic and the Mainland Scandinavian languages to a difference in adverb-placement that has to be stipulated and receives no independent support, a move that is conceptually unattractive. Finally, an additional and equally unsupported stipulation is needed in Platzack's and Holmberg's account to capture the behavior of the Mainland Scandinavian languages with respect to Object Shift. I will spend the rest of this section discussing this last problem for the V to I raising analysis in (76b), showing that no comparable problem exists for the V in situ analysis in (76a).

In Mainland Scandinavian matrix clauses, pronominal objects but not full NP objects move more or less obligatorily to the immediate left of negation or adverbs if the main verb is the highest verb. This is illustrated in (77) (based on examples in Holmberg 1986) for subject-initial matrix clauses and in (78) (= Vikner 1995a, ex. 5(36b)) for topic-initial matrix clauses.

(77)   a.   Studenterna läste inte boken/*den.
             students-the read not book-the/it
       b.   Studenterna läste den/*boken inte.
             students-the read it/book-the not
             'The students didn't read it/the book.'   (Swedish)

(78)   I går   læste Ole den uden   tvivl ikke.
       yesterday read O. it   without doubt not
       'Without a doubt, Ole didn't read it yesterday.'   (Danish)

If the subject is located in SpecIP in topic-initial matrix sentences, as seems
reasonable, then a V to I raising analysis of Mainland Scandinavian (which must
assume that negation and adverbs are I'-adjoined, cf. (76b)) is forced to the
conclusion that the pronominal object between the subject and the adverb in (78)
is itself adjoined to I'. This conclusion is problematic for the reason mentioned
above. More importantly, it fails to explain why Object Shift of the type
illustrated in (77,78) is impossible in embedded clauses that are not the asserted
complements of bridge verbs, as illustrated in (79) (again based on examples in
Holmberg 1986).

(79)   a.   Jag beklagar att studenterna inte läste boken/den.
             I   regret   that students-the not read book-the/it
       b.   *Jag beklagar att studenterna boken/den inte läste.
             I   regret   that students-the book-the/it not read
             'I regret that the students didn't read the book/it.'

                                                                    (Swedish)

The only possibly relevant difference between the grammatical (77b,78) and the
ungrammatical (79b) is the position of the verb. According to the V to I raising
analysis of Mainland Scandinavian, the verb is located in Comp in (77b,78) and
in Infl (or the highest inflectional head) in (79b). I will show below that the V
to I raising analysis is not able to derive the contrast between these two examples from general locality requirements on XP-movement such as the ECP or
Shortest Move. In the absence of an independent explanation, the contrast
between (77b,78) and (79b) has to be stipulated. According to the V in situ
analysis of Mainland Scandinavian, the verb is located in Comp in (77b,78) and
in V (or one of the lower inflectional heads) in (79b). I will show below that the
V in situ analysis is able to derive the contrast between these two examples from
the ECP or Shortest Move and no recourse to stipulation is necessary.[23]

Both the ECP and Shortest Move prohibit movement of a complement or specifier across a filled specifier unless the head of the phrase that minimally contains the intervening specifier has itself moved out of that phrase. To see this, consider the structures in $(84)^{24}$ in light of the ECP definitions in (20) and (21) (repeated for your convenience below as (80) and (81)) and the Shortest Move Definitions in (82) and (83).[25]

(80)   Barrierhood:
        Let D be the smallest maximal projection containing A.
        Then C is a BARRIER between A and B iff C is a maximal projec-
        tion that contains B and excludes A and either
        a.   C is not [IP, VP or θ-marked], or
        b.   the head of C is distinct from the head of D and selects some
              XP equal to or containing B.   (Baker 1988:56)

(81)   Distinctness:
        X is **distinct** from Y only if no part of Y is a member of a (move-
        ment) chain containing X.   (Baker 1988:64)

(82)   Minimal Domains of Head Chains:
        For any head chain $(\alpha_1,...,\alpha_n)$, the minimal domain $\text{Min}(\alpha_1)$ of
        $(\alpha_1,...,\alpha_n)$ is the smallest subset K of S, S the set of nodes contained
        in the least full-category maximal projection dominating α_1 that are
        distinct from and do not contain α_i, such that for any $\gamma \in$ S, some
        $\beta \in$ K reflexively dominates γ.
                           (after Chomsky 1992 [1995]: 178–180)[26]

(83)   Shortest Move:
        For any α_i in a XP-movement chain $(\alpha_1,...,\alpha_n)$, there is no filled
        target position β such that β c-commands α_{i+1} but does not c-com-
        mand α_i, unless α_i and β are in the same minimal domain (and
        hence "equidistant" from α_{i+1}).
                           (after Chomsky 1992 [1995]: 184)

(84)

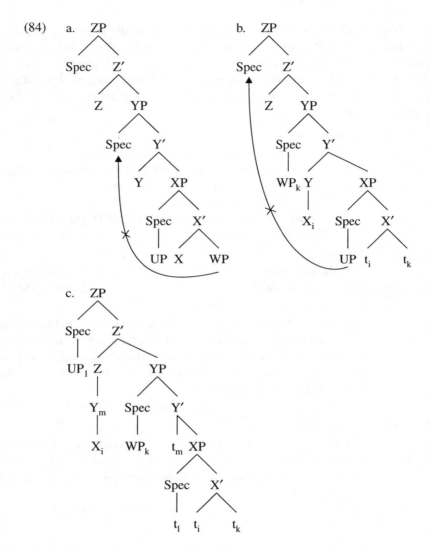

When X remains in situ, its complement WP cannot move to SpecYP across UP in SpecXP (cf. (84a)) because this movement violates both the ECP (XP, whose head is distinct from the head of YP, constitutes a barrier between SpecYP and WP) and Shortest Move (SpecXP is a filled target position which c-commands WP but does not c-command SpecYP, yet SpecXP and SpecYP are in different minimal domains, i.e. those of X and Y, respectively). When X moves to Y, WP can move to SpecYP across UP (cf. (84b)) because now this movement does not violate either the ECP (XP, whose head is not distinct from the head of YP, does not constitute a barrier between SpecYP and WP) or Shortest Move (SpecXP and SpecYP are in the same minimal domain, i.e. that of (X_i, t_i)). However, UP cannot move to SpecZP across WP in SpecYP in this structure because YP, whose head is distinct from the head of ZP, constitutes a barrier between SpecZP and UP (ECP) and because SpecYP is a filled target position which c-commands UP but does not c-command SpecZP, yet SpecYP and SpecZP are in different minimal domains, i.e. those of Y and Z, respectively (Shortest Move). Only when Y moves to Z can UP move to SpecZP across WP in SpecYP (cf. (84c)) because this time the movement satisfies both the ECP (YP, whose head is not distinct from the head of ZP, does not constitute a barrier between SpecZP and UP) and Shortest Move (SpecYP and SpecZP are in the same minimal domain, i.e. that of (Y_m, t_m)).

Let us now turn to the contrast between Object Shift in Mainland Scandinavian matrix clauses (cf. (77,78)) and lack of Object Shift in Mainland Scandinavian embedded clauses (cf. (79)). According to the V to I raising analysis of Mainland Scandinavian (cf. (76b)), the grammatical sentence in (77b) has the structure in (85), where IP represents the highest inflectional projection and lower inflectional projections do not play a role.

(85)

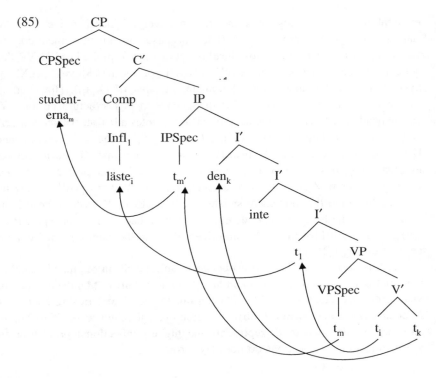

The structure in (85) is equivalent to that in (84c) in all relevant aspects: Movement of the object from its base position as the complement of V across the subject in SpecVP to its surface position as the adjunct of I′ satisfies both the ECP (VP, whose head is not distinct from the head of IP, does not constitute a barrier between den_k and t_k) and Shortest Move (den_k and SpecVP are in the same minimal domain, namely that of ($läste_i,t_i$) before movement of Infl to Comp). Movement of the subject from its base position as the specifier of VP across the I′-adjoined object to its derived position as the specifier of IP also satisfies both the ECP (for the reason mentioned above) and Shortest Move (the I′-adjoined object does not qualify as an intervening filled target in the sense of (83) because it commands SpecIP (cf. note 13) and because both are in the same minimal domain, namely that of Infl before movement of Infl to Comp). It is easy to see that further movement of the verb from Infl to Comp and the subject from SpecIP to SpecCP is likewise unproblematic.

The V to I raising analysis of Mainland Scandinavian assigns the ungrammatical sentence in (79b) virtually the same structure as the grammatical sentence in (77b), i.e. (85) minus verb movement from Infl to Comp and subject movement from SpecIP to SpecCP. As should be clear from the discussion in the previous paragraph, this structure satisfies both the ECP and Shortest Move and the V to I raising analysis therefore has no way to derive the ungrammaticality of (79b) from general locality requirements on XP-movement. Instead, it has to stipulate that Object Shift is unavailable in embedded clauses that are not the asserted complements of bridge verbs.

Lower inflectional projections do have the potential to play a role in the V in situ analysis of Mainland Scandinavian (cf. (76a)). Let us assume a fleshed-out clause structure like that in (i) in note 1 of Chapter 1 or that in (55) in this chapter, with the difference that the negation marker is an adjunct rather than being the head or specifier of its own phrase between AgrSP and TP. For the sake of the discussion, let us assume that it is adjoined to AgrO'. Let us further assume that Object Shift moves the object to SpecAgrOP, perhaps in order to remove the object from the LF-domain of existential closure (i.e. VP) and to allow it thus to receive a specific interpretation, as proposed by Diesing and Jelinek (1993). Following Jonas and Bobaljik (1993), I will now show that given these or similar assumptions,[27] the V in situ analysis of Mainland Scandinavian in conjunction with the ECP or Shortest Move can explain the distribution of Object Shift as follows. The situation in matrix clauses is illustrated in (86), the S-structure of (77b).

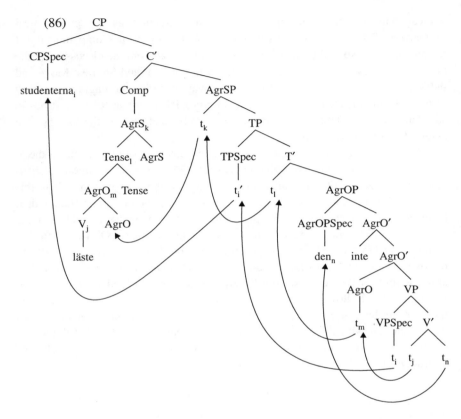

Just like (85), (86) is equivalent to (84c) in all relevant aspects: Verb movement to AgrO renders the heads of AgrOP and VP non-distinct, voiding barrierhood of the latter, and puts SpecAgrOP and SpecVP in the same minimal domain, making them equidistant from the object in its underlying position as the complement of V. The object can therefore move across the subject in SpecVP to its surface position in SpecAgrOP without violating either the ECP or Shortest Move. Similarly, movement of the Verb-AgrO complex to Tense voids barrierhood of AgrOP and makes SpecTP and SpecAgrOP equidistant from the subject in its underlying position as the specifier of VP. The subject can therefore move across the object in SpecAgrOP to its derived position in SpecTP. As before, further movement of the verb to Comp and the subject to SpecCP is unproblematic.

The situation is different in embedded clauses that are not the complements of asserted bridge verbs. In (87), the V in situ structure of (79), it has been left open whether the verb stays in its underlying position inside VP or undergoes "short" verb movement to AgrO. Remember that either case falls into the category "V in situ", understood throughout this book to mean "failure to undergo 'long' verb movement to the highest inflectional head".

(87)

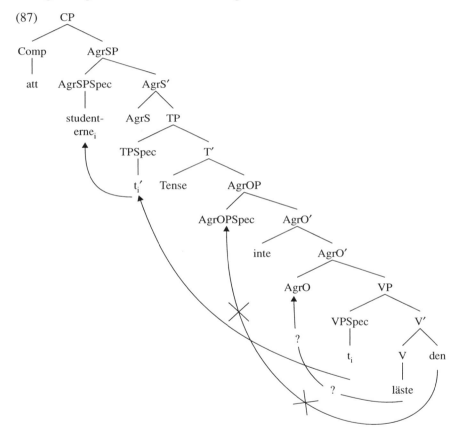

Let us first assume that the verb does not move from its underlying position inside VP. In this case, the head of AgrOP and the head of VP are distinct and SpecAgrOP and SpecVP are in different minimal domains. Since VP is a barrier for the object and SpecAgrOP and SpecVP are not equidistant from the object,

movement of the latter across the subject to SpecAgrOP would violate both the'
ECP and Shortest Move. (87) without any verb movement at all thus instantiates
(84a). Let us next assume that the verb moves to (and no further than) AgrO. In
this case, the head of AgrOP and the head of VP are non-distinct, voiding
barrierhood of the latter, and SpecAgrOP and SpecVP are in the same minimal
domain, making them equidistant from the object. The object could therefore in
principle move across the subject in SpecVP to SpecAgrOP without violating
either the ECP or Shortest Move, but if it actually did move there, it would
block movement of the subject to SpecTP and SpecAgrSP: In the terms of the
ECP, the head of TP and the head of AgrOP are distinct and the latter is hence
a barrier for the subject in SpecVP. In the terms of Shortest Move, SpecTP and
SpecAgrOP are in different domains and hence not equidistant from the subject
in SpecVP. In neither theory can the subject move from SpecVP across the
object in SpecAgrOP to SpecTP and SpecAgrSP. (87) with short verb movement
thus instantiates (84b). Since the subject must move to SpecAgrSP in order to
check Case and agreement, the object cannot move to SpecAgrOP and Object
Shift is impossible in Mainland Scandinavian embedded clauses that are not the
asserted complements of bridge verbs.[28,29]

Above I have shown that the V to I raising analysis of Mainland Scandinavian has to stipulate the difference between matrix clauses, in which pronominal
Object Shift applies, and embedded clauses, in which pronominal Object Shift
does not apply. I have further shown that the V in situ analysis of Mainland
Scandinavian does not have to stipulate this difference but can instead derive it
from general locality requirements such as the ECP or Shortest Move. This
constitutes a strong argument in favor of the V in situ analysis, which has other
advantages (cf. the paragraph below (76)). I conclude that Mainland Scandinavian does not have V to I raising.

Unlike their English counterparts (cf. (74)), Mainland Scandinavian auxiliaries and modals never precede sentential negation or adverbs in subordinate
clauses that are not the complements of asserted bridge verbs, cf. (11f) repeated
below in (88a). In fact, while there is good reason to believe that in English,
auxiliaries, modals and main verbs belong to separate syntactic categories, it
appears that they are all members of the same category 'verb' in Mainland
Scandinavian. I will come back to this topic in Chapter 4.

(88)   a.   Vi tenkte ikke at   han aldri *ville* ha   penger.
              we thought not that he   never would have money

b. *Vi tenkte ikke at han *ville* aldri ha   penger.
we thought not that he would never have money
'We didn't think that he would never have any money.'
(Norwegian, based on ex. in Taraldsen 1986)

In this section, I have presented evidence against verb raising beyond AgrO in Mainland Scandinavian. The evidence for verb movement up to AgrO is, as far as I know, scant to non-existent. It seems safe to conclude that when the Mainland Scandinavian verb does not move to Comp, it either does not move at all or moves only to one of the lower inflectional heads but not the highest inflectional head.

2.4.2.3 *Faroese*

Most speakers of Faroese allow embedded Verb Second only in the complements of asserted bridge verbs, but not in other subordinate sentences (cf. Vikner 1995a). For these speakers, V2 is for example excluded from relative clauses such as the one in (11c), repeated below in (89). As in the case of Mainland Scandinavian, I take the obligatory pre-verbal position of sentential negation and adverbs in these sentences to indicate that V to I raising is in general not available in Faroese.

(89) a. Har vóru nógv fólk, eg *ikki* **kendi**.
here were many people I not knew
b. *Har vóru nógv fólk, eg **kendi** *ikki*.
here were many people I knew not
'There were many people I didn't know.'
(Faroese, Lockwood 1964:156, and Vikner 1995a, ex. 5(44a))

A minority of Faroese speakers however seems to at least marginally allow embedded Verb Second outside the bridge verb context (cf. (90) and (91a–93a)), although non-V2 is always an option (cf. (91b–93b)). Examples (90) and (91) come from Lockwood (1964:88,157) and examples (92) and (93) come from Barnes (1987:ex.1–2) and Barnes (1989:ex.2f), respectively.

(90) a. Við tað at stríðið   við bygdarmenninar **linkað**   *ikki*
with it that quarrel-the with villagers-the   diminished not
av...
from
'Since the hostilities with the villagers didn't die down...'
(Faroese)

      b.   Steinurin var so stórur, at   hann **kundi** *ikki* berast   av
          the-stone was so large   that he   could not be-carried by
          høkrum manni.[30]
          any   man   (Faroese)

(91)   a.   Eg segði tað, at   hann **skuldi** *ikki* havt nakað.
          I   said it   that he   should not have anything
      b.   Eg segði tað, at   hann *ikki* **skuldi** havt nakað.
          I   said it   that he   not should have anything
          'I said that he shouldn't have anything.'   (Faroese)

(92)   a.   Tey nýttu fleiri   or,   sum   hon **hevði** *ikki* hoyrt fyrr.
          they used several words which he   had   not heard before
      b.   Tey nýttu fleiri   or,   sum   hon *ikki* **hevði** hoyrt fyrr.
          they used several words which she not had   heard before
                                               (Faroese)

(93)   a.   Hann spyr, hví tað   **eru** *ikki* fleiri tílíkar samkomur
          he   asks why there are not more such   meetings
      b.   Hann spyr, hví tað   *ikki* **eru** fleiri tílíkar samkomur
          he   asks why there not are more such   meetings (Faroese)

This situation contrasts sharply with the one found in the (standard) Mainland Scandinavian languages, where Verb Second is always ungrammatical in similar constructions (compare (90a) with (94a) = Vikner 1994, ex. (ia) from fn. 3 and (93a) with (94b) = Vikner 1991, ex. 2(92b)).

(94)   a.   *Bara för det att vi **ville**   *inte* följa   honom.
          just for that that we would not follow him
          'Just because he would not follow him.'   (Swedish)
      b.   *Jeg ved hvorfor koen   **står** *altid* inde i huset
          I   know why   cow-the stands always inside in house-the
          'I don't know why the cow always stands inside the house.'
                                             (Danish)

I take the post-verbal position of sentential negation and adverbs in (90a–93a) to indicate that a minority of speakers of Faroese has residual V to I raising. These residues of V to I raising in Faroese may just represent archaic style, a pocket of resistance against the otherwise completed loss of V to I raising, as suggested in Barnes (1989) and Vikner (1995a). This would be an especially plausible hypothesis if one could show that V to I raising was lost in Faroese more recently than in Mainland Scandinavian, but unfortunately this question cannot be answered conclusively because the relevant Faroese data are lacking. In Section 3.5, I will tentatively propose a different explanation for residual V to I raising that is in line with the theory developed in sections 3.3 and 3.4. What is most important to keep in mind is that Modern Faroese does in general not allow V to I raising.

2.4.2.4 *Icelandic*

Icelandic requires Verb Second in all types of finite embedded clauses, including those that are not the complements of asserted bridge verbs. This is illustrated by examples (11b) and (13b), repeated below as (95a, b).[31]

(95)　a.　Það var gott að Jón **keypti** *ekki* bókina.
　　　　　　it   was good that J.   bought not book-the
　　　　　　'It was good that John didn't buy the book.'
　　　　　　　　　　　　　(Icelandic, Holmberg 1986, ex 6(172c))

　　　b.　Jón harmar að þessa bók **skuli** ég hafa lesið.
　　　　　　J.   regrets that this book should I   have read
　　　　　　'John regrets that I should have read this book.'
　　　　　　　　　　　　　(Icelandic, Vikner 1995a, 4(20a))

(96)　a.　*Það var gott að Jón *ekki* **keypti** bókina.
　　　　　　it   was good that J.   not bought book-the
　　　　　　'It was good that John didn't buy the book.'
　　　　　　　　　　　(Icelandic, based on Holmberg 1986, ex 6(172c))

　　　b.　*Jón harmar að þessa bók ég **skuli** hafa lesið.
　　　　　　J.   regrets that this book I   should have read
　　　　　　　　　　　(Icelandic, based on Vikner 1995a, 4(20a))

Most of the numerous analyses that have been proposed to account for Verb Second in Icelandic embedded clauses that are not the complements of asserted bridge verbs fall into one of the following three types. The first type of analysis, which I will call the 'Uniform IP Analysis', assumes that both the embedded subject in (95a) and the embedded topic in (95b) have moved to SpecAgrSP (or the specifier of the highest inflectional projection) and that in both sentences, the embedded finite verb has moved to AgrS (or the head of the highest inflectional projection), as shown in (97). In other words, Icelandic SpecAgrSP has the special property of being a possible landing site for A'-movement. Analyses of this type have been proposed in Cardinaletti & Roberts (1991), Diesing (1990),

Kosmeijer (1991), Platzack (1984), Rögnvaldsson (1984), Rögnvaldsson & Thráinsson (1990), Santorini (1994) and Thráinsson (1985, 1993).

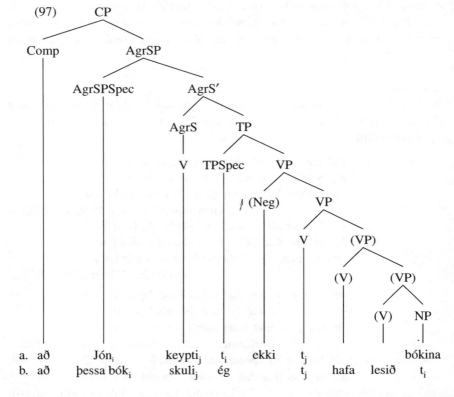

(97)

a. að   Jón$_i$ keypti$_j$ t$_i$ ekki   t$_j$ bókina
b. að   þessa bók$_i$ skuli$_j$ ég   t$_j$ hafa lesið   t$_i$

The second type of analysis, which I will call the 'Uniform CP Analysis', assumes that both (95a) and (95b) involve CP-recursion with movement of the subject or topic to SpecCP and movement of the finite verb to Comp, as shown in (98). In other words, Icelandic has the special property of allowing 'free' CP-recursion in (almost) all embedded clauses, not just those that are complements of asserted bridge verbs. An analysis of this type has been proposed in Vikner (1994, 1995a).

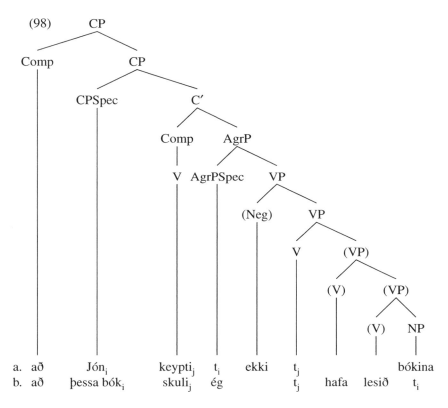

The third type of analyses, which I will call 'Mixed IP/CP Analyses' and which I will adopt below, assumes that all subject-initial embedded V2 clauses that are not the complements of bridge verbs like (95a) are simple CPs and have the structure in (97a) and that all topic-initial embedded V2 clauses like (95b) are recursive CPs and have the structure in (98b). Analyses of this type have been proposed in Hornstein (1991), Jónsson (1991b) and Ottósson (1989).

According to both the Uniform IP Analysis and the Mixed IP/CP Analysis, Icelandic has visible V to I raising, either in all embedded V2 clauses that are not complements of asserted bridge verbs (Uniform IP Analysis) or in subject-initial embedded V2 clauses that are not complements of asserted bridge verbs (Mixed IP/CP Analysis). According to the Uniform CP Analysis, putative V to I raising would never be visible in Icelandic since verb movement always continues to Comp. Since structures involving verb movement to Comp may involve either cyclic head movement or direct V to C plus adjunction of intermediate heads to the verb in Comp (cf. the discussion in Section 2.3), we do not have any evidence for V to I raising in Icelandic under the Uniform CP Analysis.

There is however evidence against the Uniform CP Analysis. Let me first mention an argument against it that I do not consider to be especially convincing, but that is nevertheless potentially interesting. Free CP-recursion is motivated by cases of topicalization in embedded clauses that are not complements of asserted bridge verbs, yet recall that it is a matter of debate how good or bad examples like (95b) really are (cf. note 5). But recall also that in Dutch, embedded topicalization is ungrammatical even when CP recursion is clearly available, i.e. under verbs that allow embedded subject-initial V2 clauses (compare (7h) with (9h)). The variable acceptability of Icelandic embedded topicalization outside the bridge verb context might therefore be due to reasons that are independent of the question whether these clauses are IPs or CPs. More conclusive evidence against the Uniform CP Analysis comes from long extraction from asserted complements of bridge verbs. As noted by Holmberg (1986), this construction is possible in the Mainland Scandinavian languages only if verb movement to the lower embedded Comp has not taken place (cf. (99a)). It is impossible in both subject-initial (cf. (99b)) and topic-initial (cf. (99c)) embedded Verb Second clauses.[32]

(99) a. Vilken fest sa   hon att vi inte skulle köpa roliga hattar till?
          which party said he   that we not should buy funny hats for
      b. *Vilken fest sa   hon att vi skulle inte köpa roliga hattar till?
          which party said he   that we should not buy funny hats for
      c. *Vilken fest sa   hon att roliga hattar skulle vi inte köpa till
          which party said he   that funny hats   should we not buy for
          'Which party did he say that we shouldn't buy funny hats for?'
                                        (Swedish, Holmberg 1986, ex. 4(84a–c))

The contrast in (99) constitutes the basis for one of the original arguments for CP-recursion in Mainland Scandinavian embedded V2 clauses presented in Platzack (1986b). In current terms, (99b,c) are ruled out because they violate Shortest Move (or Relativized Minimality, cf. Rizzi 1990): As shown in (100), the wh-element would have to skip the lower embedded SpecCP filled with the subject (in (99b)) or the topic (in (99c)) in order to get to the higher embedded SpecCP and from there to the matrix SpecCP. But since the two embedded SpecCPs are in different minimal domains and hence not equidistant from the base position of the wh-element, such skipping of the lower embedded SpecCP violates Shortest Move (cf. (82,83)), ruling out (99b,c).

(100)

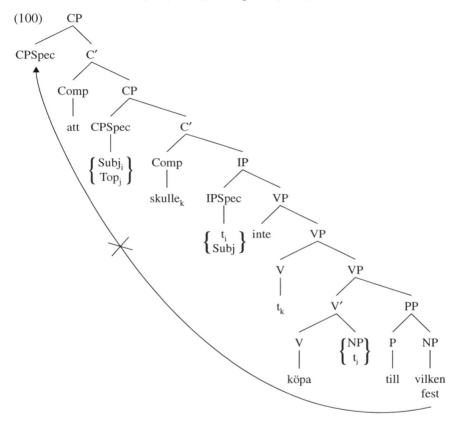

No violation of Shortest Move occurs in (99a) with the structure in (101). Here the wh-element has to skip the embedded SpecIP filled with the subject in order to get to the single embedded SpecCP and from there to the matrix SpecCP. Although the embedded SpecIP and the single embedded SpecCP are in different minimal domains and hence not equidistant from the base position of the wh-element, such skipping of the embedded SpecIP does not violate Shortest Move since SpecIP, an A-position, is not a target position in the sense of (83) for wh- or other A'-movement.

(101)

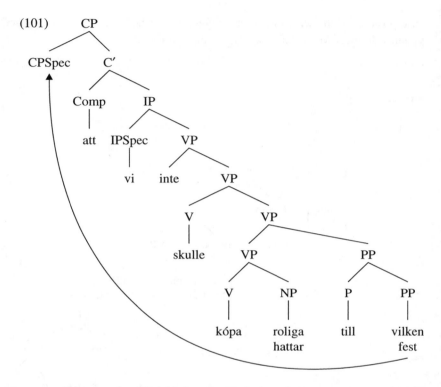

Long extraction out of topic-initial embedded clauses is as ungrammatical in Icelandic as it is in Mainland Scandinavian (compare (102b) with (99c)), even for speakers who otherwise freely allow embedded topicalization.[33] Long extraction out of subject-initial embedded V2 clauses on the other hand is grammatical in Icelandic, whereas it is ungrammatical in Mainland Scandinavian (compare (102a) with (99b)). The examples are again taken from Holmberg (1986).

(102) a. Hvaða bók sagðir þu að Jón   vildi   ekki gefa Haraldi?
            which book said   you that J.(NOM) wanted not give H.(DAT)
       b. *Hvaða bók sagðir þu að Haraldi vildi   Jón   ekki gefa?
            which book said   you that H.(Dat) wanted J.(NOM) not give
            'Which book did you say that John didn't want to give to Harald?'   (Icelandic, Holmberg 1986, ex. 4(86a, b))

Given the discussion around the Swedish examples above, the grammaticality of long extraction in (102a) strongly suggests that Icelandic subject-initial embedded V2 clauses have a structure without CP-recursion in which the subject remains in SpecIP, leaving SpecCP open for wh-movement. The finite verb that follows the subject and precedes negation then surfaces in Infl (cf. (103), the structure of (102a)). In Icelandic subject-initial embedded V2 clauses, there is then no CP-recursion and V2 takes place inside IP, contra the Uniform CP Analysis.

(103)

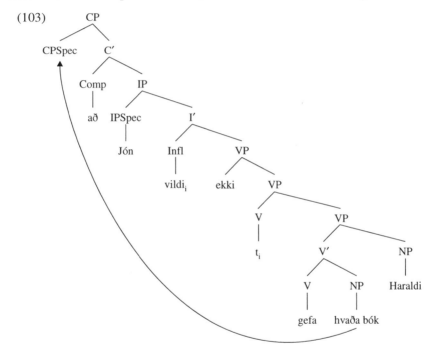

If we assume a fleshed-out clause structure for Icelandic with AgrSP, TP and AgrOP, the grammaticality of (102a) is in principle compatible with an analysis according to which embedded verb movement stops in AgrO or Tense instead of moving to the highest inflectional head, AgrS. Although such an analysis has to my knowledge never been proposed, I want to quickly show that it could not be maintained.

The distribution of Object Shift in Icelandic shows that the verb moves at least to Tense (i.e. past AgrO and thus farther than in Mainland Scandinavian) when it does not move all the way to Comp. As in Mainland Scandinavian (cf. (77)), movement of pronominal objects to the immediate left of sentential negation and adverbs is more or less obligatory in Icelandic main clauses where the main verb is the highest verb (cf. (104)). A comparison of the examples in (104) with those in (77) reveals that unlike Mainland Scandinavian, Icelandic allows optional Object Shift of full NPs, a difference that will be addressed in Section 5.4. What is crucial here is another difference: Whereas Object Shift in embedded clauses that are not the complements of bridge verbs is impossible in Mainland Scandinavian (cf. (79b)), it is possible in Icelandic (cf. (105)). Given the discussion of the ungrammatical Swedish example (79b) and its structure in (87), the verb must move at least as far as Tense in the grammatical Icelandic example (105b) (where, as we have just shown, it does not move all the way to Comp) in order to make SpecTP and SpecAgrOP equidistant from SpecVP and allow movement of the subject from SpecVP across the object in SpecAgrOP to SpecTP and ultimately to SpecAgrSP where it must check Case and agreement.

(104) a. Jón keypti ekki bókina/ ?*hann.
           J. bought not book-the/it
       b. Jón keypti bókina/ hann ekki.
           J. bought book-the/it   not
           'John didn't buy the book/it.'

(105) a. Það var gott að Jón keypti ekki bókina/ ?*hann.
           it was good that J. bought not book-the/it
       b. Það var gott að Jón keypti bókina/ hann ekki.
           it was good that J. bought book-the/it   not
           'It was good that John didn't buy the book/it.'
                              (Icelandic, Holmberg 1986, ex. 6(172a–d))

It is harder to come by clear evidence showing that the verb moves past Tense to AgrS, but I think the following sentence (inspired by an example from Rögnvaldsson 1984 and constructed with the help of Jóhannes Jónsson) provides such evidence.

(106) Þessa bók tel   ég að það hafi sumir menn ekki lesið.
       this book believe I that there have some men not read
       'I believe that some men haven't read this book'   (Icelandic)

Let us make the reasonable assumptions that the indefinite subject *sumir menn* in (106) is in a specifier position and not, for example, adjoined to VP, and that this specifier cannot not be SpecAgrOP since at LF, the object or its trace must occupy this specifier in order for the object agreement features to be checked. Moreover, the expletive subject *það* must be in the specifier of an inflectional projection (i.e. an A-specifier) since it does not block long topicalization.[34] Taken together, this means that the expletive is in SpecAgrSP and the indefinite Subject is in SpecTP. It follows that the finite verb between the expletive and the indefinite subject is in AgrS. We arrive at the following structure for (106).

(107)

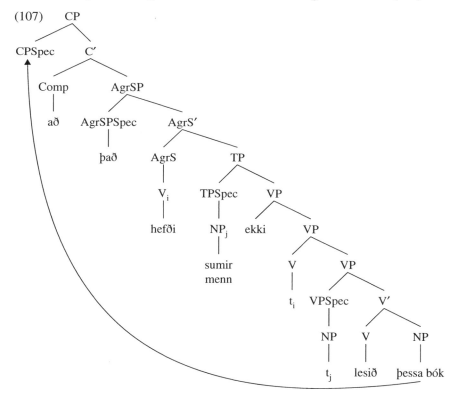

(107) thus constitutes positive evidence that the finite verb moves to the highest inflectional head in at least some Icelandic subject-initial embedded clauses. In the absence of evidence to the contrary, I will assume that V to I raising occurs in fact in all Icelandic finite clauses.

Let us now turn to topic-initial embedded V2 clauses. The ungrammaticality

of long extraction in (102b) can be straightforwardly explained if this sentence
has (nearly) the same structure as its Swedish counterpart in (99c), namely (100),
i.e. if all Icelandic topic-initial embedded clauses necessarily involve CP-
recursion with topic- and verb-movement to the lower SpecCP and Comp,
respectively. The Uniform IP Analysis can account for the contrast in (102) if
SpecIP counts as an A-specifier when occupied by the subject and as an A'-
specifier when occupied by a topic. We will however see in the next section that
in Yiddish, extraction is possible not only from subject-initial, but also from
topic-initial embedded V2 clauses. The Uniform IP Analysis cannot explain this
fact if a topic in SpecIP turns this specifier into an A'-position and the embedded
clause into an island for extraction.

It seems that the Mixed IP/CP analysis is best suited for the Icelandic data.
All subject-initial embedded V2 clauses are simple CPs with visible V to I
raising and all topic-initial embedded V2 clauses involve CP-recursion with verb
movement to Comp. What is most important here is that there is empirical
evidence that Icelandic has V to I raising or verb movement to the highest
inflectional node.

Positioning the highest embedded verb to the left of sentential negation and
adverbs is not restricted to finite clauses, but is also possible in some infinitival
clauses, i.e. the complements of control verbs (cf. (108)) and epistemic modals
(cf. (109)). In the complements of root modals, this order is excluded (cf. (110a),
but this fact may not say anything about verb raising, since these clauses do not
allow adverbs to adjoin to the left of VP (cf. (110b)) and require them instead to
adjoin to the right (cf. (110c)). All of the infinitival constructions mentioned so
far share the presence of the infinitival marker *að*. Bare infinitival clauses that do
not exhibit this marker like Exceptional Case Marking (cf. (111)) or raising verbs
(cf. (112)) never allow the verb to precede sentential negation or adverbs.

(108) a.   María lofaði   að *lesa ekki* bókina.
             M.   promised to read not   book-the
       b. *María lofaði   að *ekki lesa* bókina
             M.   promised to not   read book-the
             'Mary promised not to read the book.'

                                                        (Icelandic, Hornstein 1990)

(109) Ég kann að *elda ekki* mat.
      I   may to cook not food
      'It is possible that I won't cook.'
                                   (Icelandic, Sigurjónsdottir 1988, ex. (34a))

(110) a. *Risgarnir eiga   að *éta oft*   ríkisstjórnir.
           giants-the ought to eat frequently governments
      b. *Risgarnir eiga   að *oft*   *éta* ríkisstjórnir.
           giants-the ought to frequently eat governments
      c. Risgarnir eiga   að *éta* ríkisstjórnir *oft*.
           giants   ought to eat governments frequently
           'The giants should frequently eat governments.'
                    (Thráinsson 1993, ex. (27d), (i) from fn. 21 & (28))

(111) a. Ég talði   Mariu   *alltaf lesa*   bókina.
           I   believed M.(ACC) always read(INF) the-books
      b. *Ég talði   Mariu   *lesa   alltaf* bókina.
           I   believed M.(ACC) read(INF) always books-the
                           (Icelandic, Hornstein 1990)

(112) *Jón virðist lesa   *hægt* bókina.
     J.   seems read(INF) slowly the-book
     'John seems to read the book slowly.'
                         (Icelandic, Jónsson 1991b, ex. (9a))

If the infinitival marker *að* is located in Comp as claimed in Sigurjónsdóttir (1989) or a clitic generated in the highest inflectional head and the post-verbal position of the negation marker in (108a) and (109) indicates verb movement to that highest inflectional head, these example are problematic for the theory in Pollock (1989) according to which such movement is excluded from infinitivals. This was first pointed out in Hornstein (1990). Conversely, if raising complements include inflectional projections and if the ungrammaticality of (112) indicates that the verb has not moved to the lowest inflectional projection, this example is again problematic for Pollock's theory since it predicts such movement to be possible in all languages with verb movement to the highest inflectional head in finite clauses. This was first pointed out in Johnson (1992b). But (108a), (109) and (112) do not have to be analyzed this way. Thráinsson (1993) argues that the infinitival marker is a free morpheme (blocking adjunction to it) generated in AgrS in control complements and in Tense in root modal complements and that the non-finite verb therefore raises only to Tense in control complements while it does not leave VP at all in root modal complements. The absence of the infinitival marker in the complements of ECM and raising verbs suggests that these clauses do not contain (all) functional projections. Overall, the correct analysis of Icelandic infinitives is an issue that is far from resolved. Either Icelandic infinitives undergo 'short' verb movement to Tense only, in which case they fall outside the scope of this work (cf. the case of French infinitives discussed in Section 5.2.2; see in particular note 4), or they undergo 'long' verb movement to AgrS, in which case they do so by virtue of the infinitival marker being part of a full affixal paradigm (cf. the case of Italian infinitives discussed in Section 5.2.2; see in particular note 3).

2.4.2.5 *Yiddish*
Yiddish has obligatory Verb Second in both subject- and topic-initial embedded clauses that are not the complements of asserted bridge verbs, cf. (11a) repeated below as (113a) and (13a) and (14a) repeated below as (114a, b). Embedded topicalization is freer (i.e. fully acceptable to most if not all speakers) in Yiddish than it is in Icelandic.

(113) a. Avrom bedoyert az Max *shikt* nit avek dem briv.
           A.   regrets   that M.   send not away the letter
       b. *Avrom bedoyert az Max nit *avekshikt*   dem briv.
           A.   regrets   that M.   not away-sends the letter
           'Abraham regrets that Max doesn't mail the letter'

(114) a. Es iz a shod   vos hayntike tsaytn *kenen* azoy fil   mentshn
           it is a shame that today's   times can   so   many people
           afile nit leyenen.
           even not read
       b. *Es iz a shod   vos hayntike tsaytn azoy fil   mentshn *kenen*
           it is a shame that today's   times so   many people can
           afile nit leyenen.
           even not read
           'It is a shame that nowadays so many people can't even read.'   (Yiddish)

Unlike Icelandic, Yiddish allows extraction not only from subject-initial, but also from topic-initial embedded Verb Second clauses and it does so even where the embedded clause is not the complement of an asserted bridge verb.[35] Compare the contrast between the Icelandic examples in (102) with the absence of a similar contrast between the Yiddish examples in (115).

(115) a. Vemen   hot er nit gevolt az mir   zoln di
        who(DAT) has he not wanted that we(NOM) should the
        bikher   gebn?
        books(ACC) give

     b. Vemen   hot er nit gevolt az ot   di bikher   zoln
        who(DAT) has he not wanted that PART the books(ACC) should
        mir   gebn?
        we(NOM) give
        'Who didn't he want that we should give the books?'
        (Yiddish, Diesing 1990, ex. (30))

The same type of reasoning that surrounded the Swedish examples in (99b,c) and the Icelandic examples in (102) leads me to reject the Uniform CP and Mixed IP/CP Analyses for Yiddish and adopt instead the Uniform IP Analysis for this language. In other words, I take it that the Yiddish examples in (113a) and (114a) share a structure that resembles the one in (97) and has visible V to I raising. This proposal was already made on essentially the same grounds in Diesing (1990). Diesing assumes that in (115b), the topic-filled specifier of the embedded IP is an A'-position, but in this case it should constitute a target position for wh- and other A'-movement. Since SpecCP and SpecIP are non-equidistant from the indirect object, wh-movement of the latter across the topic in SpecIP to the embedded (and ultimately the matrix) SpecCP should be blocked as a violation of Shortest Move. Since the movement in question is in fact possible, SpecIP must be an A-position even when filled by a topic. I assume that all specifiers that are potential sites for Case-checking or theta-assignment are A-positions and that only specifiers that are never sites for Case-checking or theta-assignment are A'-positions. According to this assumption, the embedded SpecIP in (115b) is an A-position as required.

In this section, I have presented arguments (parasitic on those from the previous section) to the effect that Yiddish shows overt V to I raising in embedded clauses.[36]

2.5 Conclusion

The main goal of this chapter was to establish in which Germanic languages V
to I raising or verb movement to the highest inflectional head occurs. The
findings in this respect are summarized for the convenience of the reader in
Table 2.3.

Table 2.3: *V to I raising in the Germanic languages*

	D-structure		S-structure	
	I^Neg^V^O	Neg^O^V^I	**V to I**	**V in Situ**
Yiddish	✓		✓	
Icelandic	✓		✓	
Faroese	✓			✓
Mld. Sc.	✓			✓
English	✓			✓
German/Dutch		✓	?	?

Notes

1. I am abstracting from certain grammatical cases of V1. In Icelandic 'Narrative Inversion' for
   example, the finite verb can introduce a matrix clause containing a 'topical', definite NP
   (cf. (i)). The fact that Narrative Inversion is excluded from embedded clauses (cf. (ii)) indicates
   that, like matrix V2, it involves verb movement to Comp. See Sigurðsson (1990) for a
   discussion of this construction.

   (i)   *Kom* Ólafur seint heim.
         came O.   late home
         'Olaf came home late.'

   (ii) *Ég vissi ekki að *færu* skipin   til Grænlands.
         I knew not that went ships-the to Greenland
         'I didn't know that the ships went to Greenland.'

                                                        (Icelandic, Sigurðsson 1990)

2. Certain adverbs allow V2 in subject-initial clauses, provided that the verb does not take an NP-
   object (cf. (i)). Clauses that start with a quote also allow V2, again with the provision that the
   verb does not take an NP-object (cf. (ii)). See Section 2.4.2.1 for a discussion of these cases.

    (i)   Mary *looked* attentively at the screen.

    (ii)   "I liked the movie", *said* Mary to John.

Topic-initial clauses involving an 'affective' topic show the same residual Verb Second as complement questions (compare (iii) with (6c)).

    (iii)   Under no circumstances *would* Mary watch trashy movies.

3.   Bridge verbs differ from other verbs in that they allow extraction out of their finite sentential complements. Many of the syntactic details vary from dialect to dialect. The following German examples (including judgments) are taken from Grewendorf (1988: 81).

    (i)   a.   Wen, glaubt   Peter, liebt Maria?
               who   believes P.   loves Mary
         b.   [?]Wen, glaubt   Peter, daß Maria liebt?
               who   believes P.   that M.   loves
               'Who does Peter believe that Mary loves?'

    (ii)   a.   *Wen, weiß   Peter, liebt Maria?
               who   knows P.   loves M.
         b.   *[?]Wen, weiß   Peter, daß Maria liebt?
               who   knows P.   that M.   loves
               'Who does Peter know that Mary loves?'   (German)

Vikner (1995a: 70 fn.7) claims that "there are many bridge verbs in this sense that do not allow sentential complements with V2", though he gives no examples. Below, I will continue to use the term 'bridge verbs' to refer to verbs that allow embedded V2 in all Scandinavian languages.

4.   Dutch allows subject-initial embedded V2 only with a sub-set of the bridge verbs, namely verbs of saying (cf. Weerman 1989). Thus although (7h) is grammatical, (i) is not.

    (i)   *Jan geloofde Marie *zou*   naar huis gaan.
         J.   believed M.   would to   home go
         'John believed that Mary would go home.'   (Dutch, Peter Ackema, p.c.)

A similar restriction in Norwegian might be the reason why Taraldsen (1986) judges (7f) to be only marginally acceptable.

5.   A few cautionary notes are in order. First, judgments on non-bridge verb embedded topicalization in Icelandic range from perfect to ungrammatical. Thus (11b) is perfect according to Vikner's (1995a) informants while Jónsson (1991a) finds this sentence "a lot worse" than its counterpart with an asserted bridge verb in the matrix clause. Ottóson (1991) observes that Yiddish allows embedded topicalization more freely than Icelandic, cf. his examples (11a, b) reproduced below in (i).

    (i)   a.   Ikh veys nit tsi ot   dos bukh hot er geleyent.
               I   know not if PART that book has he read   (Yiddish)
         b.   *Ég veit ekki hvort þá bók hefur hann lesið.
               I   know not if   that book has he   read
               'I don't know if he has read that book.'   (Icelandic)

Second, Richard Kayne (p.c.) points out that the German example in (11c) might involve scrambling instead of topicalization. In that case, none of the languages without V2 in non-bridge verb complements have topicalization in that environment.

Third, some speakers of Faroese seem to at least marginally allow V2 in embedded clauses that are not the complements of asserted bridge verbs (cf. Section 2.4.2.3).

Finally, Reinholtz (1989) is singular in the literature in claiming that V2 generalizes to (almost) all embedded clauses in Danish, cf. her example in (ii) with V2 in an extraposed sentential subject.

> (ii) Det var en overraskelse at paa det punkt *var* de slet ikke uenige.
> it   was a surprise   that on that point were they at all not disagreed
> 'It was a surprise that on that issue, they didn't disagree at all.'

(Danish, Reinholtz 1989, ex. (7h))

Vikner (1995a) also finds (ii) acceptable but notes that the sentence becomes much worse without embedded topicalization (cf. (iii) = Vikner 1995a, ex. 4(170b)) and that examples like (iv) (= Vikner 1995a, ex. 4(160a)) do not improve under topicalization (cf. (v) = Vikner 1995a, ex. 4(161a)).

> (iii) ??Det var en overraskelse at de *var* slet ikke uenige paa det punkt.
> it   was a surprise   that they were at all not disagreed on that point
> 'It was a surprise that they didn't disagree on this issue at all.'   (Danish)

> (iv) *Hun bekræftede at hann *kunne* ikke have begået   den forbrydelsen.
> he   confirmed that she could not have committed that crime   (Danish)

> (v) *Hun bekræftede at den forbrydelsen *kunne* hann ikke have begået.
> he   confirmed that that crime   could she not have committed
> 'He confirmed that she could not have committed that crime.'   (Danish)

In spite of the yet to be explained relative acceptability of (ii), Danish then does not in general allow V2 in subordinate clauses that are not the complements of asserted bridge verbs.

6. According to Richard Kayne (p.c.), (i) is better than (15b):

> (i) I was shocked by Mary's claim that under no circumstances would she watch artsy movies.

It is not clear to me what is responsible for this difference, if it indeed exists. See note 32 for further discussion.

7. Alternatively, V2 has been analyzed as V to I raising and XP to SpecIP movement in both topic- and subject-initial clauses (e.g. von Stechow & Sternefeld 1988, for German, Travis 1988; Rögnvaldsson & Thráinsson 1990 and Kosmeijer 1991 for Icelandic and Diesing 1990 for Yiddish) and as V to I raising and XP to SpecIP movement in subject-initial and V movement to Comp and XP movement to SpecCP in topic-initial clauses (e.g. Ottóson 1989 and Hornstein 1991 for Icelandic and Travis 1984 and Zwart 1991).

8. Travis (1984) argues the verb must move to matrix Comp in order to eliminate an ungoverned empty category, a violation of the Empty Category Principle (ECP). Taraldsen (1986), citing Kayne (1982), claims that matrix clauses, being non-arguments, have to be headed by a non-

nominal elements such as verbs and that embedded clauses, being arguments, have to be headed by nominal elements such as complementizers. A similar theory is developed in Holmberg (1986). Rizzi (1990b) and Kosmeijer (1991) propose that (V to) I to C movement occurs to let the tense specification c-command (cf. note 13) the event feature [+I] in matrix Comp (Rizzi) or the subject in SpecIP (Kosmeijer). Anderson (1993: 89) maintains that "the principle involved [in V2] is the same as that which I suggested motivates clitic placement: Locate the formal reflection of a linguistic unit's relational properties by reference to a prominent position in that unit (here, immediately following the initial constituent)." For an overview over Verb Second explanations, see Vikner (1995a: 51–64)).

9. I take distinctness to be a symmetric and transitive relation: If X is distinct from Y, Y is distinct from X and if X is distinct from Y and Y is distinct from Z, X is distinct from Z.

10. I assume that each substitution and each adjunction count as one step in the derivation.

11. Other arguments concerning V to I Raising in the Germanic OV languages such as those involving the position and scope of adverbial PPs (cf. Reuland 1990; Haider 1993; Sabel 1994; and Neeleman 1996) either base themselves on questionable judgments or rely heavily on theory-internal assumptions. In the interest of space, I will refrain from discussing them here.

12. If it is instead assumed that extraposition adjoins the relative clause to the highest VP in (34) before the lower VP containing the trace of the extraposed clause is moved to SpecCP and that the resulting ECP-violation is subsequently repaired by adjunction of the extraposed clause to SpecCP (cf. the next paragraph in the main text), then this theory (which requires V in situ) becomes indistinguishable from the theory to be developed below (which allows V to I) and relative clause extraposition no longer bears on the issue of V to I raising. Notice that it cannot be assumed that in (34), the highest VP has been moved to SpecCP (together with the extraposed clause that is adjoined to this VP) after the highest verb has moved to Comp, since this analysis not only violates the ECP, but also fails to derive the word order in (i) where there is no reason to assume that the intermediate verb *wollen* has moved out of the highest VP:

    (i)   Einem Kind helfen das nach Hilfe ruft wird doch wohl jeder   wollen.
          a   child help   that for help calls will PART PART everybody want
          'Everybody would want to help a child that is calling for help.'

13. I am using a definition of c-command according to which A c-commands B iff A excludes B and every branching category that dominates A also dominates B, where a category C dominates D if every segment of C dominates D. In Minimalist terms, the dependency between the extraposed clause and its trace in the topicalized VP violates Superiority (cf. Manzini 1994) in (37) and obeys it in (34) with the structure in (38). The ECP-based analysis in the text can therefore be directly translated into Minimalist terms.

14. (42) is not an exact paraphrase of (41): It reflects the totality- and antisymmetry restriction imposed on linear orderings, but not the transitivity restriction. It is however easy to see that the latter restriction could be omitted from the formal version of the Linear Correspondence Axiom without any practical consequences.

15. The structures in (43) differ from those given in Kayne (1994) in not containing an abstract beginning node. It is easy to show that the assumption of such a node has no consequences for the issue at hand: All it can possibly lead to is the replacement of one stipulation ("asymmetric

c-command translates always into precedence") by two ("there is an abstract beginning node" and "asymmetric c-command translates either always into precedence or always into sub-sequence").

16. Notice that in order to rule in any of the trees in (43), including the desired SVO tree in (43a), Kayne has to assume that specifiers (e.g. subjects) are adjuncts and, more importantly, that simplex (i.e. mono-morphemic) arguments have complex (i.e. multi-leveled) projections. The latter assumption is incompatible with a central axiom of Minimalist theory according to which each level of projection is licit only if it is required to accommodate syntactic material (cf. Chomsky 1995). The Minimalist version of the VP in (43a) given below in (i) does not satisfy the Linear Correspondence Axiom because neither $\langle v,n_2 \rangle$ nor $\langle n_2,v \rangle$ is in d(A). This contradiction between Antisymmetry and Minimalism is often overlooked in attempts to integrate the former into the latter.

(i)
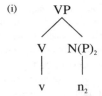

17. The right-headed approach does not face this problem, even in the case of the reordering required by the verb (projection) raising that is possible in some configurations:

   (i)   Die Eltern bedauern,
         the parents regret
         (a)   daß Kaspar seine Suppe nicht essen wollen hat.
               that K.   his   soup not eat   want has
         (b)   daß Kaspar seine Suppe nicht hat essen wollen.
               that K.   his   soup not has eat   want
         'The parents regret that Kaspar didn't want to eat his soup.'

Optional right-adjunction of this type resembles extraposition, a well-established process, and is therefore less problematic than assumption c). The facts of verb (projection) raising are complex (and its details differ in Dutch and German) and cannot be adequately addressed here.

18. Recall that in declarative sentences, English main verbs do not undergo V2, and (i,ii) show that the same is true for English auxiliaries. In (48a), the dummy auxiliary *did* (which is often regarded as a pure realization of inflection) is therefore located in (clause-medial) Infl rather than in Comp.

   (i)   *This movie did Sue not see.

   (ii) This movie Sue did not see.

19. Branagan and Collins (1997) argue that English adverbs attach to AgrOP or higher, an assumption that is incompatible with the analysis of (51a) in (52). Branigan and Collins (1993,

1997) also argue that Quotative Inversion (cf. (i)) should be analyzed as an instance of verb movement to AgrO in English.

    (i)   "I'm so happy", said Mary to John.

Quotative Inversion is restricted to literary English and probably reflects an earlier stage of the language. As such, it cannot be used as an argument for verb movement to AgrO in Modern (colloquial) English. See footnote 3 in Rohrbacher (1994b) for discussion.

20. The exact adjunction site of the extraposed PP is irrelevant with respect to the topic of this section. The concrete choice of AgrSP in (61) should not be mistaken for a theoretical claim, especially in light of the fact that below I will adjoin extraposed PPs to T/AgrOP where this is more convenient.

21. The following remarks grew out of discussions with Michael Hegarty and Tony Kroch.

22. As in the case of extraposition (cf. note 20), the target location of Heavy NP-Shift is irrelevant with respect to the topic of this section and the concrete choice of AgrSP in (73) should not be mistaken for a theoretical claim.

23. The (un)availability of Object Shift in a particular construction has often been linked to the (un)availability of main verb movement in that construction ("Holmberg's Generalization", cf. Holmberg 1986). One piece of evidence that is supposed to show this link is the apparent unavailability of Object Shift in complex tenses where the main verb has not moved to Comp (cf. (i)).

    (i)   a.   Studenterna har   inte läst boken/den.
                  students-the have not read book-the/it
          b.   *Studenterna har   boken/den inte läst.
                  students-the have book-the/it not read
                  'The students haven't read the book/it.'

Zwart (1994) however points out that it is reasonable to assume that in complex tenses, negation and adverbs attach to the higher VP headed by *har* "have" and Object Shift targets an inflectional projection associated with the lower VP headed by *läst* "read". In this case, (ia) may in fact involve Object Shift (as well as short main verb movement), as shown in (ii).

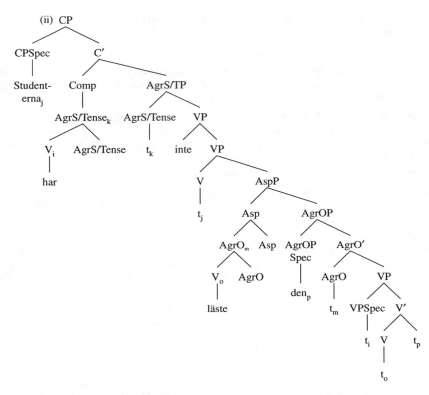

Another piece of evidence that is supposed to show the link between Object Shift and main verb movement is the unavailability of Object Shift in embedded clauses that are not the asserted complements of bridge verbs (cf. (79b)). But as I point out below, within the V in situ analysis this unavailability of Object Shift in embedded clauses is in fact compatible with main verb movement to one of the lower (but not the highest) inflectional head. (Remember that I use the term "V in situ" in this way throughout this book, cf. note 1 of Chapter 1.) There is thus no simple link between the (un)availability of Object Shift and the (un)availability of main verb movement. Holmberg's Generalization can however be restated as a link between the (un)availability of Object Shift and the (un)availability of main verb movement out of the phrase that provides the landing site for Object Shift. See the following discussion for clarification.

24. For the sake of concreteness, (84) and the other structures in this section assume cyclic head movement throughout, but bear in mind the discussion in Section 2.3.

25. In (82) and (83), I have chosen Chomsky's original formulation of Shortest Move rather than Manzini's reformulation in (23)—(25). The difference between the two formulations is immaterial for the argument in the text. If however Object Shift adjoins Mainland Scandinavian

pronominal objects to a phrase such as VP as suggested in note 29 rather than moving them to a specifier such as SpecAgrOP as assumed in the text, then only Chomsky's original formulation but not Manzini's reformulation will yield the desired results. Since the details are of little interest for the matter at hand, I will not discuss them here.

26. The notion "head chain" includes trivial, one-membered head chains formed by unmoved heads in which $\alpha_1 = \alpha_i = \alpha_n$. The notion "reflexively dominates" includes domination of each category in a tree by itself.

27. I would like to stress that the specific assumptions in the main text are made solely in order to facilitate the exposition of the argument. In fact, both are probably incorrect: Adjunction to X′ may be generally ruled out by structure preservation (cf. above) and Mainland Scandinavian may not even have AgrOP, let alone movement to its specifier (cf. sections 3.4 and 5.4). Note 29 recasts the argument in terms of adjunction of both negation and object to VP, and one can think of any number of still different assumptions that would keep the reasoning in the text valid.

28. Unlike subject movement, Object Shift is thus not an absolute requirement that must always be fulfilled, but rather a preferred option that is chosen whenever possible. This situation is problematic within Minimalism (see Zwart 1994 for discussion).

29. In sections 3.4 and 5.4, I adopt a proposal made by Bobalijk (1995) according to which the Mainland Scandinavian languages lack AgrOP. If this is correct, pronominal Object Shift of the kind discussed here cannot target SpecAgrOP. One solution is to adjoin the object pronoun to VP. The argument in the text goes through without changes, provided that the VP-adjoined position counts as a target position for movement of the subject.

30. Beatrice Santorini (p.c.) points out that Verb Second in the complement of degree phrases such as (90b) might have to be analyzed as involving CP-recursion instead of V to I raising, since parallel examples are found in Frisian (cf. (i) from de Haan and Weerman 1986), an OV-language with presumably right-peripheral Infl where embedded V2 cannot be the result of V to I raising alone.

    (i)   Hy is sa meager dat hy kin wol   efter   in reid skûlje.
            he is so skinny that he can PART behind a cane hide
            'He is so skinny that he can hide behind a cane.'   (Frisian)

Note that Frisian does not in general allow CP-recursion outside the complements of asserted bridge verbs. The availability of CP-recursion in the complements of degree phrases is therefore construction-specific and does not motivate a CP-recursion (i.e. non V to I raising) analysis of Verb Second in other Faroese embedded clauses that are not the complements of asserted bridge verbs such as (90a–93a).

31. Icelandic embedded V2 is sometimes obscured by other processes. Thus superficial Verb First is possible with indefinite subjects of passivized or unaccusative verbs. This is shown in (i), where the specifier of the phrase headed by the moved verb (i.e. SpecIP) is presumably occupied by a *pro*.

(i)   Ég efast um   að *verði* ekki keyptar margar bækur.
       I   doubt PART that will be not bought many   books
       'I doubt that many books will not be bought.'   (Icelandic)

Crucially, the verb moves to Infl in all finite embedded clauses, including those displaying V1
(cf. the post-verbal position of the negation marker in (i)).

32. Richard Kayne (p.c.) finds the following English example "fairly acceptable":

     (i)   The person who I think that not once has she told the truth to...

If the fronting of affective elements in English involves topicalization (i.e. movement to
SpecCP) as suggested earlier in the discussion of (15a, b), (i) should have the same status as
(99b,c). Together with the fact that the fronting of affective elements in complementizer-
introduced non-bridge verb complements is sometimes better than expected (cf. (i) in note 6),
the relative acceptability of extraction from clauses with fronted affective elements might be
taken as an indication that the fronting of affective elements involves a mechanism other than
movement to SpecCP.

33. The judgments range from "usually bad" (Rögnvaldsson 1984) over "almost impossible"
     (Rögnvaldsson and Thráinsson 1990) to "clearly blocked" (Jónsson 1991a). Rögnvaldsson
     (1984) finds (i) "reasonably good" and cites it as a counter-example to this generalization.

     (i)   Þessar bækur hélt   ég að þér   myndi ekki nokkur maður   lána.
            these books thought I that you(DAT) would not any   man(NOM) lend
            'I thought nobody would lend you these books.'   (Icelandic)

Holmberg (1986) however points out that here the fronted object pronoun *þer* is probably not
topicalized, but stylistically fronted (i.e. left-adjoined to Infl, cf. Jónsson 1991). Stylistic
Fronting is licensed in (i) by the subject gap which results from leaving the indefinite subject
in its d-structure position in SpecVP. According to this analysis, the embedded clause in (i) has
the structure in (ii) and the example does not cause a problem for the generalization that long
extraction from topic-initial embedded clauses is ungrammatical in Icelandic.

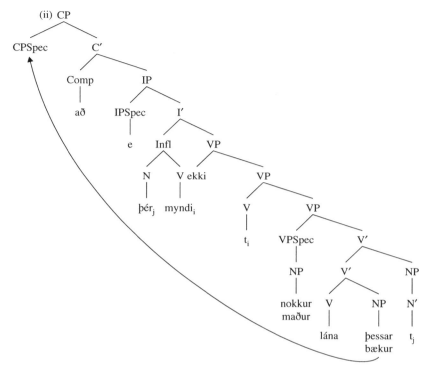

Surprisingly, long topicalization out of wh-islands (cf. (iii) = Jónsson 1991a, ex. (19)) is only "mildly ungrammatical" according to Jónsson (1991a) and hence much more acceptable than long wh-extraction out of a topic-island (cf. (102b)).

(iii) ?Mariu   veit ég hvaða hring Ólafur   lofaði.
       M.(DAT) know I which ring O.(NOM) promised
       'I know which ring Olaf promised to Mary.'   (Icelandic)

Jónsson assumes that in (102b), the higher of the two recursively embedded CPs does not have a specifier and long extraction crosses two CP-barriers, resulting in a strong subjacency violation. In (iii), there is only one embedded CP and crossing it results only in a weak subjacency violation. Recasting this explanation for the difference between (102b) and (iii) in Minimalist terms is a non-trivial matter which I will not address here.

34. Thráinsson (1992) argues that *það* is in fact never in SpecCP and always in SpecAgrSP since (among other things) it occurs more freely in embedded clauses than topicalization (cf. Magnússon 1990). See also Hornstein (1991).

35. According to Lisa Travis (p.c.), extraction from topic-initial embedded V2 clauses is possible in Yiddish only if the topicalized element is an adverb or if it is accompanied by the particle *ot*. The latter case is illustrated in (115b).

36. Geilfuß (1990) argues that Yiddish is an OV and not, as assumed here, a VO languages. His argument is based on the alternation in (i) (= Geilfuß 1990, ex. (2a, b)) and others like it.

>   (i)   a.   matones zaynen gevorn gebrakht.
>   presents are   became brought
>   b.   matones zaynen gebrakht gevorn
>   presents are   brought became
>   'Presents have been brought.'   (Yiddish)

Geilfuß derives the $V_1V_2V_3$ order in (ia) (typical of VO languages) from an underlying $V_3V_2V_1$ order (typical of OV languages) with the help of V2–style finite verb movement to Comp of V_1 and non-finite Verb (Projection) Raising of V_3 to the right of V_2. In (ib), verb movement to Comp but not Verb Raising has applied and the example thus reveals the underlying clause-final position of verbs. But Geilfuß also notes that in Yiddish, Verb Raising is obligatory except with the verb *vern* "become". In other words, the OV-typical $V_1V_3V_2$ order in (ib) optionally surfaces only where V_3 is a form of one particular verb and the VO-typical $V_1V_2V_3$ order in (ia) obligatorily surfaces where V_3 is a form of any other verb. In my view, this severely weakens Geilfuß' argument. But even if Yiddish is in fact underlyingly OV, there is still no question that Yiddish Infl is generated clause-medially (as in the VO-language Icelandic) and not clause-finally (as in the OV-language German) and that Yiddish has V to I raising. To see this, reconsider (113a) and (115). The post-verbal position of the negation marker *nit* to the left of the separable verb particle *avek* shows that negation is adjoined to the left of VP and that the verb *shikt* has moved out of VP in (113a). The grammaticality of extraction from embedded clauses shows that the embedded subject or topic is in SpecIP and not SpecCP and therefore that the verb is in Infl and not Comp in (115).

CHAPTER 3

Agreement Morphology in the Syntax and the Lexicon

3.1 Introduction

The previous chapter established that in the absence of V to C movement, Yiddish and Icelandic move the finite verb out of VP into Infl (or AgrS, the highest inflectional head), whereas English, standard Faroese and the Mainland Scandinavian languages Swedish, Danish and Norwegian leave the verb in situ inside VP. In Section 3.2 below, these facts constitute the background for a discussion of several previously proposed theories of V to I raising which correlate this type of movement with properties of negation (cf. Section 3.2.1), Case marking (cf. Section 3.2.2) and number agreement (cf. Section 3.2.3). Various shortcomings of these theories lead me to reject them and to focus instead on the central role of person agreement: V to I raising occurs in exactly those languages which distinctively mark the person features [1ST] and [2ND] in either the singular or the plural of at least one tense (cf. Section 3.3). This descriptive generalization then serves as the point of departure for the development of an explanatory theory of V to I raising: All and only those languages that minimally distinctively mark both referential agreement features have lexically listed agreement affixes which syntactically project AgrSP and trigger verb movement to the head of this projection (cf. Section 3.4). The chapter closes with some speculative remarks concerning residual V to I raising in Faroese (cf. Section 3.5).

3.2 Previous Accounts for V to I Raising

3.2.1 *Negation (Ouhalla 1990, 1991; Benmamoun 1991)*

According to Pollock (1989), the negation marker (e.g. English *not*) is a syntactic head (Neg) that projects a phrase of its own (NegP) which intervenes between IP and VP. Ouhalla (1990, 1991) and Benmamoun (1991) point out that in this case, the Head Movement Constraint of Travis (1984) prescribes that head movement from a position α below Neg (e.g. V) to a landing site β above Neg (e.g. Infl) cannot proceed in one step, crossing Neg (as in (1a)) and must instead be broken up into two steps, with Neg functioning as an intermediate landing site (as in (1b)).

(1)   a.

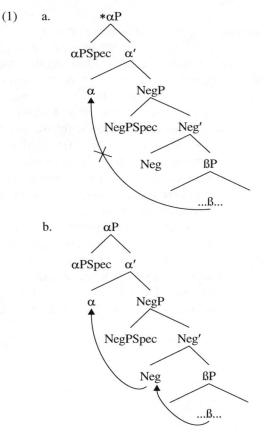

   b.

The structures in (1a) and (1b) have all the relevant properties of the structures in (18) and (19) of Chapter 2. The same reason that rules out direct head movement of the verb to Comp across Infl in (18) of Chapter 2 also rules out direct head movement of β to α across Neg in (1a) above: This movement violates both the ECP (because it crosses NegP, a barrier by virtue of having a head that is distinct from α; cf. (20,21) of Chapter 2) and Shortest Move (because it puts α and β in non-adjacent minimal domains separated by the minimal domain of Neg; cf. (23–25) of Chapter 2). Just like head movement of the verb must land in Infl on its way to Comp as in (19) of Chapter 2, head movement of β must land in Neg on its way to α as in (1b) above: This movement satisfies both the ECP (because no movement step crosses a barrier) and Shortest Move (because each movement step involves adjacent minimal domains).[1]

Ouhalla and Benmamoun assume that head movement may land in Neg (or any other X^0 position) only when the latter is filled by a bound morpheme or altogether empty, but not when it is filled by a free morpheme. Given what was said above, the grammaticality or ungrammaticality of V to I raising in a certain language now follows (at least in negated clauses) from the realization of Neg through a bound or free morpheme in that language. Thus V to I raising is grammatical in languages like French, where negation is a bound morpheme and Neg is therefore available as an intermediate landing site for verb movement (cf. the sentence in (2a) and its structure in (2b), an instance of (1b)). V to I raising is on the other hand ungrammatical in languages like English, where negation is a free morpheme[2] and verb movement would have to cross over Neg and move directly to Infl (cf. the sentence in (3a) and its structure in (3b), an instance of (1a)).

(2)   a.   Jean n'**aime**   *pas*   Marie.
        J.   NEG-likes PART M.
        'John doesn't like Mary.'   (French)

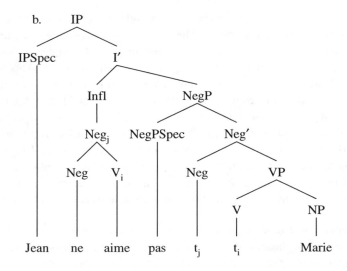

(3)   a. *John **likes** *not* Mary.

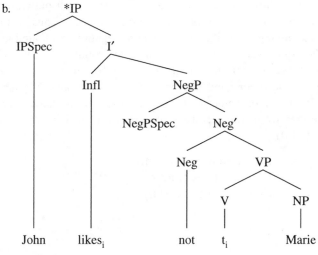

This explanation for V to I in French versus V in situ in English however does not carry over to affirmative clauses, where a similar contrast exists even though negation is absent:[3]

(4) a. Marie **embrasse** *souvent* Jeanette.
         M.   embraces often   J.   (French)
     b. Mary *often* **embraces** Jean.

Even though it is sometimes argued that English main verbs raise out of VP to some lower inflectional head it has as far as I know never been proposed that they raise to the highest inflectional head in affirmative clauses (cf. Section 2.4.2.1). French affirmative clauses on the other hand are standardly assumed to involve verb movement to the highest inflectional head (cf. Section 5.2.2). Ouhalla therefore assumes that in affirmatives, the relative 'richness' of agreement (in the sense of sections 3.2.3 and 3.3 below) determines the position of the verb. But in this case, it is unclear why 'richness' of agreement does not suffice to account for the position of the verb in negated sentences, too. To prove that the status of negation as a free or bound morpheme plays a role in the licensing V to I raising, one would have to adduce a language which is like French in that it has 'rich' agreement while at the same time being like English in having a free negation marker between IP and VP. Such a language would be expected by Ouhalla's theory to exhibit V to I raising in non-negated sentences and V in situ in negated sentences. I am not aware of any language that unequivocally meets this description.[4]

In addition, there are other empirical problem with Ouhalla's and Benmamoun's theory. Thus Icelandic and Yiddish exhibit V to I raising (cf. Chapter 2) although negation is a free morpheme which is not bound by the verb, as shown for example by the fact that in question sentences like those in (5), the subject may intervene between the verb and the negation marker after movement of the verb to Comp.

(5) a. **Þekki** Jón *ekki* Ingiríði?
         knows J. not I.
         'Doesn't John know Ingrid?'
                                            (Icelandic, Holmberg 1986, ex. 4(3a))
     b. Far vos **shmekt** ir *nit* dos esn?
         why tastes her not the food
         'Why has she lost her appetite?'
                               (Yiddish, based on Santorini 1989, ex. (24b) & (45c))

Ouhalla's and Benmamoun's account can be maintained if we assume that like French *pas* but unlike English *not*, Icelandic *ekki* and Yiddish *nit* are in fact the specifier and not the head of NegP. Icelandic and Yiddish Neg then remains

empty at D-structure and is hence available for verb raising through it at S-structure (cf. (6), the S-structure of (5a)).

(6)

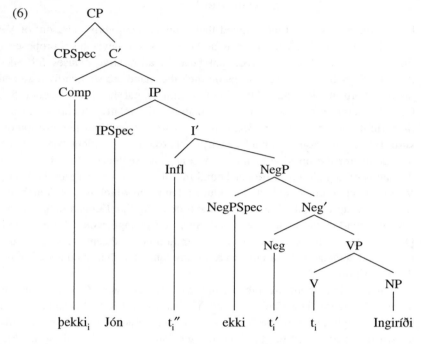

But now the following problem arises with respect to Mainland Scandinavian.
Like Icelandic and Yiddish, Mainland Scandinavian also has verb movement to
Comp despite the fact that negation is realized by a free morpheme. To see this,
compare the Icelandic example in (5a) with its entirely parallel Swedish counterpart in (7).

(7)   **Känner** Johan *inte* Ingrid?
       knows   J.   not   I.
       'Doesn't John know Ingrid?'

                                        (Swedish, Holmberg 1986, ex. (2a))

In order for Ouhalla's and Benmamoun's story to go through, we have to assume
that in Swedish, too, the negation marker *inte* is base-generated in SpecNegP and
V to C raising makes a stop-over in the underlyingly empty Neg. On the basis
of this assumption, we however wrongly predict that Swedish should allow V to

I raising. In other words, if sentence (7) has an S-structure that is, with the exception of the terminal string, identical to the one in (6), then the grammatical S-structure in (9) should be available for the in fact ungrammatical embedded clause in (8a). The actually attested word order is given in (8b) for comparison.

(8)   a.   *Jag beklagar att   jag **träffade** *inte* henne.
             I   regret   that I   met   not her
             'I regret that I didn't meet her.'
        b.   Jag beklagar att jag *inte* **träffade** henne
                                     (Swedish, based on Holmberg 1986, ex. (19cd))

(9)

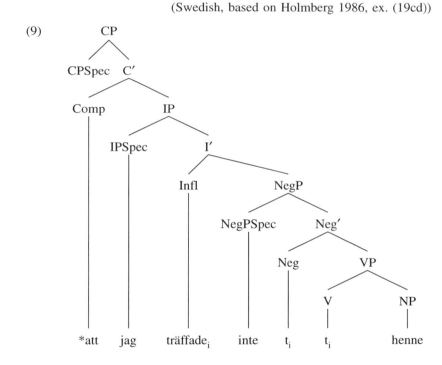

It will not do to assume that Mainland Scandinavian and Icelandic instantiate different settings of Ouhalla's Neg Parameter in (10). If Icelandic negation selects VP as shown in (6) whereas Swedish negation selects IP as shown in (11), then V to I raising results in the correct order of verb and negation in both languages, i.e. V^*ekki* in Icelandic and *inte*^V in Mainland Scandinavian embedded clauses that are not the complements of asserted bridge-verbs. But if

NegP dominates IP in Mainland Scandinavian, the subject in SpecIP is predicted
to follow the negation marker in SpecNegP (cf. (11)), contrary to fact (cf. (8b)).[5]

(10)   Neg Parameter
       i.   Neg c[ategory]-selects VP
       ii.   Neg c-selects Agr/Tense [=Infl]   (Ouhalla 1991: 138)

(11)   CP

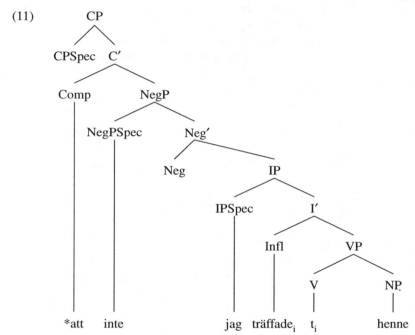

It is at least possible that in Mainland Scandinavian, the filled specifier of NegP
prevents Comp from governing and assigning Nominative Case to the subject in
SpecIP, thus triggering adjunction of the subject to NegP and resulting in the
correct word order. But Ouhalla's theory has at least two other drawbacks.

       First, this theory attributes the difference in Scandinavian embedded word
order to a difference in parameter setting that is, in the case of Scandinavian, not
independently motivated. Ouhalla's claims to the contrary notwithstanding, the
Neg Parameter does not "provide us with a principled motivation for base-
generating Neg in different positions" (Ouhalla 1991: 138); instead, it merely
describes this variation. This is generally the fate of parameters in the Principles

and Parameters framework: they describe that which cannot be explained in a principled way. Surely it would be preferable to be able to give a more explanatory account for the problem at hand. In Section 3.4, I will propose that V to I occurs in languages that have separate lexical entries for their agreement affixes and that V in situ occurs in languages that do not have separate lexical entries for their agreement affixes. I will further claim that the choice between these two options is not parametrically governed, but follows from the (in-) ability of the agreement affixes to refer (depending on the (non-) distinctive marking of the referential agreement features [1ST] and [2ND]) in conjunction with the characterization of the lexicon as a list of referential elements.

Second, Ouhalla's theory does not extend to Scandinavian embedded affirmative clauses that are not the complements of asserted bridge-verbs and that exhibit essentially the same differences as negative clauses (i.e. post-verbal adverbs or V to I raising in Icelandic (cf. (95) of Chapter 2) versus pre-verbal adverbs or V in-situ in Mainland Scandinavian (cf. (75) of Chapter 2). Like the analogous contrast between French and English affirmatives (cf. (4)), this difference makes it unlikely that the status of negation as a free or bound morpheme plays a role in V to I raising.[6] A unified explanation for V to I raising in both negative and affirmative sentences is clearly desirable. In Section 3.4, I will show that such a unified theory is in fact possible.

What emerges is that Ouhalla's and Benmamoun's Theory cannot handle the Scandinavian data in a satisfactory fashion. It is therefore unlikely that the status of the negation marker (or other markers) as either a free or a bound morpheme, a head or a specifier, plays a role in the licensing of V to I raising.

3.2.2 Case (Trosterud 1989)

Trosterud (1989) argues that the presence of overt morphological nominative Case-marking in Icelandic (cf. (12a) from Haugen 1976) and the absence of this marking in Mainland Scandinavian (cf. (12b) based on Haugen 1976 and James Cathey, p.c.) explains why V to I raising is possible in Icelandic and impossible in Mainland Scandinavian.

(12)   a.   Icelandic   b.   Swedish
              arm- 'arm'   *arm-* 'arm'
              (MASC CLASS 1)   (MASC CLASS 1)

	SG	PL	SG	PL
NOM	arm-ur	arm-ar	arm	arm-ar
ACC	arm	arm-a	arm	arm-ar
DAT	arm-i	örm-um	arm	arm-ar
GEN	arm-s	arm-a	arm-s	arm-ar-s

Trosterud assumes that phonetically realized NPs need either overt morphological case or abstract Case, and that nominative Case is assigned by the finiteness feature [+F]. This feature, which can be located either in Comp or in Infl,[7] functions as an event operator and must therefore bind an appropriate (i.e. event-) variable such as the trace of V or Infl. Let us consider these options in turn. I will focus on embedded clauses where verb movement to Comp is impossible, since only these are relevant in our context.

If the finiteness feature [+F] is located in Infl, the operator-variable relation is created by V to I raising: After this movement, Infl and the verb trace t_i are non-distinct (in the sense of (21) in Chapter 2) and [+F] in Infl can hence properly bind t_i. At the same time, Agr in Infl absorbs the abstract nominative Case from [+F] and this Case can no longer be assigned to the subject in SpecIP which must therefore bear whatever overt morphological case is available in this position. It follows that [+F] can be located in Infl only in languages like Icelandic which have overt morphological nominative case. All this is indicated in (13), the schematic S-structure that Trosterud's theory would assign to an Icelandic embedded clause that is not the complement of an asserted bridge verb.

(13)

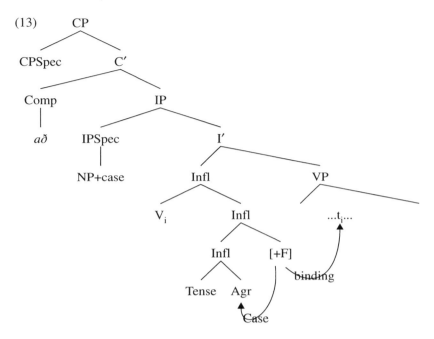

If, on the other hand, [+F] is located in Comp (which is the only option for languages like Mainland Scandinavian without overt morphological nominative Case), V to I raising results in ungrammaticality: The event operator [+F] in Comp cannot establish an operator-variable relation with the verb trace t_i in VP because t_i is already bound by the verb in Infl (cf. (14)), and no other potential variable is at hand.

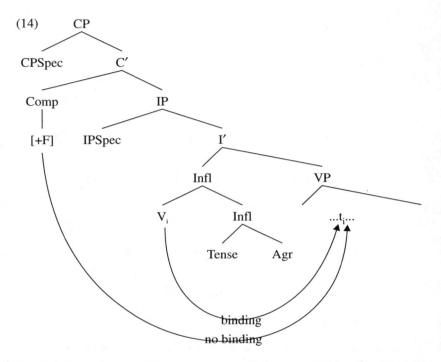

The remaining option, [+F] in Comp in combination with V in situ and Infl-lowering, does not give rise to similar problems: The event operator [+F] in Comp can establish the required operator-variable relation with t_i, the as yet unbound trace of the lowered Infl. Moreover, [+F] can assign abstract nominative Case to the subject in SpecIP, since [+F] and Agr are not structurally adjacent and the latter does therefore not absorb abstract nominative Case from the former. It follows that [+F] can be located in Comp in languages like Mainland Scandinavian that do not have overt morphological nominative case.[8] All this is indicated in (15), the schematic S-structure that Trosterud's theory would give to a Swedish embedded clause that is not a complement of an asserted bridge verb.

(15)

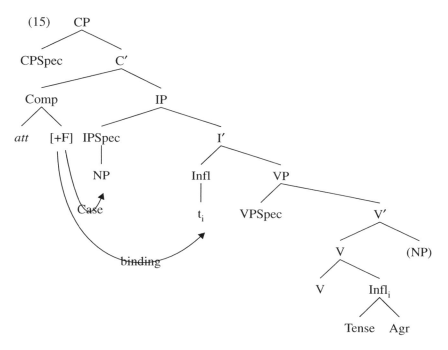

In short, Trosterud's theory predicts that all and only those languages that have overt morphological nominative case allow ([+F] in Infl and) V to I raising. This prediction is however incorrect. Faroese has overt morphological nominative case (cf. (16) from Lockwood (1964:28–29)), yet the language does not allow V to I raising (cf. Chapter 2).

(16)   Faroese
              arm- 'arm'
              (MASC CLASS 1)
              SG   PL
NOM   arm-ur   arm-ar
ACC   arm   arm-ar
DAT   arm-i   ørm-um
GEN   (arm-s)   (arm-a)[9]

Note that unlike Icelandic (cf. (12a)), Faroese has distinctive nominative marking only in the singular and never in the plural. It is however unlikely that this gap in the paradigm explains the lack of V to I raising in Faroese, since the V to I raising language Icelandic does not always distinctively mark nominative Case either. In Icelandic (and Faroese) neuter and strong feminine nouns, nominative case is never morphologically distinguished from accusative case (cf. (17) from Haugen 1976). Yet this gap in the paradigm does not have any consequences for V to I raising in Icelandic.

(17)   a.   Icelandic   b.   Icelandic
                 sól- 'sun'   *aug-* 'eye'
                 (FEM CLASS 1)   (NEUT WEAK)

	SG	PL		SG	PL
NOM	sól	sól-ir		aug-a	aug-u
ACC	sól	sól-ir		aug-a	aug-u
DAT	sól	sól-um		aug-a	aug-um
GEN	sól-ar	sól-a		aug-a	aug-n-a

I conclude that overt morphological nominative case is not responsible for V to I raising.

3.2.3   Number Agreement (Roberts 1993; Falk 1993)

Already Pollock (1989) suggested that the relative "richness" of overt subject-verb agreement morphology is somehow responsible for the presence versus absence of V to I raising. As a point of departure, consider Table 3.1 which shows the relation between word order and overt subject-verb agreement in part of a sample of 50 of the world's languages chosen by Perkins (1980) "in such a way that no two languages are from the same phylum...and no two are from the same cultural or geographic area" (Bybee 1985: 25).

Table 3.1: *Word order and Agreement in a sample of the world's languages (after Bybee 1985)*

	No Agreement	Agreement
SOV	11 (52%)	10 (48%)
SVO	7 (64%)	4 (36%)
VOS	1 (100%)	0
VSO	1 (12%)	7 (88%)

What is interesting in Table 3.1 is that SOV and SVO languages are more or less evenly split between those that do not have overt subject-verb agreement and those that do have agreement. This correlates with the fact that these word orders can be straightforwardly derived with or without V to I raising, as shown in (18a, b). VSO languages on the other hand have a strong tendency to have subject-verb agreement. This correlates with the fact that given standard assumptions of clause structure, this word order can be easily derived only with V to I raising, as shown in (19).

(18)   a.

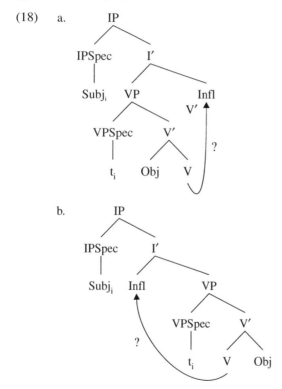

b.

(19)

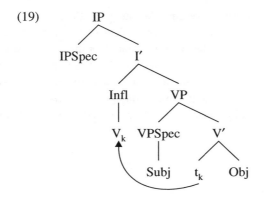

While the facts in Table 3.1 support Pollock's idea that V to I raising is linked to the "richness" of overt subject-verb agreement, it is clear that the simple presence of (any amount of) overt subject-verb agreement is not enough to trigger V to I raising. To see this, take a look at (20–22), the verbal paradigms of the languages that are the main topic of discussion in this book. The V to I raising languages Yiddish (cf. (20a)) and Icelandic (cf. (20b)) show lots of agreement and the V in situ language Swedish (cf. (21b), and standard Mainland Scandinavian in general) does not show any agreement, but the V in situ languages English (cf. (21a)) and Faroese (cf. (22)) also show some agreement.

(20) a. Yiddish *loyf-n* 'run'   b. Icelandic *segj-a* 'say'

	IND PRES		IND PRES	
	SG	PL	SG	PL
1ST	loyf	loyf-n	segi	segj-um
2ND	loyf-st	loyf-t	segi-r	seg-ið
3RD	loyf-t	loyf-n	segi-r	segj-a

(21) a. English throw   b. Swedish *bit-a* 'bite'

	IND PRES		IND PRES	
	SG	PL	SG	PL
1ST	throw	throw	bit-er	bit-er
2ND	throw	throw	bit-er	bit-er
3RD	throw-s	throw	bit-er	bit-er

(22)   Faroese *kast-a* 'throw'

                         IND PRES

                         SG   PL
     1ST   kast-i   kast-a
     2ND   kasta-r   kast-a
     3RD   kasta-r   kast-a

It is nevertheless true that if the number of different endings in the verbal paradigm of a language is used to measure the amount of agreement in that language, each of the V to I raising languages has more agreement than any of the V in situ languages. But the mere number of affixes is bound to be theoretically uninteresting: while counting inflectional endings may eventually yield an accurate descriptive generalization, it cannot be expected to serve as the basis for an explanation. For the latter, we have to look beyond quantity and at the qualitative relation between agreement morphology on the one hand and the syntactic features it represents on the other hand.

Roberts (1993) makes a step in this direction and proposes that V to I raising occurs in those languages which postulate Agr^{-1} (i.e. a category with a subcategorization frame requiring the incorporation of a verbal stem) and that

(23) Agr^{-1} is postulated if there is overt distinct morphological plural
         marking[10]   (Roberts 1993: 267)

where 'overt' means non-empty and "'distinct' means 'distinct from the singular form(s)'" (Roberts 1993: 267).

Number agreement plays a similar if less central role in Falk (1993). According to Falk, V to I raising is possible if and only if Infl is a governor for the verb trace and affix lowering is possible if and only if the overt content of Infl (tense and/or number agreement and/or person agreement) is recoverable by the finiteness feature [+F] in Comp. Infl is a governor in exactly those languages that have overt agreement in number and/or person. Tense and number agreement are recoverable by [+F], but person agreement is not.[11] It follows that V to I raising is obligatory in languages with person agreement, optional in languages with number agreement but without overt person agreement, and ungrammatical in languages with neither person nor number agreement between subject and verb.

Below, I will focus my critique on Robert's theory, but this critique covers Falk's theory as well insofar as overt distinct number agreement will be shown not to be a sufficient licenser for V to I raising.

The V to I raising languages Yiddish (cf. (20a)) and Icelandic (cf. (20b)) have overt distinct morphological plural marking in the sense of (23). This is shown by a comparison of for example the second person singular and plural affixes, which are *-st* and *-t* in Yiddish and *-r* and *-ið* in Icelandic. The two language postulate Agr^{-1} and V to I raising is triggered. The V in situ languages English (cf. (21a)) and Mainland Scandinavian (cf. (21b)) on the other hand do not have overt distinct plural marking. The English plural marker is distinct in the third person, but not overt, (cf. singular *-s* versus plural *-Ø*). The opposite is true in Mainland Scandinavian, where the plural markers are overt but not distinct (cf. singular *-er* versus plural *-er*). Neither language postulates Agr^{-1} and both disallow V to I raising.

The situation is more complex in Faroese. In this language, verbs of the first weak class generally have the following inflectional pattern (All Faroese paradigms in this chapter are taken from Lockwood 1964)

(24)　Faroese (weak class 1)

INF *kasta* 'throw'

		SG	PL
IND PRES 1ST		kast-i	kasta
	2ND	kasta-r	kasta
	3RD	kasta-r	kasta
IND PRET		kasta-ði	kasta-ðu
PRET PART		kasta-ður	
IMP		kasta	kast-ið

Note that in (24), the plural form *kasta* is identical to the infinitive and the imperative singular. This form moreover appears intact in all other verb forms except for the first person singular present indicative and the imperative plural. If we assume in accordance with the traditional analysis for this class of Scandinavian verbs that *kasta* represents in fact the stem (cf. Haugen 1982: 144), we can derive the first person singular indicative present and the imperative plural as shown in (26) by applying the vowel truncation rule in (25) which deletes a short stem-final vowel in front of a suffix-initial vowel. This is well-known from Icelandic (cf. Orešnik 1972).

(25)　$\begin{matrix} \mu \\ | \\ V \end{matrix} \rightarrow \varnothing / \_\#V$

(26)　a.　/kasta+i/ → kast-i　b.　/kasta+ið/ → kast-ið

Roberts concludes that the present indicative plural forms are bare stems (plus possibly a Ø-suffix) and that while the indicative preterit has overt distinct morphological plural marking (cf. singular *kasta-ði* versus plural *kasta-ðu*), the indicative present lacks it. Thus generalization (23), if understood to require the relevant marking to be observable in all tenses, seems to be compatible with the absence of V to I raising in Faroese.

A look at the agreement paradigms of the other Faroese verb classes however reveals that the indicative present, too, exhibits overt distinct morphological plural marking.

(27) Faroese (weak class 2)
      INF *nevn-a* 'name'

		SG	PL
IND PRES	1ST	nevn-i	nevn-a
	2ND	nevn-ir	nevn-a
	3RD	nevn-ir	nevn-a
IND PRET		nevn-di	nevn-du
PRET PART		nevn-dur	
IMP		nevn	nevn-ið

(28) Faroese (weak class 3)
      INF *krevj-a* 'require'

		SG	PL
IND PRES	1ST	krevj-i	krevj-a
	2ND	krev-ur	krevj-a
	3RD	krev-ur	krevj-a
IND PRET		krav-di	krav-du
PRET PART		krav-dur	
IMP		krev	krevj-ið

(29) Faroese (strong)
      INF *strúk-a* 'strike'

		SG	PL
IND PRES	1ST	strúk-i	strúk-a
	2ND	strýk-ur	strúk-a
	3RD	strýk-ur	strúk-a
IND PRET		streyk	struk-u
PRET PART		strok-in	
IMP		strúk	strúk-ið

In these paradigms, the imperative singular is not identical with and in fact shorter than the infinitive and the present indicative plural (e.g. *nevn* vs. *nevna*). It is this shorter form visible in the imperative that surfaces in the preterit indicative singular and plural and the preterit participle (e.g. *nevndi, nevndu, nevndur*). Here the respective suffixes clearly begin with a consonant and Vowel Truncation Rule (25) cannot be invoked to delete a putative underlying stem-final vowel. Remember that class 1 weak verbs, where such a stem-final vowel is well motivated, do in fact not delete this vowel before the preterit suffixes (cf. *kastaði, kastaðu, kastaður*). The traditional assumption (cf. Haugen 1982: 144) that the stems of class 2 and 3 weak verbs and strong verbs are identical with the imperative singular (i.e. *nevn-, krev(j)-, strúk-*) directly accounts for these facts. The plurals *nevna, krevja* and *strúka* and the plurals of the roughly 60% of all Faroese verbs that pattern similarly then require the overt distinct morphological plural marker -*a*. This analysis is again in line with traditional assumptions (cf. Haugen 1982: 146) and can be straightforwardly extended to class 1 weak verbs. The derivation of the present indicative plural *kasta* now involves the stem *kasta-*, the regular plural suffix -*a* and Vowel Truncation Rule (25) as shown in (30).

(30)   /kasta+a/ → kast-a

This means that all Faroese verbs have overt distinct morphological plural marking in the sense of generalization (23). Hence Roberts's and Falk's theories incorrectly predict obligatory (Roberts) or optional (Falk) V to I raising in Faroese.[12]

Robert's theory would be compatible with the Faroese data if "distinct" referred to distinctness not only from the singular forms, but also from the infinitive. But his theory would then no longer correctly predict that 14th century Middle English, with identical forms for the infinitive and the indicative present plural (cf. (31), after Wyld 1927), had V to I raising (cf. Chapter 4).

(31)   Middle Midland English: INF cast-en

	SG	PL
IND PRES 1ST	cast-e	cast-en
2ND	cast-est	cast-en
3RD	cast-eþ	cast-en

It then appears that overt and distinctive number agreement is not sufficient to license V to I raising.

3.3 Person Agreement

Platzack and Holmberg (1989) were the first to propose that person agreement is responsible for V to I raising:

(32)   If a language L has overt S-V person agreement, then L has Agr.
(Platzack & Holmberg 1989: 72)

As it stands, this generalization is incorrect: While the V to I raising languages Yiddish and Icelandic clearly have person agreement (cf. (20a, b)) and the V in situ language Swedish (and standard mainland Scandinavian in general) clearly does not have person agreement (cf. (21b)), the V in situ language English arguably has agreement for third person singular (cf. (21a)) unless -*s* only marks singular (cf. Kayne 1989) and, more importantly, the V in situ language Faroese clearly has agreement for first person singular (cf. (27–29)). Neither can it be said that V to I raising languages show distinctive person agreement on all forms of their paradigms, since the Yiddish first and third person plural forms and the Icelandic second and third person singular forms are homophonous and probably reflect only number agreement.

There is however an important sense in which person agreement in the V to I raising languages Yiddish and Icelandic is "richer" than person agreement in the V in situ languages English, Mainland Scandinavian and Faroese: Only the former overtly distinguish all three persons from each other in either the singular (Yiddish, cf. (20a)) or the plural (Icelandic, cf. (20b)). Faroese, the only V in situ language in our sample that clearly has some person agreement, does not overtly distinguish second from third person in either singular or plural (cf. (27–29)), except for ca. twenty irregular verbs to be discussed in Section 3.5.

It is however not enough to have three different forms in either the singular or the plural, since this would not explain why English lost main verb movement to Infl in the 16th century after the language had gone from the Middle English paradigm in (33a) to the Early Modern English paradigm in (33b). Both paradigms have three distinct affixes that mark the three persons in the singular, yet Middle English still had main verb movement to Infl (cf. (34)) and Early Modern English no longer had it (cf. (35) and the discussion in Section 4.2.1).

(33)   a.   Middle English   b.   Early Modern English
               sing-en   *cast-Ø*
               IND PRES   IND PRES

	SG	PL		SG	PL
1ST	sing-e	sing-en		cast-Ø	cast(-e)
2ND	sing-est	sing-en		cast-est	cast(-e)
3RD	sing-eþ	sing-en		cast-eþ	cast(-e)

(34)   Wepyng and teres **counforteth** *not* dissolute laghers.
       weeping and tears comfort   not dissolute laughers
       'Weeping and tears don't comfort dissolute laughers.'
                         (Middle English 1400–1450 [Love *Lyf of Jesu Christ*],
                                                     Roberts 1993, ex. 3(25a))

(35)   ... bycause the nobylyte ther commynly dothe *not* **exercyse** them in
       the studys therof.
                         (Early Modern English 1534–38 [Starkey *Dialogue*],
                                                        Kroch 1990, ex. (20b))

Neither will it do to require that each of the three person affixes not only be the
distinct from the other two, but also overt. This requirement would correctly
predict V in situ in Early Modern English, where the first person singular marker
is non-overt, but it also would incorrectly predicts V in situ in Yiddish, where
the first person singular marker is likewise non-overt (cf. (20a)).

I think that what is responsible in paradigm (33b) for the loss of V to I
raising in Early Modern English is not the fact that the first person singular
marker is empty, but rather the fact that it is identical with the infinitival affix.
This of course presupposes that in Early Modern English, the two markers no
longer differed in their underlying phonological shape, a claim that can (and
should) be maintained in the absence of phonological evidence to the contrary.
Requiring that all three person agreement affixes in question must not only be
distinct from each other, but also from the infinitival affix, will again not do,
since this would wrongly predict V in situ in Icelandic, where the forms for the
infinitive and the third person plural are identical (cf. (20b)). Why then does
homophony of a first person marker with an infinitival marker result in loss of
V to I raising, but homophony of a third person marker with an infinitival
marker does not? It is important to note in this connection that cross-linguistically, third person does not have the same status as first (and second) person. Thus
Beard (1991) observes that "Third Person is ... the morphologically unmarkered

... person in virtually all languages which have some null markered finite form of the verb".[13] This is illustrated in (36) with the help of four unrelated languages, to which many others (including Italian from Romance and both Arabic and Hebrew from Semitic) could be added. In Czech (Slavic, (36a) after Lee and Lee 1959), Hungarian (Finno-Ugric, (36b) after Spencer 1991), and Turkish (Altaic, (36c) after Lewis 1967), only the forms for the third person singular do not bear an overt subject agreement marker. In Yuma (Hokan, (36d) after Anderson 1992), where subject and object agreement are expressed simultaneously by the same marker, only the combination of a third person subject with a third person object does not co-occur with any overt agreement marker on the verb.[14]

(36)   a.   Czech 'know'   b.   Hungarian 'read'
            IND PRES   IND PRES

            SG   PL   SG   PL
      1ST   zna:-m   zna:-me   olvas-ok olvas-nuk
      2ND   zna:-š   zna:-te   olvas-ol olvas-tok
      3RD   zna: zna:-yi: olvas   olvas-nak

       c.   Turkish 'come'   d.   Yuma 'see'
            IND PRET   NON-FUT SG

            SG   PL   S\O 1ST   2ND   3RD
      1ST   geldi-m   geldi-k n^y-ayúk   ?-ayúk
      2ND   geldi-n   geldi-niz   ?an^{y}m-ayúk   m-ayúk
      3RD   geldi   geldi-ler n^y-ayúk m-ayúk   ayúk

Beard assumes that in languages where a feature such as "person" is represented both by overt and by non-overt morphology, overt morphology represents the marked value(s) of the feature and zero morphology represents the unmarked value of the feature. The systematic absence of overt morphology from the third person (singular) then suggests that universally, third person is the unmarked value of the feature "person". This view is standardly translated into the assumption that "person" falls into two features, [1ST] and [2ND], whose positive values are marked and whose negative values are unmarked (cf. for example Beard 1992, Jensen and Stong-Jensen 1984 and Lieber 1992). First and second correspond to the marked feature combinations [+1ST,−2ND] and [−1ST,+2ND], respectively.[15] Third person corresponds to the unmarked feature combination [−1ST, −2ND]. In fact, it should not be viewed as an independent "third" person, but rather as the absence of person. To make this even more evident, I will use the privative features [1ST] for first person and [2ND] for second person and the absence of any person marking for "third" person (as well as uninflected infinitives).

Further evidence for the absence of person marking in the "third" person comes from some *pro*-drop languages like Modern Hebrew and Finnish, where referential *pro* drop is restricted to first and second person (compare (37a, b) and (38a) with (37c) and (38b)). If, as proposed above, the inflected verb bears person marking in the first and second but not in the "third" person, and if, as discussed in Section 4.3, person marking is necessary for the recoverability of the content of referential *pro*, then this contrast is less than mysterious: In (37a, b) and in (38a) but not (37c) or in (38b) can the content of a missing referential subject be recovered by the inflection on the verb.[16]

(37) a. (ʾani) ʾaxalti ʾet   ha-banana.
         (I)   ate-1SG ACC the-banana
      b. (ʾatem) ʾaxaltem ʾet   ha-banana.
         (you-p) ate-2PL ACC the-banana
      c. *(hu) ʾaxal   ʾet   ha-banana.
         (he) ate-3SG ACC the-banana.
         'I/y'all/he ate the banana.'
                        (Modern Hebrew, Borer 1984, ex. 6(17a,18a,19ab))

(38) a. (Minä) jään   kotiin, jos (sinä) pyydät kauniisti.
         (I)   stay-1SG home   if (you) ask-2SG nicely
         'I'll stay home if you ask nicely.'
      b. Jukka lähtee,   jos *(hän) saa   kutsun.
         J.   leave-3SG if (he)   get-3SG invitation
         'Jukka will go if he gets an invitation.'
                        (Finnish, after Vainikka & Levy 1995, ex. (9a, b))

We can now formulate the following descriptive generalization regarding the connection between "richness" of person agreement and V to I raising:

(39) **The Paradigm-Verb Raising Correlate**
      A language has V to I raising if and only if in at least one number of one tense of the regular verb paradigm(s), the person features [1ST] and [2ND] are both distinctively marked.

A privative feature such as [1ST] or [2ND] is distinctively marked if and only if the forms bearing this feature are distinct from the forms lacking this feature. Accordingly, a language has V to I raising if its regular verbs distinguish the forms for first and second person in at least one number of one tense from each other as well as from the forms for "third" person in that tense/number combination and from the form for the infinitive. I will refer to such a paradigm as a "Full Paradigm" with "minimally distinctive marking" of the person features.

It is easy to see that minimal distinctive marking of [1ST] and [2ND] is present in the Yiddish singular (cf. (20a)) and in the Icelandic plural (cf. (20b)). Note that the fact that "third" person plural and infinitive are identical in Icelandic and that first person singular is marked by a phonetically empty affix in Yiddish is irrelevant with respect to the Paradigm-Verb Raising Correlate.

Consider next the Early Modern English paradigm in (33b). Here first person singular and infinitive are identical (as are the plural forms), [1ST] is not distinctively marked and V to I raising is not triggered. In the Middle English paradigm in (33a) on the other hand, the singular forms and the infinitive all differ from each other, [1ST] and [2ND] are distinctively marked and V to I raising is triggered.

Turning to Faroese, observe that in the regular weak class two paradigm in (27), second and "third" person are identical in both the singular and the plural. The situation is the same for the other regular verb classes, i.e. weak class one (cf. (22)), weak class three (cf. (28)) and strong verbs (cf. (29)). Regular Faroese verbs therefore do not distinctively mark the person feature [2ND] and V to I raising is, at least for the majority of speakers, not triggered. In Section 3.5, I will offer a principled account for residual V to I raising in the language of a minority of Faroese speakers that is based on the Paradigm-Verb Raising Correlate and the existence of a few (but very frequent) irregular Full Paradigms in Faroese.

A look at Mainland Scandinavian concludes this cursory evaluation of the Paradigm-Verb Raising Correlate with respect to its descriptive adequacy. The situation is straightforward in the standard languages: Swedish ((21b)), distinctively marks neither [1ST] nor [2ND] and V to I raising is not triggered. The situation is the same in Danish and Norwegian.

Things get a little more interesting in a number of Mainland Scandinavian Dialects. Hallingdalen Norwegian has different forms for singular and plural but does not distinctively mark [1ST] and [2ND] (cf.(40) after Trosterud 1989). The pre-verbal position of the negation marker in embedded clauses that are not the asserted complements of bridge verbs (cf. (41) from Platzack & Holmberg 1989) indicates that this dialect lacks V to I raising.

(40) a.   Hallingdalen Norwegian b. Hallingdalen Norwegian
              kastæ 'throw' (WEAK)   *taka* 'take' (STRONG)
              IND PRES   IND PRES
              SG   PL   SG   PL
      1ST   kasta   kastæ   tek   taka
      2ND   kasta   kastæ   tek   taka
      3RD   kasta   kastæ   tek   taka

(41) Noko gamlæ mænna som *ikji* **haddæ** vore mæ   ve kyrkja.
      some old   men   who not had   been along at church
      'Some old men who hadn't come along to church.'
                                          (Hallingdalen Norwegian)

Älvdalen Swedish distinctively marks the person features [1ST] and [2ND] in the
plural of the indicative present (cf. (42) after Vikner 1994) and the verb raises
over negation to Infl as predicted by the Paradigm-Verb Raising Correlate
(cf. (43) from Platzack and Holmberg 1989).

(42)   Älvdalen Swedish
              kasta 'throw'
              IND PRES
              SG   PL
      1ST   kasta-r   kasta-um
      2ND   kasta-r   kasta-er
      3RD   kasta-r   kasta

(43) Ba fo dye at   uir **uildum** *int* fy.
      just for that that we wanted not follow
      'Just because we didn't want to follow.'   (Älvdalen Swedish)

Kronoby Swedish, a dialect spoken in Finland, does not conform to the Paradigm-Verb Raising Correlate. Its inflectional paradigm resembles the Standard
Swedish one in (21b) in the relevant aspects (i.e. it lacks minimal distinctive
marking of both [1ST] and [2ND]), yet V to I raising seems to be attested
(cf. (44)).

(44) He va bra et   an **tsöfft** *int* bootsen.
      it was good that he bought not book-the
      'It was good that he didn't buy the book.'
                        (Kronoby Swedish, Platzack & Holmberg 1989, ex. (43))

Many of the relevant facts about Kronoby Swedish are unavailable. A priori, it is at least conceivable that in this Finland-Swedish dialect, V to I raising is due to influences from Finnish. Finnish has a complete verbal paradigm (cf. (45a) after Lehtinen 1964), and Mitchell (1991) argues that it has V to I raising, too. The latter fact is obscured in negated sentences, where negation is realized by an auxiliary (cf. (45b) after Lehtinen 1964) that (like e.g. Icelandic temporal auxiliaries) blocks movement of the main verb. But V to I raising is visible in asserted sentences, where the verb precedes sentential adverbs. Negated and asserted Finnish word order is illustrated in the examples (46) taken from Trosterud 1992.

(45)　　　　　Finnish *laula-a* 'sing' IND PRES

　　a.　　　AFF　　　　　　　　b.　NEG

	SG	PL	SG	PL
1ST	laula-n	laula-mme	e-n laula	e-mme laula
2ND	laula-t	laula-tte	e-t laula	e-tte laula
3RD	laula-a	laula-vat	e-i laula	ei-vätt laula

(46)　a.　Tytöt eivät　　　ostaneet　　　kirjaa.
　　　　　girls　AUX(NEG) bought-PART book
　　　　　'The girls didn't buy the book.'

　　　b.　Anna **näki** kerran *yllättäen*　　　suden.
　　　　　A.　saw once　unexpectedly wolf
　　　　　'Once Anna unexpectedly saw a wolf.'　　　(Finnish)

Attributing V to I raising in Kronoby Swedish to influences from Finnish is an unattractive solution since it seriously weakens the restrictiveness of the theory: There is now no longer a single trigger for V to I raising.[17] If, as I will claim in the next section, the correlation between distinctive person marking and V to I raising amounts to more than a merely descriptive generalization, it is hard to see how external factors such as language contact could play a role. Note also that other Finland-Swedish dialects behave exactly like Swedish in correlating the absence of a full paradigm with V in situ. Given that Kronoby Swedish is the only counter-example within the Germanic VO languages to the strong (bi-conditional) version of the Paradigm-Verb Raising Correlate in (39) I am aware of (with the possible exception of Middle Scots, cf. Section 4.2.1) and given that this dialect is equally problematic for all other morphology-based theories of V to I raising that have been proposed, it might be preferable to maintain that distinctive marking of [1ST] and [2ND] is a necessary and sufficient trigger for

V to I raising and to let Kronoby Swedish stand as an unresolved problem for this approach.[18]

The correlation between minimal distinctive marking of the person features on the one hand and V to I raising on the other hand in the Germanic VO languages is summarized in Table 3.2. Already included in this summary are the facts from earlier stages of English and the Mainland Scandinavian languages which I will discuss in the next chapter.

Table 3.2: *Minimal distinctive marking of the person features and V to I raising in the Germanic VO languages*

	[1ST]	[2ND]	V to I
Faroese	✓		
Hallingdalen Norwegian			
Early Modern English		✓	
English			
Danish			
Norwegian			
Swedish			
Yiddish	✓	✓	✓
Icelandic	✓	✓	✓
Middle English	✓	✓	✓
Old Danish	✓	✓	✓
Old Norwegian	✓	✓	✓
Old Swedish	✓	✓	✓
Älvdalen Swedish	✓	✓	✓
Kronoby Swedish			✓

Overall, the reformulated Paradigm-Verb Raising Correlate has proven to be an adequate descriptive generalization: It describes the potentially important fact that V to I Raising seems to depend on the minimal distinctive marking of the person features [1ST] and [2ND]. But it does not yet explain this correlation and is hence of limited theoretic significance, at least until such an explanation can be found. Before I turn to this issue in the next section, I want to discuss the precise content of the Paradigm-Verb Raising Correlate in more detail.

One question that arises in this connection is whether minimal distinctive marking of the number feature(s) should be added to (39) as a prerequisite for V to I raising. The answer to this question appears to be "no". To see this, we have to address the nature of the number feature(s). Notice that in each of the paradigms in (36), the morphologically unmarked form representing the unmarked abstract feature values is the "third" person *singular*. This indicates not only that, as argued earlier, "third" is the unmarked value for person, but also that "singular" is the unmarked value for number. We can capture the latter conclusion in the by now familiar way, i.e. by using the privative feature [pl] for plural and the absence of any number marking for singular. It now becomes obvious why minimal distinctive marking of [pl] cannot be a prerequisite for V to I raising: If it were, Middle English (cf. (33a)) should not have had V to I raising since the plural forms and the infinitival form are identical and [pl] is hence not minimally distinctively marked. In the other Germanic VO languages, minimal distinctive marking of the person features implies minimal distinctive marking of the number feature. This is in fact a very strong crosslinguistic tendency. Nichols (1992) reports about her representative sample of 174 languages from all of the worlds major language families that "there is only one language in my sample that has verb agreement in some category but not in number: West Futuna (Oceania), which has agreement in person but not in number" (Nichols 1992: 150). Similarly, only 12 (or 5%) of the 237 languages in the sample of the world's languages analyzed in Siewierska and Bakker (1994) have an agreement system of this kind. My own inquiries have turned up only a handful of other languages of this type, mostly from the Americas. The available information on these languages is often slim and the word order tests developed in connection with (mostly) Indo-European languages cannot always be applied to them. However, at least one of these languages supplies additional evidence in support of the conclusion that minimal distinctive marking of [pl] is not required in order for a paradigm to qualify as a Full Paradigm. Miskitu, a Language spoken in Nicaragua, has minimal distinctive marking of person agreement but no overt number agreement (cf. (47)). Information about V to I raising in Miskitu is unavailable, but the language has referential *pro*-drop (cf. (48)).[19] In Section 4.3 I will argue that *pro*-drop, like V to I raising, is possible only in languages with a Full Paradigm. If this is indeed correct, minimal distinctive marking of [pl] should not be added to the Paradigm-Verb Raising Correlate in (39).

(47)　　　Miskitu *atk-aia* 'to buy'

	PRES		PAST		FUT	
	SG	PL	SG	PL	SG	PL
1ST	atk-isna	atk-isna	atk-ri	atk-ri	atk-amna	atk-amna
2ND	atk-isma	atk-isma	atk-ram	atk-ram	at(k)-ma	at(k)-ma
3RD	atk-isa	atk-isa	atk-an	atk-an	at(k)-bin	at(k)-bin

(48)　　　Yang [*e* plun atk-ram　　　] ba piak-amna.
　　　　　I　　　food buy-2ND.pst　the cook-1ST.fut
　　　　　'I will cook the food you bought.'　　　　　　　　　　　　(Miskitu)

Since I first proposed the Paradigm-Verb Raising Correlate in Rohrbacher (1994),[20] Vikner (1995) and Bobaljik (1995) have made alternative proposals that link V to I raising to agreement morphology in different ways. Vikner (1995) argues for the descriptive generalization in (49) for which he however gives no theoretical explanation.

(49)　　　An SVO-language has V^0-to-I^0 movement if and only if person morphology is found in all tenses.　　　　　　　(Vikner 1995: 14)

The empirical coverage of the generalization in (49) is very similar to that of the Paradigm-Verb Raising Correlate, although Vikner claims that it is better equipped to handle some facts in the history of English (cf. Section 4.2.1).[21] To see how (49) works, consider again the paradigms of the Germanic VO languages in (20–22) which are repeated (with the addition of the preterit indicative) below in (50–52).

(50)　a.　　　Yiddish *loyf-n* 'run'　　　b.　Icelandic *kast-a* 'throw'

	IND PRES			IND PRES	
	PL	SG		PL	SG
1ST	loyf	loyf-n		kasta	köst-um
2ND	loyf-st	loyf-t		kasta-r	kast-ið
3RD	loyf-t	loyf-n		kasta-r	kasta

	IND PRET			IND PRET	
	PERIPHRASTIC:			PL	SG
	PRES AUX		1ST	kasta-ði	köstu-ðum
	+ (INVARIANT)		2ND	kasta-ðir	köstu-ðuð
	PERF PART		3RD	kasta-ði	köstu-ðu

(51) a.   English *walk*   b.   Swedish *smaka* 'taste'

IND PRES   IND PRES

	PL	SG		PL	SG
1ST	walk	walk		smaka-r	smaka-r
2ND	walk	walk		smaka-r	smaka-r
3RD	walk-s	walk		smaka-r	smaka-r

IND PRET   IND PRET

	PL	SG		PL	SG
1ST	walk-ed	walk-ed		smaka-de	smaka-de
2ND	walk-ed	walk-ed		smaka-de	smaka-de
3RD	walk-ed	walk-ed		smaka-de	smaka-de

(52)   Faroese *nevna* 'name'

IND PRES

	PL	SG
1ST	nevn-i	nevn-a
2ND	nevn-ir	nevn-a
3RD	nevn-ir	nevn-a

IND PRET

	PL	SG
1ST	nevn-di	nevn-du
2ND	nevn-di	nevn-du
3RD	nevn-di	nevn-du

The Yiddish preterit (cf. (50a)) is expressed in a periphrastic construction and does therefore not constitute a tense in the sense of (49). Since person morphology is found in the Yiddish present tense, the language has V to I raising. Person morphology is also found in the present and preterit of the V to I raising language Icelandic (cf. (50b)). The V in situ language Swedish (cf. (51b) and Mainland Scandinavian in general) does not have person morphology in any tense. English (cf. (51a)) and Faroese (cf. (52)) have person morphology in the present, but not in the preterit, and both accordingly lack V to I raising.

Bobaljik (1995) argues that V in situ languages have a fused Agr/Tense head that projects a single inflectional phrase and that V to I raising languages have separate Agr and Tense heads that project two inflectional phrases. He assumes that the features of a head can not only be checked against the features of (adjuncts to) adjuncts to that head or against the features of its specifier, as proposed by Chomsky (1992), but also against the features of its complement.

He further assumes that the features of a phrase are those of its head, in line with Chomsky (1995). In languages with a fused Agr/Tense head, the V-features [+f] of Agr can be checked against the V-features that VP, the complement of Agr/Tense, inherits from its head V (cf. (53)). V to I raising for feature checking purposes is therefore unnecessary and, given Economy of Derivation, ungrammatical in languages with a fused Agr/Tense head.[22]

(53)

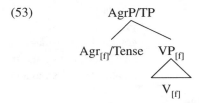

In languages with separate Agr and Tense heads, the V-features of Agr cannot be checked against the V-features of the verb when the latter stays in situ (cf. 54a)) or moves only to Tense (cf. (54b)) because in both case, the V-features of the verb are in the checking domain of Tense but not in that of Agr. Only when the verb moves to Agr (cf. (54c)) can the V-features of Agr be checked against the V-features of the verb because only in this case is the verb in the checking domain of Agr. Accordingly, languages with separate Agr and Tense heads must have V to I raising.

(54)   a.   b.

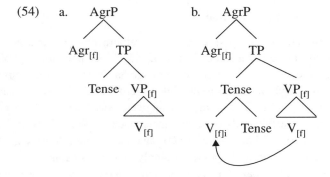

c.

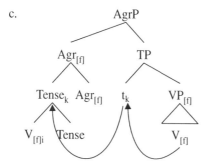

Bobaljik at first claims that the overt morphological tense and agreement system of a language determines whether that language has separate or fused Tense and Agr heads (and hence whether it has V to I raising or V in situ), although he later reverts the causality in the relation between morphology and syntax and comes to regard the overt morphological tense and agreement system of a language as a consequence of (rather than the reason for) this language having separate or fused Tense and Agr heads. Note that under the later view, we are left without an explanation for V to I raising. The earlier view is summarized in (55).

(55) *Evidence for Fusion*
      If the appearance of Tense morphology blocks the appearance of Agreement morphology, then Tense and Agreement Vocabulary Items are in complementary distribution, and T and Agr must be fused.   (Bobaljik 1995: 48)

(55) works pretty much like (49), although the fact that Faroese has both agreement and tense morphology in the preterit (cf. (52)) is a problem for Bobaljik. In the next section, I will accept Bobaljik's suggestion that V to I raising languages have separate agreement projections while V in situ languages do not have separate agreement projections. However, I will reject Vikner's generalization in (49) as well as Bobaljik's generalization in (55) and maintain instead that the Paradigm-Verb Raising Correlate in (39) is the correct generalization. The reason for this choice is that while Vikner's generalization cannot explain children's early acquisition of V to I raising in French and Bobaljik's generalization cannot explain children's early acquisition of V in situ in English, the Paradigm-Verb Raising Correlate straightforwardly explains the early acquisition of verb placement in both child languages.

      Vikner (1995b:24) correctly states that according to his theory, "the child must assume the absence of V^0 to I^0 movement unless she finds 'that all core tenses are inflected for person'". Children acquiring V to I raising languages such as French however do not seem to make this assumption. The example in (56) and the data in Table 3.3 show that already in the earliest stages, children acquiring French consistently place finite verbs before negation and non-finite verbs after negation, indicating that they have acquired an adult-like grammar with V to I raising for finite verbs and V in situ for non-finite verbs (cf. The discussion of (2) above and Section 5.2.2).[23] The problem for Vikner's theory is that in these early stages, children have not yet learnt all 'core' tenses of French and should therefore still assume that V to I raising is absent from this language.

(56)

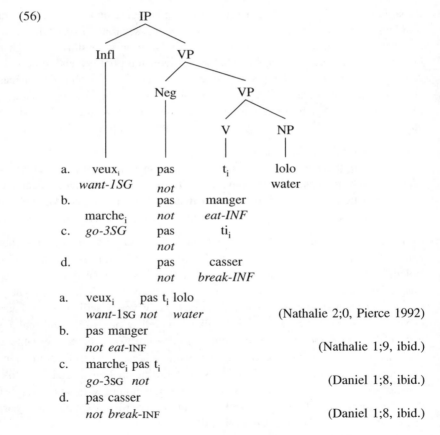

a.   veux$_i$ pas   t$_i$ lolo
      want-1SG   *not*   water
b.   pas   manger
      marche$_i$ *not*   *eat-INF*
c.   *go-3SG*   pas   ti$_i$
                      not
d.   pas   casser
                      not   *break-INF*

a.   veux$_i$ pas t$_i$ lolo
      want-1SG not   water   (Nathalie 2;0, Pierce 1992)
b.   pas manger
      not eat-INF   (Nathalie 1;9, ibid.)
c.   marche$_i$ pas t$_i$
      go-3SG not   (Daniel 1;8, ibid.)
d.   pas casser
      not break-INF   (Daniel 1;8, ibid.)

Table 3.3: *Relative order of negation and finite and non-finite verbs in child French (Pierce 1992)*

| | Nathalie (1;9–2;3) | | Daniel (1;8–1;11) | |
	+ finite	− finite	+ finite	− finite
Verb-Neg	68	0	53	1
Neg-Verb	3	82	3	36

Bobaljik does not make any explicit statements regarding language acquisition but the logic of his generalization dictates that children must assume the presence of V to I raising unless they acquire tense morphemes whose appearance blocks that of agreement morphemes. Children acquiring V in situ languages such as English however do not seem to make this assumption. It is well-known that many children acquiring English learn the "third" person present tense marker *-s* before the past tense marker *-ed* (cf. for example Sarah in Brown 1973). Bobaljik's theory predicts that at the stage at which these children have already mastered the present tense but not yet the past tense, they should exhibit V to I raising since their single tense has person agreement and since they do not know any tense morphology whose appearance blocks the appearance of agreement morphology. This prediction is however wrong: All available reports converge on the conclusion that children acquiring English "correctly stop short of producing sentences in which the verb precedes the negative elements", indicating that "they have correctly set the parameter which excludes main verb raising in English" (Pierce (1992: 61)).[24]

The Paradigm-Verb Raising Correlate on the other hand makes the right predictions for the acquisition of both French and English: Whichever tense a child acquiring French or English acquires first, that tense has minimal distinctive marking of the person features in French but lacks such marking in English, and therefore all children acquiring French correctly move their first (and all subsequent) finite verbs to Infl and all children acquiring English correctly leave their first (and all subsequent) main verbs in situ. Given that the theory developed here can explain the early acquisition of verb placement in English and French and that the theories developed in Vikner (1995b) and Bobaljik (1995) cannot, my theory is to be preferred over its competitors.

3.4 The Representation of Inflectional Affixes

In the previous section, we saw that V to I raising occurs in all and only those languages whose regular verbal paradigm(s) minimally distinctively mark(s) the person features [1ST] and [2ND]. In this section, I will address the question why it is just these features to the exclusion of all others that trigger V to I raising. My central claim is that the person features play a special role in syntax because they have the special ability to refer to entities in the discourse: If distinctively marked by overt subject-verb agreement, the person features by themselves establish whether the subject refers to the speaker(s), the addressee(s), or other(s). Other features often expressed by subject-verb agreement do not have this ability: Distinctive number marking tells the hearer only whether the subject is a one-membered or a multi-membered set, and distinctive gender marking tells the hearer only whether the subject is a feminine, masculine, or neuter entity. Whereas the discourse universe typically contains only one speaker (or group of speakers) and one addressee (or group of addressees), it may contain any number of one- or multi-membered sets and feminine, masculine or neuter entities. Person marking therefore tells us much more about the subject then number or gender marking. It has referential abilities that the other two lack. At least in the case of gender, the general inability to refer is compounded by the tendency to be purely 'grammatical' (i.e. arbitrarily determined) instead of 'natural' (i.e. determined by the actual gender of the object referred to). Cross-linguistic variation (cf. (57)) and alterability (cf. (58)) may suffice to illustrate this point.[25]

(57) a. la   lune   le   soleil
          the-FEM moon   the-MASC sun   (French)

      b. der   Mond   die   Sonne
          the-MASC moon   the-FEM sun   (German)
          'the sun'   'the moon'

(58) a. der   Junge   die   Magd
          the-MASC boy   the-FEM maid
          'the boy'   'the maid'

      b. das   Jüngelchen   das   Mädchen
          the-NEUT boy-DIM   the-NEUT girl-DIM   (German)
          'the young boy'   'the young girl'

Person and number are often singled out as referential features, as for example in Rizzi's postulate in (59).

(59)   An NP is referential only if it has the specification of person and
        number.   (Rizzi 1986a: 543)

Rizzi postulated (59) to explain the distribution of referential *pro*: *pro* receives
its specifications from Infl and given (59), it can be referential only if Infl is
specified for person and number. In the last section, we already discussed an
example which shows that (59) cannot be entirely correct: Miskitu has referential
pro (cf. (48)) although it does not have number marking (cf. (47)). (59) should
therefore be restated as in (60):

(60)   An NP is referential only if it has the specification of person.

We may in fact say that Infl itself is referential if it has the specification of
person, i.e. if it distinctively marks [1ST] and [2ND] in some fashion to be
defined below.

(61)   Infl is referential if and only if it has the specification of person.

I would now like to propose that it is exactly the members of referential
categories (i.e. substantive elements with non-grammatical meanings such as
nouns or verbs and Infl-affixes in those languages where Infl has the specification of person) which are listed in the lexicon. Members of non-referential
categories (i.e. functional elements with only grammatical significance such as
complementizers and Infl-affixes in those languages where Infl does not have the
specification of person) do not have lexical entries. Instead, they are phonetic
spell-outs of feature bundles that are abstractly represented on syntactic nodes.
The distinction between lexical, referential categories on the one hand and non-
lexical, non-referential categories on the other hand is reminiscent of (but not
identical with) the familiar distinction between major and minor categories. It
follows the general intuition that the lexicon is ultimately responsible for the
referential meaning of a sentence and that a linguistic expression refers to an
object or property of the real world ("giraffe"), a possible world ("unicorn") or
even an impossible world ("square circle") because that expression contains
certain lexical elements. Bouchard (1983) observes that this domain D of real,
imagined and unimaginable objects "stands at the interface between real world
and 'linguistic world'" because "individuals in domain D have grammatical
features". We are now saying something similar, i.e. that lexically listed inflectional affixes refer to individuals of domain D by virtue of being specified for
the grammatical feature person.

In a nutshell, we want lexically listed Infl-affixes to trigger V to I raising, and Infl-affixes that merely are phonetic feature spell-outs not to affect the position of the verb. With this in mind, let us now return to the question of what degree of distinctive feature marking renders Infl a referential category. Remember that distinctive feature marking requires the phonological matrixes of forms bearing the feature in question to be distinct from the phonological matrixes of forms lacking that feature. 'Maximal' distinctive marking (with distinctive person marking in the singular and plural of all tenses) cannot be involved, since this would restrict V to I raising to languages like Finnish (where, as shown in (62a), [1ST], [2ND] distinctively marked in both the singular and the plural of the indicative present), and exclude it from languages like Yiddish (where, as shown in (62b), [1ST] is not distinctively marked in the first person plural of the indicative present because the relevant affix is identical to the third person plural marker.

(62) a.   Finnish *laula-a* 'sing'   b.   Yiddish *loyf-n* 'run'
                IND PRES   IND PRES

                SG   PL   SG   PL
      1ST   laula-n   laula-mme   loyf-Ø   loyf-n
      2ND   laula-t   laula-tte   loyf-st   loyf-t
      3RD   laula-a   laula-vat   loyf-t   loyf-n

Instead of 'maximal' distinctive marking, it seems to be 'minimal' distinctive marking (with distinctive person marking in either the singular or the plural of one tense) that is required for the referentiality of the category Infl. Yiddish (as well as Finnish) meets this weaker requirement, since [1ST] and [2ND] are both distinctively marked in the singular of the indicative present. Let us capture this in the following principle governing the referentiality of Infl and hence the lexicality of Infl-affixes.

(63)   **Referentiality of Infl/Lexicality of Infl-Affixes**
       Infl is a referential category with lexically listed affixes in exactly
       those languages where regular subject-verb agreement minimally
       distinctively marks the referential Infl-features such that in at least
       one number of one tense, the person features [1ST] and [2ND] are
       distinctively marked.

Crucial for the status of Infl as a referential, lexical category is its general ability to refer by virtue of being able to distinctively mark each of the referential Infl-features. This ability in itself clearly depends on minimal and not on maximal distinctive marking of these features. It follows that it may be of secondary importance whether a specific Infl-affix actually distinctively marks all referential Infl-features (and thus has unique reference) or not. In case a verbal paradigm minimally distinctively marks all referential Infl-features, Infl is a referential category and all affixes of that paradigm are lexically listed, including those (if they exist) without distinctive marking of a relevant referential Infl-features (and hence without unique reference). Thus in Yiddish, where Infl is referential due to the distinctive marking of [1ST] and [2ND] in the uniquely referential first and second person singular affixes (cf. (62b)), the first person plural marker is lexically listed, too, although its fails to distinctively mark [1ST] (and thus fails to have unique reference) due to its homophony with the third person plural marker. Accordingly, V to I raising in Yiddish extends to verbs inflected for first person plural (cf. (64)).

(64)   Avrom bedoyert az   mir *shikn nit* avek dem briv.
         A.   regrets   that we send not away the   letter
         'A. regrets that we don't mail the letter.'

                              (Yiddish, based on Diesing 1990, ex. (3b))

Similarly in the opposite case: If a verbal paradigm fails to minimally distinctively mark a referential Infl-feature, Infl is non-referential and no affix of that paradigm is lexically listed, including those (if they exist) with distinctive marking of the relevant referential Infl-feature (and hence with unique reference). Thus in Faroese, where Infl is non-referential because [2ND] is never distinctively marked in the regular paradigms (cf. (65)), the first person singular marker is not lexically listed, either, although it distinctively marks [1ST] (and has unique reference). Accordingly, Faroese verbs inflected for first person singular do not raise to Infl (cf. (66))., just like verbs inflected (but not distinctively marked) for second person

(65)   Faroese
                  nevn-a 'name'
                  IND PRES
                         SG   PL
         1ST   nevn-i   nevn-a
         2ND   nevn-ir   nevn-a
         3RD   nevn-ir   nevn-a

(66)   Jón er keddur av at   eg *ekki havi* lisið hesa bók.
      J.   regrets   that I   not   have read this book
      'J. regrets that I haven't read this book.'

                                        (Faroese, based on Vikner 1994, ex. (44b))

Let us now see how this proposal works. The Icelandic inflectional paradigm is listed in the lexicon as (partially) shown in (67) because the referential Infl-features are minimally distinctively marked by the first and second person plural markers. Inserted under Infl at D-structure, these affixes are required by Lasnik's Filter[26] to be bound at S-structure. Assuming, as is by now standard, that lowering of the affix to the verb ("Affix Hopping") is not an option, either because it violates the ECP (cf. Ouhalla 1990, contra Chomsky 1989) or a version of Extend Target (cf. Chomsky 1995), the verb must raise to Infl at S-structure as shown in (68). Under this view, Icelandic inflectional morphology takes place in syntax, a proposal that is familiar from 'weak lexicalist' theories of inflection such as the one developed in Lieber (1992) where morphology is syntactically represented.

(67)   **Lexicon:**

[pres]	[1ST]	[2ND]	
	-*V*	-*Vr*	-*Vr*
[pl]	-*um*	-*ið*	-*a*

(Icelandic)

(68)   **SYNTAX:**

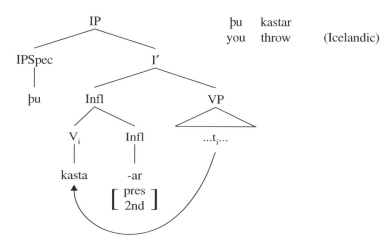

In Faroese, where [2ND] is never distinctively marked on regular verbs, the inflectional affixes are not listed in the Lexicon. At D-structure, a verb stem bearing abstract inflectional features is inserted in V. In Rohrbacher (1994), I also assumed that there is an Infl-head which remains radically empty. Although I will reject this assumption shortly, let us stick with it for now. Since Lasnik's Filter does not apply, the verb does not need to and, given Economy of Derivation (cf. Chomsky 1989), is therefore not allowed to move to Infl at S-structure, as shown in (69). Note that in (69), no overt inflectional morphology is present at any point during the syntactic derivation.

(69)   **SYNTAX:**

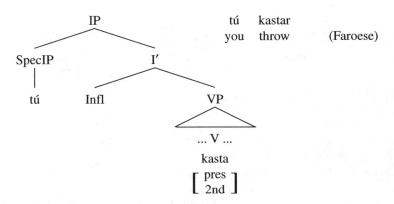

In Phonetic Form, Faroese has the spell-out rules in (70) of which the abstractly inflected verb undergoes the most specific one it is compatible with, i.e. the spell-out rule mentioning the largest subset of the features on the verb.

(70)
Phonetic Form:

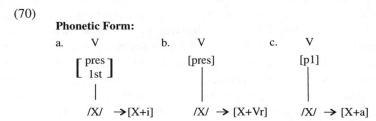

In the case of the syntactic structure in (69), the verb is compatible only with the phonetic spell-out rule in (70b): (70a) and (70c) mention the features [1ST] and [pl], respectively, neither of which is found on the verb. (70b) is therefore chosen as the spell-out rule for the verb in (69) as shown in the PF derivation in (71). Note that it is only at this post-syntactic point that overt inflectional morphology is introduced, as in the 'interpretativist' approaches to inflectional morphology of Anderson (1992) and Beard (1991).

(71)   V
           [pres]
            | (70b)   (25)
        tú kasta → tú kasta-ar → tú kastar

Let us now return to the question of the IP headed by a radically empty Infl in
(69). This phrase is projected from an abstract label rather than a terminal
element drawn from the lexicon, a possibility ruled out in the Bare Phrase
Structure framework of Chomsky (1995). In this framework, there are no labels
other than those based on the featural content of particular terminal elements
drawn from the lexicon. A "DP" for example, which is traditionally represented
as shown in (72a), is now represented as shown in (72b), i.e. without abstract
labels (after Chomsky (1995:246)). It follows that although we may continue to
use the labels like Infl and IP as a convenient shorthand notation standing in for
e.g. "pres 2ND (phrase)" (or "-*ar*(P)") as in the Icelandic structure in (68), we
may not use them in cases where they are not given concrete featural content by
a terminal element as in the Faroese structure in (69).

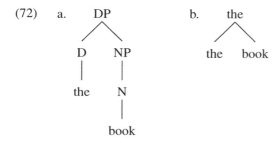

(72)   a.   DP   b.   the
             / \   /   \
           D   NP   the   book
           | |
          the   N
                 |
               book

It is nevertheless clear from examples like (11c) of Chapter 2 (repeated below as
example (73)) that there is an inflectional projection in Faroese (and other V in
situ languages). The specifier of this projection serves as a landing site for the
subject which has moved from its base position in SpecVP, as indicated by its
position to the left of negation.

(73)   Har vóru nógv fólk,   eg ikki kendi.
        here were many people I not knew
        'There were many people I didn't know.'

                                    (Faroese, Lockwood 1964:156)

Let us assume that all languages have a TP headed by the abstract tense features which are essential for the interpretation of the sentence at LF and which are therefore always structurally represented in syntax. The abstract subject-verb agreement features on the other hand are not essential for the interpretation of the sentence at LF and are therefore structurally represented in syntax only if the paradigm expressing them is referential and hence listed in the lexicon (from which syntactic heads are drawn) by virtue of minimally distinctively marking the referential agreement features [1ST] and [2ND]. Thus only languages of the latter type have an AgrP. Since Faroese is not among them, we arrive at the S-structure in (74) instead of the one in (69). The derivation remains virtually unchanged: The verb is abstractly specified for tense and agreement. Since the abstract tense features in Tense are non-affixal, the verb does not have to move overtly to this position and can instead stay in situ at S-structure. At LF, the verb must covertly move to Tense to check its abstract tense specification against that on Tense and its abstract agreement specification against that on the subject in SpecTP. A principle such as Procrastinate (cf. Chomsky 1992) ensures that the verb moves as late in the derivation as possible, i.e. only at LF but not already at S-structure. At PF, the abstract tense and agreement specifications are spelled out by rule (70b). As before, it is only at this post-syntactic point of the derivation that inflectional morphology is introduced.

(74)

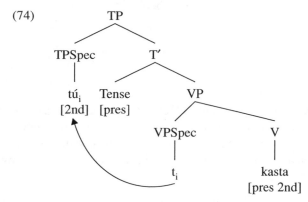

It is clear from examples like (106) of Chapter 2 (repeated below as example (75)) that there are two inflectional projections in Icelandic (and other V to I raising languages). The specifier of the higher inflectional projection is occupied

by the expletive subject and the specifier of the lower inflectional projection
serves as a landing site for the thematic subject.

(75) Þessa bók tel   ég að það hafi sumir menn ekki lesið.
      this book believe I that there have some men not read
      'I believe that some men haven't read this book.'   (Icelandic)

Since the Icelandic verbal agreement paradigm minimally distinctively marks
both [1ST] and [2ND], it is referential and hence listed in the lexicon. At D-structure, one agreement affix is selected from the paradigm and projects AgrP, a
second, language-particular inflectional projection in addition to the universal TP.
We arrive at the structure in (76) instead of that in (68). The derivation is again
virtually unchanged: At S-structure, the verb must overtly move to Agr via Tense
in order to bind the agreement affix, satisfying Lasnik's Filter. In this configuration, the abstract tense and agreement features can also be checked.

(76)

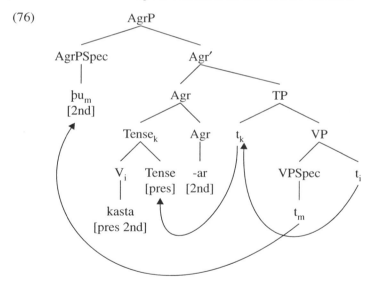

The idea that V to I raising languages have an inflectional projection that is
absent in V in situ languages is by no means new. Such a proposal was first
made in Åfarli (1991) and more recently in Bobaljik (1995). Bobaljik links the
absence or presence of this inflectional projection not only to the (im)possibility
of V to I raising, but also to the (im)possibility of full NP object shift and
transitive expletive constructions (cf. (75)). In Section 5.4, I will adopt Bobaljik's

reasoning concerning the latter two construction types. Bobaljik and I however differ with respect to the reasons for the presence of the additional inflectional projection in V to I raising languages. Recall that Bobaljik ends up rejecting his earlier suggestion that AgrP is posited unless the appearance of tense morphology blocks the appearance of agreement morphology (cf. (55)) in favor of the view that AgrP is the result of an arbitrarily determined parameter setting. In this book, I am defending the position that AgrP is projected whenever the agreement paradigm minimally distinctively marks the referential features [1ST] and [2ND] and is hence itself referential and as such listed in the lexicon. This position is summarized in (77), a revised version of (63).

(77)   **Referentiality of Agr/Lexicality of Agr-Affixes**
        Agreement is a referential category with lexically listed affixes (projecting AgrP in syntax and triggering overt verb movement) in exactly those languages where regular subject-verb agreement minimally distinctively marks the referential agreement features such that in at least one number of one tense, the person features [1ST] and [2ND] are distinctively marked.

I have adopted an approach to inflectional morphology that is in part 'weak lexicalist' (for V to I raising languages with minimally distinctive marking of both referential agreement features, cf. (78a)) and in part 'interpretativist' (for V in situ languages without minimally distinctive marking of both referential agreement features, cf. (78b)).

(78)   a.   V to I languages   b.   V in situ languages

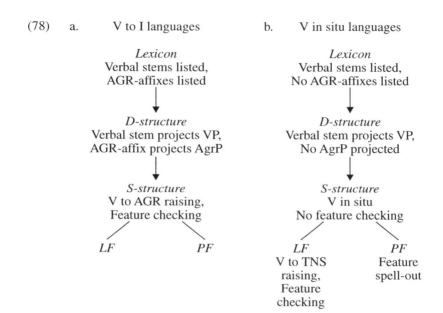

Lexicon	*Lexicon*
Verbal stems listed,	Verbal stems listed,
AGR-affixes listed	No AGR-affixes listed

D-structure	*D-structure*
Verbal stem projects VP,	Verbal stem projects VP,
AGR-affix projects AgrP	No AgrP projected

S-structure	*S-structure*
V to AGR raising,	V in situ
Feature checking	No feature checking

LF	*PF*	*LF*	*PF*
		V to TNS	Feature
		raising,	spell-out
		Feature	
		checking	

In adopting this model, I reject a 'strong lexicalist' approach to inflectional morphology according to which verbs are already overtly inflected when they are taken out of the lexicon and inserted in D-structure and that syntax merely checks abstract inflectional features. Such a view, familiar from Jensen and Stong-Jensen (1984) and others, has been the standard one since Chomsky (1992, 1995). Chomsky assumes that V to I raising languages have 'strong' abstract Infl-features which either are illicit (or 'visible') PF elements (Chomsky 1992) or simply have to be deleted as soon as they are introduced (Chomsky 1995) and which therefore have to be eliminated already at S-structure via checking against the corresponding features on the verb. It follows that in languages with 'strong' Infl-features, V to I raising takes place overtly at S-structure to establish this checking relationship (cf. (79a)). Chomsky further assumes that V in situ languages have 'weak' abstract Infl-features which either are licit (or "invisible") PF elements (Chomsky 1992) or are simply tolerated throughout overt syntax (Chomsky 1995) and which therefore do not have to be eliminated until LF. It follows that in languages with 'weak' Infl-features, V to I raising takes place covertly at LF (cf. (79b)).

(79)   a.   V to I languages   b.   V in situ languages

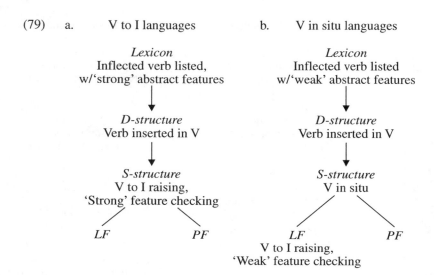

Empirically, (79) makes the same predictions as (78) if languages with complete paradigms have 'strong' agreement features and languages with incomplete paradigms have 'weak' agreement features. But I would like to argue that the strong lexicalist approach has to stipulate this difference between V to I and V in situ languages. In contrast, I have tried to show above that in my framework, the lexical listing of complete paradigms versus the post-syntactic generation of incomplete paradigms follows from the way in which inflectional elements refer (i.e. via distinctive marking of the person features). If this is correct, we have reason to prefer (78) over (79).

Chomsky's proposal would have considerable appeal if the invisibility of 'weak' agreement features would translate into their de facto absence in lexicon and syntax, but this is not the case. Consider for example the fact that in the V to I raising language Icelandic and in the V in situ language Faroese alike, present tense verb forms that can co-occur with first person singular subjects cannot co-occur with any other type of subject (cf. (80)). To guarantee this result, the strong lexicalist approach has to assign Icelandic and Faroese first person singular indicative present verb forms lexical representations that are identical in all relevant aspects except perhaps for abstract feature 'strength' (cf. (81)). Note in particular that 'weak inflectional features' do not translate into 'fewer inflectional features' in Faroese.

(80)   a.   ég / *þu   / *hún / *við / *þið / *þær segi ...
              I   / *you / *she / *we / *you / *they say ...   Icelandic

        b.   eg / *tú   / *hon / *vit / *tit   / *tær krevji ...
              I   / *you / *she / *we / *you / *they require ...   Faroese

(81)   a.   segi   b.   krevji
              $\begin{bmatrix} \text{pres} \\ \text{(-pl)} \\ \text{1st} \end{bmatrix}$ $\begin{bmatrix} \text{pres} \\ \text{(-pl)} \\ \text{1st} \end{bmatrix}$

There is then no independent difference between the lexical entries of 'weakly' and 'strongly' inflected verb forms that would distinguish them and explain their different syntactic behavior. Nor does the 'strength' versus 'weakness' of the agreement features have any other consequences apart from requiring the verb to move to Infl already in overt syntax or allowing postponement of this movement until LF.[27] In other words, the distinction between 'strong' and 'weak' features is not independently motivated and although it correctly describes the facts, it does not (yet) explain them.

Within the weak lexicalist-interpretativist model proposed above, such an explanation seems possible: The lexicon contains all and only referential elements. *Pro*-drop theory independently attests that referentiality requires overt person marking. It is therefore plausible to assume that a paradigm of agreement affixes is referential and hence listed in the lexicon iff person agreement is (minimally) distinctively marked. Lexically listed, referential agreement affixes project AgrP in syntax and trigger V to Agr raising via Lasnik's Filter. Lexically unlisted, non-referential agreement affixes do not project AgrP. Rather, they are introduced post-syntactically and do therefore not affect the position of the verb. If this reasoning goes through, the weak lexicalist-interpretativist model offers a more principled account for V to I raising than the strong lexicalist model.

3.5   Residual V to I Raising in Faroese

In closing this chapter, let me address the question of residual V to I raising in Faroese. I would like to propose a solution for this problem which supports the claim I made earlier in this section that languages which minimally distinctively mark the referential agreement features list all Agr-affixes in the lexicon, including those without unique reference. Recall that in Faroese, [2ND] is never

distinctively marked in regular agreement morphology (cf. (65)). We expect
Faroese verbs to be only abstractly inflected in syntax and (overt) V to I raising
to be absent. This expectation is confirmed by the fact that most speakers allow
the negation marker only in preverbal position in embedded clauses that are not
the complements of asserted bridge verbs (cf. (82a)), indicating obligatory V in
situ where V to C movement cannot apply. However, I mentioned in Chapter 2
that a minority of speakers seems to also allow post-verbal negation in this
context (cf. (82b)), suggesting a residue of optional V to I raising.

> (82)   a.   Hann spyr, hví tað   *ikki eru* fleiri tílíkar samkomur.
>   he   asks why there not are more such   gatherings
>   b.   Hann spyr, hví tað   *eru ikki* fleiri tílíkar samkomur
>   he   asks why there are not more such   gatherings
>   (Faroese [Barnes 1989, ex. 2f])

Residual V to I raising in Faroese is usually attributed to archaic style, a pocket
of resistance against the otherwise completed change to V in situ (cf. Barnes
1989, Vikner 1994). This analysis is supported by the existence of parallel cases
in Mainland Scandinavian. 19th century Danish for example did in general no
longer allow V to I raising, yet V to I raising is evident in the following sentence
from a 19th century version of a Danish Folk tale.

> (83)   Prindsessen havde faaet Vulle saa kjær, at   hun *vilde   ikke* have
>   princess-the had   got   V.   so fond that she would not have
>   Kongen.
>   king-the
>   'The princess had gotten so fond of Vulle that she wouldn't have the
>   king.'   (Danish, 19th century [Vikner 1994: fn. 6 ex. (i)])

An analysis of cases of residual V to I raising as archaisms might well be on the
right track. Yet such an analysis is not very exciting from a theoretical point of
view. It also runs into a problem already mentioned in Section 3.3: Like reducing
V to I raising in Kronoby Swedish to influence from Finnish, explaining
(marginal) V to I raising in Faroese as reflecting archaic style severely weakens
the restrictiveness of the system because it essentially abolishes the idea that
there is a single trigger for V to I raising.[28] In the following, I will offer a
principled account for residual V to I raising in Faroese that is based on the
Paradigm-Verb Raising Correlate in (63) and the Principle of Referentiality of

Agr/Lexicality of Agr-Affixes in (77) on the one hand and the existence of a few irregular complete paradigms in Faroese on the other hand.

A very limited number of Faroese verbs in fact do have a complete paradigm that minimally distinctively marks not only [1ST] and [singular], but also [2ND]. (84) and (85) list all verbs which according to Lockwood (1964) inflect as shown in (86a) and (86b), respectively. Similar patterns are found in Icelandic. In both languages, only verbs whose stems historically ended in -r (cf. (84)) or a vowel (cf. (85)) are affected (Lockwood 1983: 46; Thomson 1987: 395).

(84) *bera*   'carry'   *skera*   'cut'   *svørja*   'swear'
      fara   'go/travel'   *smyrja*   'smear'   *vera*   'be'
      gera   'do'   *spyrja*   'ask'

(85) *búgva*   'live'   *grógva*   'grow'   *sláa*   'strike'
      doyggja   'die'   *læa*   'laugh'   *spyggja*   'vomit'
      fáa   'take/get'   *rógva*   'row'   *trúgva*   'believe'
      goyggja   'bark'   *síggja*   'see'

(86) a.   Faroese   b.   Faroese
            ber-a 'carry'   *búgv-a* 'live'
            IND PRES   IND PRES

	SG	PL		SG	PL
1ST	ber-i	ber-a		búgv-i	búgv-a
2ND	ber-t[29]	ber-a		bý-rt[29]	búgv-a
3RD	ber	ber-a		bý-r	búgv-a

A comparison of regular patterns like the one in (65) with the irregular patterns in (86) shows that the latter contain an additional piece of suffix morphology, *-t*, which distinctively marks [2ND]. In other words: Unlike regular verbs, the irregular verbs in (84) and (85) have a Full Paradigm in the singular of the indicative present.

The theory of V to I raising developed above now enables us to give the following principled account for residual V to I raising in Faroese. Speakers of Faroese build their primary (and for most speakers only) linguistic system on the basis of the regular and incomplete agreement paradigms like the one in (65) which never distinctively mark the person feature [2ND]. In this primary system, agreement is not referential, the agreement affixes are not listed in the lexicon and S-structural V to I raising is therefore not triggered. I would like to tentatively suggest that in addition to this primary system, some speakers built a secondary linguistic system on the basis of the irregular and complete person agreement paradigms in (86) which minimally distinctively mark both referential agreement features. In this secondary system, agreement is referential, the agreement affixes are listed in the lexicon and overt V to I raising is hence triggered.

Implicit in this proposal is what has become known as the Double Base Hypothesis (cf. Kroch 1990; Pintzuck 1991; Santorini 1989): An otherwise monolingual speaker may realize opposite settings of one and the same parameter, thus creating two linguistic systems or a double base for what is essentially one language. Texts from Old English (Pintzuck 1991) and earlier stages of Yiddish (Santorini 1989) for example have been shown to contain both right- and left-headed IPs at the same time. In our case, individual speakers of Faroese make use of both referential and non-referential agreement since the language has both complete and incomplete paradigms.

Please note that this theory does not wrongly predict that residual V to I raising in Faroese occurs only with those verbs which have a complete paradigm. For each linguistic system, the Principle of Referentiality of Agr/ Lexicality of Agr-Affixes in (77) summarily determines on the basis of certain agreement paradigms (canonically the regular ones) whether the agreement affixes are all listed in the lexicon or all spelled out at PF. Sometimes, irregular paradigms may trigger the establishment of secondary linguistic systems. But in either case, the position of all verbs is affected, not just the position of those verbs which exhibit the paradigm in question. The behavior of Old and Early Middle English preterit-present verbs further supports this view. As mentioned above, Middle English displayed V to I raising triggered by the complete regular paradigm in (33a). Preterit-present verbs however had irregular paradigms that did not distinctively mark [1ST], cf. Chaucer's forms in (87). Nevertheless, preterit-present verbs raised to Infl like all other verbs, cf. the example in (88) taken from Chaucer's Troilus. In evaluating (88), bear in mind that until well into the Middle English period, at least some preterit-present verbs, including (pre-) modals like *connen*, acted syntactically like full verbs and where presumably base-generated inside the VP. Unlike its Modern English translation, sentence (88) therefore instantiates V to I raising instead of base-generation in an inflectional head (see Chapter 4).

(87)   Early Middle English
                        conn-en
                        IND PRES
                        SG   PL
        1ST   can   conn-e(n)
        2ND   can-st   conn-e(n)
        3RD   can   conn-e(n)

(88)   A blynde man *kan nat* juggen wel in hewis.
        a blind   man can not judge well in colors
        'A blind man cannot judge colors well.'
                              (Middle English 1387 [Chaucer *Troilus*],
                                        Roberts 1993, ex. 3(11a))

We must conclude that on the basis of the minimally distinctive marking of the
referential agreement features [1ST] and [2ND] in the regular paradigm in (33a),
not only these regular agreement affixes, but also the irregular agreement affixes
of the preterit-present verbs without minimal distinctive marking of [1ST] were
listed in the lexicon. In the next chapter, I will address the historical development of the preterit-present verbs in more detail.

Notes

1. Recall from the discussion of (22) and (27) in Chapter 2 that there is a way to salvage (1a),
    namely adjunction of Neg to α. According to Ouhalla and Benmamoun (cf. below), such
    adjunction would only be possible if α needs to be bound, which is not the case here, since α
    is already bound by β.

2. Nevertheless, *not* can contract with a preceding auxiliary or modal. This cliticization is unlikely
    to be a purely phonological phenomenon, since it affects the semantics of the sentence.
    Consider the well-known contrast between (i) with and (ii) without contraction. Negation can
    have narrow scope only in the latter.

    (i)   I can't come to the movies tonight.
    (ii)   I can not come to the movies tonight.

3. One way out would be to assume that NegP is only a specific instance of a general speech act
    phrase ΣP (cf. Laka 1990) whose head, which determines whether the content of a sentence is
    negated, asserted or questioned, is always a bound morpheme in French and always a free
    morpheme in English. But even if we make this assumption, ΣP is motivated only in negated,
    emphatically asserted and questioned sentences which require *do*-support but not in non-

emphatically asserted sentences which do not allow *do*-support (cf. Section 4.2.1). It is therefore unlikely that the pre-verbal position of adverbs in English non-emphatically asserted sentences like (4b) can be explained by appealing to a free Σ-morpheme that blocks V to I raising.

The examples in (4) and the discussion in the previous paragraph involve finite affirmatives. French and English non-finite affirmatives show the same contrast as finite affirmatives (compare (4a) with (i) and (4b) with (ii)).

    (i)   **Paraître** *souvent* triste...
          look   often   sad   (French)

    (ii)   To *often* **look** sad...

Unlike the contrast between finite affirmatives, the contrast between non-finite affirmatives can be explained by Ouhalla without the help of ΣP. He proposes that infinitival verbs precede sentential adverbs in French and follow them in English because the infinitival marker is a bound morpheme in French (allowing adjunction of the verb to this marker) and a free morpheme in English (barring adjunction of the verb movement to this marker). This is illustrated in (iii-iv), the s-structures for (i) and (ii).

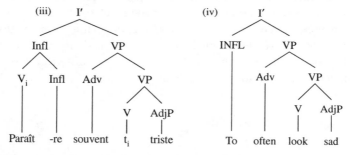

Obviously, this explanation for the contrast in (i-ii) where the inflectional morpheme is bound in French and free in English does not carry over to the contrast in (4a, b) where the inflectional morpheme is bound in French and English alike.

4.   Benmamoun claims that Standard Arabic is a case in question, but Ouhalla argues that in this language NegP dominates IP.

5.   In those (non-V2) languages for which Ouhalla explicitly argues that Neg c-selects IP, the subject in fact does canonically follow the negation marker, cf. his examples from Berber and Arabic below.

        (i)   *ur-* y- sgha *Moha* taddart.
            NEG-3MS-bought M.   house
            'Moha has not bought a house.'   (Berber)

        (ii)   *lam* ya- shtarii *Zaydun* l- bayta.
             NEG 3MS-buy   Z.   the-house
             'Zayd has not bought a house.'   (Arabic)

6. The explanation for the unavailability of V to I raising in English non-finite affirmatives outlined in note 3 does not carry over to Mainland Scandinavian non-finite affirmatives. In Swedish, there is good reason to assume that the free "infinitival" marker *att* is in fact a complementizer base-generated in Comp (cf. Platzack 1986). We would then expect the bound infinitival marker *-a* to behave like its French (rather than its English) counterpart, i.e. to be base-generated in Infl and to trigger V to I raising across sentential adverbs. Yet this is not what happens:

>   (i)   Han hade föresatt sig   att *aldrig* **slå** hunden
>   he   had   set   himself to never beat dog-the
>   'He had resolved himself on never beating the dog.'

>   (Swedish, Platzack 1986)

In general, Mainland Scandinavian has bound tense and agreement morphology and only uses periphrastic constructions where Icelandic does so, too. The status of inflection markers as free or bound morphemes can therefore not explain the word order differences in Icelandic and Mainland Scandinavian embedded affirmative clauses that are not the complement of asserted bridge-verbs.

7. Holmberg and Platzack (1995) distinguish between V2 languages where [+F] is always located in Comp and non-V2 languages where this feature is always located in Infl. In V2 languages, [+F] attracts the verb when Comp is not otherwise lexicalized, i.e. in matrix clauses and in embedded clauses that are asserted complements of bridge verbs. In embedded clauses that are not asserted complements of bridge verbs, Comp is independently lexicalized by a complementizer, and [+F] does not attract the verb. Whether a V2 language has V to I raising or V in situ in those clauses where the verb does not move to Comp is determined by the "richness" of its agreement in the sense of Section 3.2.3 and 3.3 (although Holmberg and Platzack 1995 do not precisely define this notion). In non-V2 languages, [+F] similarly attracts the verb when Infl is not otherwise lexicalized, e.g. in French (V to I raising). In English, Infl is independently lexicalized by the dummy auxiliary *do* (in negated sentences, emphatic affirmatives and non-subject wh-questions) or a phonetically empty variant of it (in all other sentences) whenever the clause does not contain a temporal or aspectual auxiliary or a modal, and [+F] does not attract the verb (V in situ). This explanation however only begs the question: Why did English develop a pair of dummy auxiliaries rather than chose the presumably unmarked and hence less costly option, i.e. V to I raising? Holmberg & Platzack do not offer any answer to this question. According to Holmberg & Platzack, English does not have V to I raising because it has *do*-support, but it is at least as plausible to say that English has *do*-support because it does not have V to I raising. I will return to this issue in Chapter 4.

8. It is less clear what forces [+F] to be located in Infl where this is possible, i.e. in languages like Icelandic with overt morphological case. One possible explanation is that syntactic Infl-lowering has to be undone via V to I raising at LF and that syntactic V to I raising triggered by [+F] in Infl is therefore more economical than Infl-lowering triggered by [+F] in Comp (cf. Chomsky 1989).

9. According to Lockwood (1964:28), "the use of the genitive is … rather limited. As a syntactic case it occurs in the spoken language only in a very few nouns, but it is found more widely in certain prepositional phrases."

10. Roberts' original formulation has "only if" instead of "if". A typing error must be the reason, since Roberts later writes that "[23] is formulated as a one-way conditional, and so it allows Agr^{-1} to exist in the absence of the relevant morphology" and that "[23] is stated so that the absence of the relevant agreement morphology is not strictly incompatible with V-to-Agr movement".

11. The recoverability of number agreement by [+F] (and hence the optionality of V to I raising in languages with number agreement) has to be stipulated. Falk (1993: 33) notes that tense in Infl and [+F] in Comp always co-occur and holds this fact responsible for the recoverability of tense by [+F]. She further mentions that "[+F] and agreement are not as closely connected", as shown by the existence of inflected infinitives, and thus explains the non-recoverability of agreement by [+F]. But at least in Portuguese, the language usually cited in this connection, inflected infinitives exhibit not only person agreement, but also number agreement (cf. (i) after Hundertmark-Santos Martin 1982). Number agreement, too, should then not be recoverable by [+F] and Falk's theory should make the stronger and more strikingly incorrect claim that V to I raising is obligatory in all languages with number agreement.

(i)	Portuguese *vend-er*	
	Inflected INF	
	SG PL	
1ST	vend-er	vend-er-mos
2ND	vend-er-es	vend-er-des
3RD	vend-er	vend-er-em

12. In Chapter 5, I will argue that Brazilian Portuguese, which has overt distinct plural marking, also lacks V to I raising. If so, Brazilian Portuguese constitutes another counterexample against Roberts' and Falk's theories.

13. Here, 'unmarkered person' means both 'person not bearing an overt person marker' and 'person not bearing an abstract person feature'. 'Unmarked person' on the other hand means 'default person'.

14. English and Yiddish appear to counter this trend. In English, third person singular is the only overtly marked form and in Yiddish, first person singular is the only overtly unmarked form. The English case is unproblematic if we follow Kayne (1989) and assume that -*s* is in fact a number and not a person marker. As for Yiddish, it is clear that historically, the unmarked first person singular form was the product of a post-syntactic phonological rule that deleted word-final unstressed schwa (*lóyf-ə* → *lóyf-Ø* V: "run" 1ST sg indicative present; "ʼ" indicates stress). But this rule is no longer active, as shown by the fact that it is restricted to the German component of the lexicon and does not extend to those items of the Hebrew component which came into the domain of schwa-deletion only after adaptation of the German stress pattern had triggered vowel reduction (*ménorá* → *menóyrə* → **menóyr* N: "menorah"). Synchronically, the Yiddish first person singular must therefore be assumed to be unmarkered already in underlying representation, thus presenting a real example of an empty affix for first person in the face of an overt affix for third person.

15. In addition, some languages have a first person inclusive corresponding to the heavily marked feature combination [+1ST, +2ND].

16. Other *pro*-drop languages such as Spanish (cf. (i)) do allow referential *pro* in the "third" person.

    (i)   (el) habla Espanol.

          he speaks Spanish.   (Spanish)

Especially puzzling is the often overlooked fact that Biblical Hebrew, which had essentially the same subject-verb agreement paradigm as Modern Hebrew, also allowed referential *pro* in the "third" person, unlike Modern Hebrew. Compare (ii) with (37c) and notice that (ii) cannot be a case of "anaphoric" Infl (cf. Borer 1989) or syntactic control and that it does not meet the syntactic and pragmatic criteria for Topic Drop that will be discussed in Section 5.3, either.

    (ii)   Vayomer   el aviv   roSi   roSi

          And-(he$_i$)-said to his$_i$-father$_k$ "my-head, my-head"

          vayomer   el hana'ar   sa'ehu   el

          and-(he$_k$)-said to the-adolescent$_l$ "carry-him$_i$ to

          imo   vayisa'ehu   vayevi'ehu

          his$_i$-mother" and-(he$_l$)-carried-him$_i$ and-(he$_l$)-brought-him$_i$

          el imo   vayeshev   al birkeha   ad

          to his$_i$-mother and-(he$_i$)-sat on her-knees until

          hacohorayim vayamot.

          noon   and-(he$_i$)-died.   (2 Kings IV 19–20)

It is not clear to me what is responsible for this difference between Biblical and Modern Hebrew.

17. Other solutions also have this or similar problems. Platzack and Holmberg (1989), who also link V to I raising to person agreement (cf. (32)), write on page 74 regarding Kronoby Swedish: "The evidence required, in the absence of overt (person) agreement, to set the [verb movement] parameter right is precisely sentences like [(44)]: given reasonable assumptions it can only be analyzed as having the finite verb moved to Agr [= Infl]." But if examples of V to I raising in the input are sufficient to trigger the acquisition of V to I raising, it is unclear why the morphological richness of person or any other agreement should play any role at all in this process.

18. Outside the Germanic VO languages, a few other problematic cases can be found. Modern Hebrew is an interesting case in question. Borer (1995) argues that the possibility of the XP^SUBJ^V order in (ii) alongside the XP^V^SUBJ order in (i) is due to the fact that V to I raising is only optional in this language (compare the structures in (iii) and (iv) although minimal distinctive person marking appears in the past and future tenses (cf. (v)). Such optionality has no place in the current system. I will have to leave the question of the right treatment of cases like (i,ii) unresolved for now.

    (i)   'et ha-yeladim limda Rina la-Sir.

          ACC the-boys   taught R.   to-sing

    (ii)   'et ha-yeladim Rina limda la-Sir.

          ACC the-boys   R.   taught to-sing

          'Rina taught the boys to sing.'   (Modern Hebrew, Borer 1995, ex. (76a, b))

(iii)

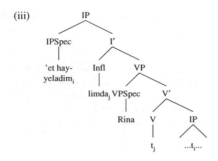

(iv)

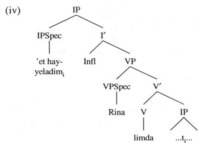

(v) Hebrew *le?exol* "eat"

a. PRES   b. PAST   c. FUT

	SG			SG	PL				SG	PL
M	oxel		1ST	M	axalti	axalnu		1ST	M	oxal	noxal
F	oxelet			F	axalti	axalnu			F	oxal	noxal
			2ND	M	axalta	axaltem		2ND	M	toxal	toxlu
	PL			F	axalt	axalten			F	toxli	toxlu
M	oxlim		3RD	M	axal	axlu		3RD	M	yoxal	yoxlu
F	oxlot			F	axla	axlu			F	toxal	yoxlu

Russian is another problematic case. On the basis of the obligatorily preverbal position of
adverbs (cf. (vi)) and the ungrammaticality of quantifier floating (cf. (vii)) in Russian,
Benedicto (1994:5) argues that Russian also lacks V to I raising although it has minimal
distinctive person marking in the present and future tenses (cf. (viii)). See also Bailyn (1995).

(vi) a. Anna bystro čitaet recepty.
         A.   quickly reads recipes
         'Anna quickly reads the recipes.'
      b. *?Anna čitaet bystro recepty.

(vii) a. Studenty vse čitajut Vojnu i   mir.
          Students all read War and Peace
          'The Students all read War and Peace.'
       b. *Studenty čitajut vse Vojnu i mir.

(viii) Russian *prixodit'/prijti* "come"

a.	PRES				b.	PAST		
		SG	PL				SG	PL
	1ST	prixožu	prixodim			FEM	prišla	prišli
	2ND	prixodiš'	prixodite			MASC	prišël	prišli
	3RD	prixodit	prixodjat			NEUT	prišlo	prišli

c.	FUT		
		SG	PL
	1ST	pridu	pridëm
	2ND	pridëš'	pridëte
	3RD	pridët	pridut

I do not know what is responsible for the apparent lack of V to I raising in Russian. In Avrutin and Rohrbacher (1997), we argue that Russian does exhibit at least one syntactic consequence of a Full Paradigm in the sense of (39), namely *pro*-drop. See Section 5.3 for the connection between the Full Paradigm and *pro*-drop in other languages.

19. Thanks to Ken Hale and Michael Walsh-Dickey for discussing the Miskitu data with me.

20. Earlier versions of the Paradigm-Verb Raising Correlate can be found in Rohrbacher (1991, 1993).

21. In addition, Vikner's generalization fares perhaps slightly better than the Paradigm-Verb Raising Correlate with respect to the languages discussed in note 18: It correctly predicts that Russian does not have any V to I raising but incorrectly predicts the same for Modern Hebrew.

22. Bobaljik argues that in languages without V to I raising, the fused Agr/Tense merges with the verb in situ under adjacency. This is problematic since in English, adjacency between Agr/Tense and V can be broken up by a VP-adjoined adverb, as shown in (i). Bobaljik acknowledges this problem but has no deep (i.e. non-stipulatory) explanation to offer.

(i)   Mary often kisses Joan.

23. The early acquisition of verb placement is not restricted to verb movement to Infl. The consistent adult-like distinction between V2 finite verbs with the possibility of topicalization and V-final nonfinite verbs without the possibility of topicalization in early child German (cf. (ia) from Poeppel & Wexler 1993 [Andreas, age 2;1], (ib,c) from Rohrbacher & Vainikka 1995 [Katrin, age 1;5 and Nicole, age 1;8], and Table I) shows that verb movement to Comp, which is typically held responsible for this distinction in the adult grammar (cf. Section 2.3), has already been acquired at this early stage.

(i)

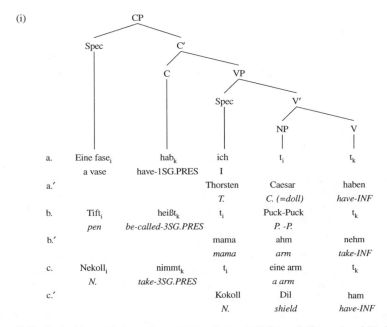

				NP	V
a.	Eine fase$_i$	hab$_k$	ich	t$_i$	t$_k$
	a vase	have-1SG.PRES	I		
a.′			Thorsten	Caesar	haben
			T.	C. (=doll)	have-INF
b.	Tift$_i$	heißt$_k$	t$_i$	Puck-Puck	t$_k$
	pen	be-called-3SG.PRES		P. -P.	
b.′			mama	ahm	nehm
			mama	arm	take-INF
c.	Nekoll$_i$	nimmt$_k$	t$_i$	eine arm	t$_k$
	N.	take-3SG.PRES		a arm	
c.′			Kokoll	Dil	ham
			N.	shield	have-INF

Table I: *Position of finite and non-finite verbs in child German (Poeppel and Wexler 1993, Rohrbacher and Vainikka 1995)*

	Andreas		Katrin		Nicole	
	+ fin	− fin	+ fin	− fin	+ fin	− fin
V2	19(95%)	6 (14%)	68(77%)	2 (3%)	71(77%)	6 (5%)
Vf	11 (5%)	37(86%)	0	6 (5%)	4 (4%)	24(21%)

Note that most of Katrin's and Nicole's non-finite clauses are ambiguous and could be analyzed either as V2 or as V-final structures. By contrast, all of Andreas's non-finite clauses are unambiguous and must in their overwhelming majority be analyzed as V-final structures. The difference is due to the fact that whereas Katrin and Nicole are for the most part still in the two-word stage, Andreas is already in the multi-word stage. In the two-word stage of a SOV V2 language, the order VX clearly indicates that verb movement has taken place but the order XV is ambiguous between verb movement plus topicalization and V in situ. In the multi-word stage of such a language, the orders XVY and VXY clearly indicate that verb movement has taken place and the order XYV unambiguously indicates V in situ. What is most important in Katrin's and Nicole's data is that the VX order is almost always associated with finite forms, providing ample evidence for verb movement in finite clauses. These data therefore suggest that Katrin and Nicole display the same pattern as Andreas and adult speakers of German: whereas finite verbs move to C, non-finite verbs most likely stay in situ. See Rohrbacher and Vainikka (1995) for further discussion.

In Chapter 6, I will briefly mentioned that V2 poses a problem for the theory of Morphology-Driven Syntax since it is difficult to see how overt morphological properties of the complementizer system of e.g. German could be responsible for V2. In the case of early child German, this problem is even more pronounced, since at least Katrin and Nicole produce virtually no embedded clauses and arguably have not yet acquired most (if any) of the overt morphological properties of the complementizer system. Since the acquisition of verb movement to Comp goes beyond the scope of this book, which is concerned primarily with verb movement to Infl, I will have to leave this issue unresolved for now.

24. I suspect that the same argument can be made with respect to the acquisition of Faroese, but I am not familiar with the facts.

25. In some cases, number may also be argued to be grammatical´ instead of natural, as in the majestic (cf. (ia)) or (archaic) honorific (cf. (iia)) use of the German plural instead of the neutral singular (cf. (ib,iib)). Like gender marking, number marking displays crosslinguistic variation (cf. (iii)).

(i)   a.   Wir beschließen, daß die Erde flach ist.
           we determine   that the earth flat is
      b.   Ich beschließe, daß die Erde flach ist.
           I   determine   that the earth flat is
           'I determine that the earth is flat.'

(ii) a.   Ihr   seid   sehr großzügig.
           you-PL are-2PL very generous
      b.   Du   bist   sehr großzügig.
           you-SG are-2SG very generous   (German)

(iii) a.   the shears
      b.   die Schere
           the shear-SG   (German)

There are however also a few cases where person is arguably grammatical rather than natural, as in the honorific (cf. (iva)) or (archaic) contemptuous (cf. (ivb)) use of the German third person instead of the familiar second person (cf. (ivc)).

(iv) a.   Sie haben ihre Steuern noch nicht bezahlt.
           they have their taxes   still not   paid
      b.   Er hat seine Steuern noch nicht bezahlt.
           he has his   taxes   still not   paid
      c.   Du   hast deine Steuern noch nicht bezahlt.
           you-SG have your taxes   still not   paid
           'You haven't paid your taxes yet.'

26. **Lasnik's Filter**

   A morphologically realized affix must be realized as a syntactic dependent at Surface structure.   (Lasnik 1981)

27. This is often acknowledged in the Minimalist literature, cf. for example Wilder and Cavar (1994:56 fn. 14): "The only observable correlate of a strong feature is the overt movement it triggers".

28. Most Faroese dialects lost the complete paradigm before the first texts were written down at the end of the 18th century. The north-eastern dialects retained the complete paradigm until the end of the last century (cf. Krenn 1940: 94, Lockwood 1983: 45). There is however no connection between this dialectal variation and present day residual V to I raising. V^Neg is for example the normal embedded word order in the idiolect of the contemporary author Heðin Brú who comes from the central (i.e. not north-eastern) island of Sandoy (Sandqvist 1981, cited after Barnes 1987).

29. According to Lockwood (1964: 81), this second person singular affix -t is often omitted in the spoken language. At least in Icelandic, omission of the corresponding marker -ð is possible only in elevated style (see Thomson 1987: 395). Lockwood (1983: 46) claims this marker originated through cliticization of the second person singular pronoun tú "you", whereas Haugen (1982: 140) argues that it was created in analogy to the second person singular of preterit-present verbs, cf. tú skalt "you shall".

CHAPTER 4

Diachronic Germanic Syntax and the Full Paradigm

4.1 Introduction

In the previous chapter, I have shown that synchronically, V to I raising is a consequence of the Full (or Complete) Paradigm, i.e. the distinctive marking of the referential Infl-features [1ST] and [2ND] for person in the regular verbal morphology of a language. This theory predicts that diachronically, the loss of the relevant regular verbal morphology in a language should trigger the loss of V to I raising in that language. Moreover, if a language loses the crucial distinctions in the paradigms of certain irregular verbs, but maintains them with respect to regular verbs, an exceptional syntactic treatment of these irregular verbs would not come as a surprise. In this chapter, I argue that these predictions are in fact correct. English and Mainland Scandinavian lost V to I raising shortly after regular verbs ceased to distinctively marked both of the person features [1ST] and [2ND] in their inflectional morphology. On the ancestors of modern day modals, English (but not Mainland Scandinavian) lost the marking in questions at an earlier point in time when the language still preserved it on all other verbs. English pre-modals, which started out as main verbs that moved past negation and adverbs to an inflectional head, became therefore reanalyzed as functional elements that are base-generated to the left of negation and adverbs in an inflectional head. Their Mainland Scandinavian counterparts continue to function as main verbs. This explains the following well known difference between the modern languages. English modals (unlike main verbs) precede negation and adverbs, occur only in finite forms and do not take direct objects. Mainland Scandinavian modals (like main verbs) follow negation and adverbs, occur in finite and non-finite forms and may take direct objects. The analysis can be extended to account for a related difference, i.e. the position of English finite *have* and *be* in front of negation and adverbs versus the position of their Mainland Scandinavian counterparts after negation and adverbs.

4.2 On the Loss of V to I Raising in Some Germanic VO Languages

4.2.1 *English*

Old and Middle English regular verbal morphology distinctively marked all the referential Infl-features, i.e. both of the person features [1ST] and [2ND] (see for example the singular of the Middle Midland English paradigm in (1), after Wyld 1927).

(1)   Middle Midland English
                 INF *sing-en*
                 IND   PRES
                 SG   PL
        1ST   sing-e   sing-en
        2ND   sing-est   sing-en
        3RD   sing-eþ   sing-en

The theory of Chapter 3 predicts that unlike Modern English, Old and Middle English had lexical entries for their agreement affixes which projected AgrSP at D-structure and had to be bound at S-structure, hence triggering V to I raising (or verb movement to AgrS). This prediction is indeed borne out by Middle English examples like those in (2), where post-verbal negation (cf. (2a)) and sentential adverbs (cf. (2b)) indicate that the main verb has undergone V to I raising (cf. the S-structures in (3a, b)).[1] These Middle English examples should be compared with their Modern English translations, where preverbal negation and sentential adverbs indicate that the main verb stays in situ inside VP (cf. the S-structure in (3c,d) and the discussion in Section 2.4.2.1).[2]

(2)   a.   Wepyng and teres **counforteth** *not* dissolute laghers.
              'Weeping and tears do*n't* **comfort** dissolute laughers.'
                        (Middle English 1400–1450 [Love *Lyf of Jesu Christ*],
                                                      Roberts 1993, ex. 3(25a))
        b.   Quene Ester **looked** *never* with swich an eye.
              'Queen Esther *never* **looked** with such an eye.'
                        (Middle English c. 1400 [Chaucer *Merchant's Tale*],
                                                      Kroch 1990, ex. (37))

(3)

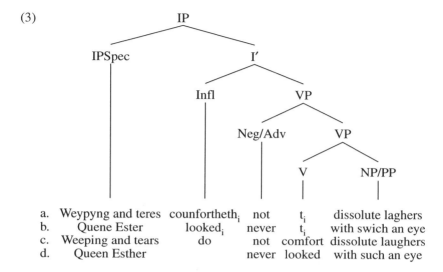

a.	Weypyng and teres	counfortheth$_i$	not	t$_i$	dissolute laghers
b.	Quene Ester	looked$_i$	never	t$_i$	with swich an eye
c.	Weeping and tears	do	not	comfort	dissolute laughers
d.	Queen Esther		never	looked	with such an eye

By the year 1500 (i.e. the beginning of the Modern English period), the in-finitival and 1ST person singular markers had practically vanished from the verbal paradigm (cf. (4), after Roberts 1993).

(4)   Early Modern Midland English

INF *cast*

IND PRES

	SG	PL
1ST	cast	cast(-e)
2ND	cast-est	cast(-e)
3RD	cast-eþ	cast(-e)

Note that in (4), the forms for the infinitive and the 1ST person singular are identical and that the person feature [1ST] is hence no longer distinctively marked. If, as I claim in this book, the availability of V to I raising depends on the distinctive marking of all referential Infl-features including [1ST], then Early Modern English should have lost V to I raising around or shortly after the year 1500. A look at the development of the position of main verbs relative to sentential adverbs and negation confirms that this is indeed what happened. The following discussion draws heavily on the data collected in Ellegård (1953) and their interpretation in Kroch (1990).

In the V to I raising languages Old and Middle English with complete paradigms like (1), finite verbs usually moved to Infl (or AgrS) and hence preceded VP-left-adjoined sentential adverbs like *never* (cf. the word order V^Adv in the Middle English example in (2b) and its S-structure in (3b)). In the V in situ language Modern English with incomplete paradigms like (51a) in Chapter 3, main verbs never leave the VP and hence follow VP-left-adjoined sentential adverbs (cf. the word order ADV^V in the gloss of example (2b) and its S-structure in (3d)). It is reasonable to assume that in the history of English, the change from V^ADV to ADV^V coincides with and dates the loss of V to I raising.

A cautionary note is however in order. Some early examples in which an adverb precedes a verbal element cannot already be due to V in situ. In some Middle English examples such as the one in (5), an adverb like *never* precedes a modal verb like *can*. Modals surface in Infl even in Modern English and did so at earlier stages of the language, too. In fact, I will argue in Section 4.3 that by the Middle English period, modals were base-generated as inflectional heads rather than as verbs. In this case, the pre-modal position of the adverb in (5) cannot be taken as an indication that the modal is located inside the VP.

(5)   For many are that *never* **kane** halde the ordyre of lufe.
       for many are that never can   hold the ordure of love
       'For there are many that can never hold the ordure of love.'
                           (Middle English c. 1350 [Rolle *Bee and Stork*],
                                                   Roberts 1993, ex. 3(31))

Roberts (1993) points out that examples like (5) can be analyzed as cases of stylistic fronting, a process that is well known from Modern Icelandic and that moves a negation marker or adverb (as well as past participles, verb particles and certain adjectives) to the immediate left of the finite verb in clauses containing a subject gap (cf. Maling 1990).

(6)   Hann er sá eini sem *ekki* **er** líklegur til að koma.
       he   is the only that not is likely   to come
       'He's the only one that isn't likely to come.'
                                   (Icelandic, Maling 1990, ex. (20a))

Following Jónsson (1991a), I will assume that stylistic fronting is due to head-adjunction of the negation marker or adverb to the left of the verb in Infl as shown in (7), the S-structure of (5). I will leave open the question why SpecIP cannot contain phonetically realized material in (7).

(7)

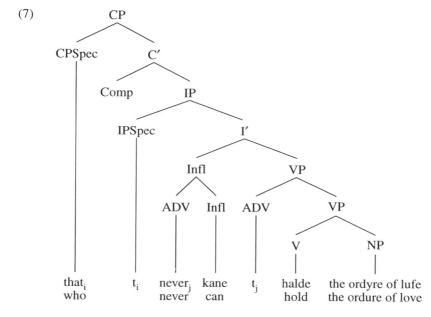

Under this analysis, sentences with a subject gap and *never* immediately preceding the finite verb are compatible with both V to I raising (in which case they involve stylistic fronting of *never*) and V in situ (in which case *never* remains in its base-generated VP-left-adjoined position). These sentences then cannot be used as evidence for or against V to I raising and should be disregarded in the context of the present discussion. Kroch (1990) estimates on the basis of concordances to 14th century literature that 16% of all sentences containing *never* exhibited stylistic fronting of this element. Table 4.1 and Figure 4.1 below trace the rise of the ADV^V order from 1425 to 1600. The raw figures include cases of stylistic fronting (assumed to be constant at 16% throughout the whole period) while the adjusted figures exclude them.

Table 4.1: *The rise of* never^*Main verb (after Ellegård 1953 and Kroch 1990)*

	all S w/ *never*		S w/ *never*^Main Verb			
	n		n		%	
	raw	adj.	raw	adj.	raw	adj.
1425–1475	154	129	55	30	35.7	23.2
1475–1500	186	156	84	54	45.2	34.6
1500–1525	109	92	81	64	74.3	69.6
1525–1535	170	143	154	127	90.6	88.8
1535–1550	152	128	139	115	91.4	89.8
1550–1575	88	74	80	66	90.9	89.2
1575–1600	163	137	158	132	96.9	96.4

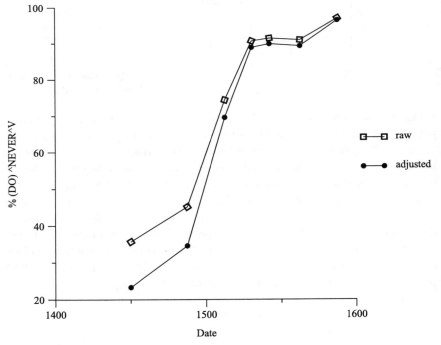

Figure 4.1: *The rise of* never^*Main verb*

Both raw and adjusted figures show the most dramatic change between periods 1475–1500 and 1525–1535: Between these periods, the percentage of preverbal *never* rose from 34.6 (adjusted) or 45.2 (raw) to 88.8 (adjusted) or 90.6 (raw). In so far as preverbal *never* reflects the absence of V to I raising, it is reasonable to assume that English lost V to I raising during this period, i.e. shortly after the year 1500. Above, I pointed out that by that same year, English had lost the minimal distinctive marking of the person feature [1ST] (cf. the Early Modern English paradigm in (4)). The diachronic data involving the relative order of main verbs and *never* thus support the hypothesis that English lost V to I raising as a result of the loss of the minimal distinctive marking of the person feature [1ST] and, more generally, that V to I raising depends on the minimal distinctive marking of both referential Infl-features as outlined in the previous chapter. Further support for this hypothesis comes from the diachronic data involving the relative order of main verbs and *not* and from a related issue, namely the historical development of *do*-support, to which I will now turn.

In Modern English negated declaratives and non-subject questions that do not underlyingly contain an auxiliary, the main verb may not simply stay in situ (cf. (8a,9a)), nor may it move out of the VP into Infl (over *not* in negated declaratives, cf. (8b)) or Comp (over the subject in non-subject questions, cf. (9b)). Instead, the periphrastic auxiliary *do* has to be inserted under Infl where in negated declaratives it surfaces in front of *not* (cf. (8c)); in non-subject questions, it must move to Comp where it surfaces in front of the subject (cf. (9c)).[3]

(8)   a.   *Tears *not comfort* dissolute laughers.
       b.   *Tears *comfort not* dissolute laughers.
       c.   Tears *do not comfort* dissolute laughers.

(9)   a.   *You *not see* how hardened his heart is?
       b.   *See* you *not* how hardened his heart is?
       c.   *Don't* you *see* how hardened his heart is?

It is clear that in this book, I cannot adopt the traditional view (expressed in Gleason 1965, Akmajian and Heny 1981, Chomsky 1989, and elsewhere), which holds that *do*-support is triggered by Lasnik's Filter (i.e. the requirement that morphological Infl-affixes be attached to a lexical base) on the one hand and the impossibility of affix-hopping (i.e. Infl-lowering) in interrogatives and negated declaratives on the other hand. Lowering processes such as affix-hopping are theoretically suspect.[4] More importantly, I have argued in the previous chapter that V in situ languages like Modern English do not have any morphological

Infl-affixes to begin with: The verb is instead abstractly inflected in situ and this, inflection is morphologically realized by post-syntactic spell-out rules (see Chapter 3). If this argument is correct, Lasnik's Filter cannot be the trigger for *do*-support in Modern English. Direct evidence against Lasnik's Filter as the trigger for *do*-support comes from the behavior of aspectual *come* and *go* (cf. Jaeggli and Hyams 1993). For independent reasons, aspectual *come* and *go* may not bear any overt inflectional morphology (cf. (10a) versus (10b)). Overt inflectional morphology cannot be rescued by *do*-support in these cases, a fact which shows that periphrastic *do* does not (primarily) serve to support stranded affixes (cf. (10c)).[5]

(10) a. I come/go play soccer every Sunday.
     b. *Mechthild comes/goes play soccer every Sunday.
     c. *Mechthild does come/go play soccer every Sunday.

In Rohrbacher (1991), I argue that *do*-support is triggered by the need for Infl (or, in current terms, Tense) to govern the verb in order to be able to assign nominative Case to the subject. The basic idea behind this requirement is that since nominative Case identifies the subject as an argument of the verb, the Case-assigner has to be linked to the verb via government, forming what might be called an identification-chain between the subject, Infl and the verb. I further assume in this earlier work that *not* and the phonetically null interrogative marker Q head a maximal projection ΣP (cf. Laka 1990) between Infl and (the verb in) VP. This maximal projection blocks government of the verb by Infl if it is not itself lexically governed (cf. (11a)).[6] *Do*-support is the last resort strategy designed to provide a lexical governor for ΣP (cf. (11b)).

(11)   a.

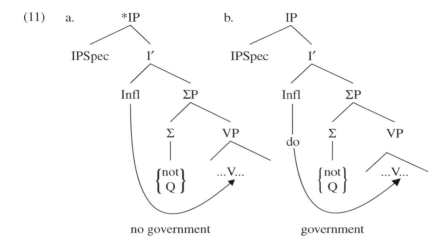

no government   government

The unavailability of *do*-support in non-emphatic declaratives containing aspectual *come* or *go* follows: In these sentences, no maximal projection intervenes between IP and VP that could prevent Infl from governing the verb (cf. (12), the S-structure of (10a)). Insertion of periphrastic *do* is not licensed (cf. (10c)), even if the sentence is later excluded on morphological grounds (cf. (10b) and example (i) of note 5).

(12)

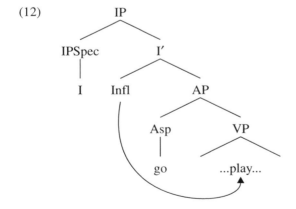

Whatever ultimately turns out to be the correct theory of *do*-support, it is most important in the present context that *do*-support is a reflex of the absence of V to I raising in Modern English.[7] The V to I raising languages Old and Middle

English employed verb movement in the same environments where *do*-support is ,
obligatory today. To see this, compare (2a) (repeated below as (13a)) with (8)
and (13b) with (9). The different structures of negative declaratives and questions in Middle and Modern English are represented in abbreviated form in (14).

(13)   a.   Wepyng and teres *counforteth not* dissolute laghers.
                weeping and tears comfort   not dissolute laughers
                'Weeping and tears don't comfort dissolute laughers.'
                        (Middle English 1400–1450 [Love *Lyf of Jesu Christ*])
        b.   *Se* ye   *not* how his herte is endurid …?
              see you not how his heart is hardened
              'Don't you see how hardened his heart is …?'
                    (Middle English 1407 [Anon. *Examinacion of Thorpe*],
                                    Roberts 1993, ex. 3(3b))

(14)

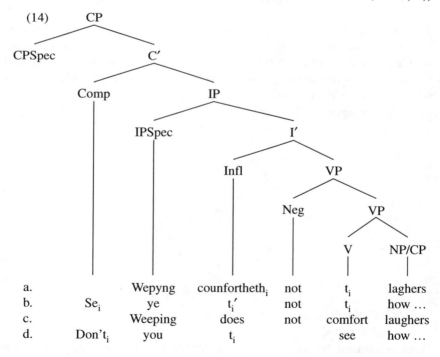

		IPSpec	Infl	Neg	V	NP/CP
a.		Wepyng	counfortheth$_i$	not	t$_i$	laghers
b.	Se$_i$	ye	t$_i'$	not	t$_i$	how …
c.		Weeping	does	not	comfort	laughers
d.	Don't$_i$	you	t$_i$		see	how …

The emergence of *do*-support should thus have coincided more or less with the
loss of V to I raising by which it was presumably triggered, and if this view is

correct, dating the emergence of *do*-support amounts to dating the loss of V to I raising.

At the beginning 15th century, periphrastic *do* occurs in 11.7% of all negative questions and nowhere else. By the middle of the 15th century, a similar percentage of affirmative transitive questions introduced by wh-adjuncts (cf. (15b)) and 1.2% of all negative declaratives (cf. (15a)) also exhibit *do*-support. These numbers increase only very slowly until the end of the 15th century, when the first cases of periphrastic *do* in affirmative wh-argument questions show up. For the next century, *do*-support is now also found (albeit much less frequently than in questions or negative declaratives) in some non-emphatic positive declaratives (cf. (15c), where the acute accent indicates stress), i.e. in an environment where it is excluded in Modern English.. Though the marginal occurrence of *do*-support in non-emphatic positive declaratives is potentially interesting,[8] I will largely disregard it here.

(15) a. … bycause the nobylyte ther commynly *dothe* not *exercyse* them in the studys therof.
(Early Modern English 1534–38 [Starkey *Dialogue*], Kroch 1990, ex. (20b))

    b. Where *doth* the grene knyght *holde* hym?
(Early Modern English 1505 [*Valentine & Orson*], Kroch 1990, ex. (20a))

    c. Thus cónscience *does make* cówards of us áll.
(Early Modern English [Shakespeare *Hamlet*], c. 1600, Roberts 1993, ex. (6a))

This development accelerates dramatically at the beginning of the 16th century, when *do*-support makes its first appearance in affirmative intransitive questions introduced by wh-adjuncts and is hence now found in all environments where it is obligatory today. In this type of questions, the percentage of periphrastic *do* immediately jumps from 0 to 21.1. At the same time (i.e. between periods 1475–1500 and 1500–1525), the percentage of periphrastic *do* in negative questions jumps from 11.1 to 59. A little later (i.e. between periods 1500–1525 and 1525–1535), *do*-support in affirmative transitive questions introduced by a wh-adjunct makes a dramatic jump from 24.2% to 69.2%. The frequency of *do*-support increases somewhat slower in affirmative wh-argument questions and negative declaratives (2% to 36% and 4.8% to 38% between periods 1475–1500 to 1550–1575). The development of *do*-support from 1400 to 1700 is summa-

rized in Table 4.2 and Figure 4.2. For the ease of the representation, the different question-types have been collapsed.

Table 4.2: *The rise of* do-*support (after Ellegård 1953 and Kroch 1990)*

	negative declaratives		questions		affirmative declaratives	
	n	% do	n	% do	n	% do
1400–1425	177	0	28	7.1	4,324	0.2
1425–1475	903	1.2	194	4.1	42,770	0.3
1475–1500	693	4.8	220	6.4	56,024	1.8
1500–1525	605	7.8	321	30.3	26,884	1.4
1525–1535	651	13.7	221	33.0	17,672	2.3
1535–1550	735	27.9	364	45.1	18,048	7.1
1550–1575	313	38.0	251	55.8	13,724	8.1
1575–1600	629	23.8	626	57.0	16,920	4.6
1600–1625	278	36.7	853	64.0	7,426	2.1
1625–1650	344	31.7	244	75.0	6,768	1.4
1650–1700	274	46.0	310	77.4	7,426	0.9

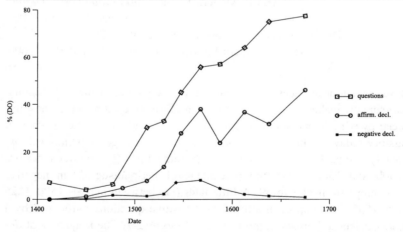

Figure 4.2: *The raise of* do-*support*

These data show that the frequency of *do*-support surged most dramatically
between periods 1475–1500 and 1550–1575, i.e. at roughly the same time at

which the most pronounced change in adverb placement occurred (cf. the discussion above). We may safely assume that (the bulk of) the loss of V to I raising took place between these periods and thus immediately followed the completion of the loss of the distinctive marking of the person feature [1ST] by the year 1500. This is of course exactly what the theory proposed in Chapter 3 of this book predicts.

Let me now address an objection raised in Schäufele (1993) against the conclusion that the loss of V to I raising in Early Modern English was triggered by the loss of distinctive person marking in the morphology of subject-verb agreement. According to the graphs in 4.1. and 4.2, V to I raising and V in situ coexisted for more than two centuries. In fact, both constructions can be found simultaneously in the same work (cf. (16)–(19) = Schäufele 1993, ex. (10,28,21, 25ab,42)), sometimes in adjacent lines (cf. (17)).[9]

(16)　a.　By thy thanks I *set not* a straw.
　　　b.　I pray you show us your intent
　　　　　In any wise, and *do not spare*.
　　　　　　　　　　(Middle English [*Everyman*], late 15th century)

(17)　a.　Nay, yet *depart not* so.
　　　b.　Though this be all, *do not* so quickly *go*.
　　　　　　　　　　(Early Modern English [Shakespeare *RII*], c. 1595)

(18)　a.　He that *knows not*, will not know nor keep God's holy com-
　　　　　mandments.
　　　b.　I know it is none of theirs, because it *does not agree* with the
　　　　　scriptures.
　　　　　　　　　　(Early Modern English [*Lord Cobham*], 16th century)

(19)　a.　He *discovers not* his whole design at once.
　　　b.　But I will be bolder, and *do not doubt* to make it good.
　　　　　　　　　　(Early Modern English [Dryden *Poetry*], 1668)

Schäufele (1993) argues that since in the history of English, V to I raising survived (if only with sharply decreased frequency) long after the impoverishment of subject-verb agreement and since in the works of authors who no longer use the older Full (or Complete) Paradigm, V to I raising nevertheless still (marginally) coexisted with V in situ, there is no correlation between richness of agreement and the position of the finite verb. I however do not think that this argument goes through, for the following reasons.

Note that there exists very little a priori reason to believe that morphologically triggered word order change should proceed in a Lightfootian catastrophic fashion within one or at most two generations. In the input of the learner, word order and morphology are in principle distinct (although clearly not independent) entities. Thus a learner who acquires only a portion of the subject-verb agreement paradigm used by the previous generation of speakers may nevertheless correctly observe the word order pattern of that generation, and this observation may retard the consequences of the learners incomplete paradigm for her (or, maybe more precisely, her generation's) word order pattern. This is not to say that for any given generation n, there are now in fact (at least) two equally relevant linguistic determinants of the position of finite verbs, namely the agreement paradigm of generation n and the word order pattern of generation n^{-1}. Instead, the acquired agreement paradigm remains the only strictly linguistic (i.e. core language[10] or UG) determinant of the position of finite verbs accessible to the Language Acquisition Device (LAD). Direct observation of word order patterns in the input is neither strictly speaking linguistic nor is it accessible to the LAD, but it is instead part of general cognitive processes (i.e. the periphery, cf. note 10). As such, it can influence the actual usage of the language and perpetuate remnants of V to I raising long after the morphological (core language or UG) trigger has vanished. Under this approach, we are not surprised to find both V to I raising and V in situ in the same Early Modern English text: At this stage, V in situ V to I raising are integrated into two different parts of the cognitive system, core language and periphery, and are triggered by two different phenomena, the new impoverished paradigm and (remnants of) the old word order.[11] Crucially, UG principles determine the bulk of the data in the short run (cf. the surge of V in situ in the fifteenth century immediately after the loss of the Complete Paradigm) and eliminate contradicting peripheral constructions in the long run (cf. the eventual disappearance of V to I raising in the eighteenth or nineteenth century).

The findings regarding the rise of preverbal *never* and the emergence of *do*-support converge on the following: V to I raising was lost in the early to mid 16th century, i.e. shortly after the distinctive marking of the referential Infl-feature [1ST] had been lost towards the end of the 15th century. The history of V to I raising in English thus confirms the theory developed in Chapter 3, according to which V to I raising depends on the distinctive marking of all referential Infl-features.

There is one historic dialect of English which followed a different pattern. Middle Scots presumably lost the distinctive marking of both [1ST] and [2ND] before the year 1400 (cf. (20), after O'Neil 1979), yet (21) shows that it continued to allow V to I raising until at least the late fourteenhundreds.

(20)   a.   Middle Scots

INF   *her-(e)*   "hear"

IND PRES

	SG	PL
1ST	her-(e)	her-es
2ND	her-es	her-es
3RD	her-es	her-es

(21)   ... quhen he trespassit nocht.
           when he trespassed not
       '... when he didn't trespass.'

(Middle Scots c. 1480 [Anon. *Unicornis Tale*],
Roberts 1993, ex. 3(55b))

O'Neil (1979) argues convincingly that the early morphological impoverishment of Middle Scots is not (as in Middle Midland English) due to (independent) simplification, but that it is rather the outcome of (conditioned) neutralization. Towards the end of the Old English period, northern England was populated not only by speakers of Old English (with the paradigm in (22a)), but also with settlers who spoke Old Norse (with the paradigm in (22b), both after O'Neil 1979). According to O'Neil, the Middle Scots paradigm in (20) is the result of

'a neutralization of the inflections brought about by the speakers of the two languages in their reaching for the inflectional common denominator by means of which they could communicate.'   (O'Neil 1979: 261)

(22)   a.   Old English   b.   Old Norse

INF *tell-an* "count"   INF *telj-ā*

IND PRES   IND PRES

	SG	PL			SG	PL
1ST	tell-e	tell-að		1ST	tel	telj-om
2ND	tel-est	tell-að		2ND	tel-R	tel-eð
3RD	tel-eð	tell-að		3RD	tel-R	telj-ā

In Old English and Old Norse, the stems were by and large very similar whereas the inflectional affixes were by and large very different. In order to facilitate communication, the different verbal affixes were replaced by the single Middle Scots affix -es, which not surprisingly corresponds to the only verbal affix found in both Old English and Old Norse, namely -eð (Old English 3RD person singular and Old Norse 2ND person plural).

A similar kind of reasoning might explain why Middle Scots retained V to I raising after the loss of distinctive [1ST] and [2ND] marking. If the changes resulting in the Middle Scots pattern were initiated in order to eradicate differences between Old English and Old Norse and thus facilitate communication between speakers of the two languages, then we do not expect to see changes in areas where Old English and Old Norse were similar or identical. Both Old English and Old Norse were V to I raising languages. A loss of V to I raising in Middle Scots would have made communication with the Scandinavian settlers harder instead of easier and V to I raising was therefore retained in spite of the morphological evidence.

This account, although feasible, creates similar problems with respect to the restrictiveness of the theory as the proposal in Section 3.3 which attributed V to I raising in Kronoby Swedish to influence from Finnish. If V to I raising is morphology-driven as claimed in this dissertation, how can sociolinguistic determinants ('facilitate communication') trigger this movement in the absence of the relevant morphology? It might be better to leave Middle Scots as an unsolved problem for future research. Notice that with respect to Middle Scots, the theory developed in Vikner (1995b) according to which V to I raising is triggered by person marking in all tenses fares better than the theory developed here, because this language had (first, but not second) person marking in the indicative present (cf. (20)) and all other tenses and unlike my theory, Vikner's theory therefore correctly predicts that it also had V to I raising. See Section 3.3 for a discussion of problems with Vikner's theory.

With the caveat of Middle Scots in mind, let me close this sub-section by saying this: In the history of English, the loss of V to I raising takes place shortly after the loss of the distinctive marking of the referential Infl-feature [1ST]. This sequence of events supports my earlier conclusion that V to I raising is triggered by the syntactic generation of affixes in Infl and that affixes are syntactically generated in Infl if and only if all of the referential Infl-features are minimally distinctively marked.

4.2.2   *Mainland Scandinavian*

Like Old and Middle English, the old Mainland Scandinavian languages distinctively marked both referential Infl-features. See for example the Old Swedish
paradigm in (23) (after Wessen 1970), where the person features [1ST] and [2ND]
are marked in the plural. The prediction is that like Old and Middle English, Old
Mainland Scandinavian had V to I raising. The Old Swedish, Old Norwegian and
Old Danish examples in (24) attest that this was indeed the case. To avoid the
V2 effect, complementizer-introduced embedded clauses that are not selected by
bridge verbs have been chosen. In each sentence, postverbal negation shows that
the verb has left the VP and moved into Infl (cf. (25), the S-structure of (24a)).[12]

(23)   Old Swedish
        INF *älsk-a* "love"
        IND PRES

	SG	PL
1ST	älsk-a(r)	älsk-um
2ND	älsk-a(r)	älsk-in
3RD	älsk-a(r)	älsk-a

(24)   a.   ... æn han *sivngær ægh* thigianda messu.
                  if he sings   not silent   mass
              '... if he doesn't sing silent mass.'
                                    (Old Swedish 1290 [*Västgöta Lagen*],
                                                Platzack 1988, ex. (29b))
        b.   Nu æf þer *skilz*   *ægi* til fullz þæsse rœde   ...
              now if you understand not to full this   speech
              'Now, if you don't fully understand this speech ...'
                                    (Old Norwegian 1240–1263 [*Konungs Skuggsiá*],
                                                Haugen 1976:238)
        c.   Wæl ær thæt oc ræt at thæn   thær gusz ræzlæ.
              good is it   and right that anyone whom god's fear
              oc rætæns ælskugh *ma æi* lokkæ til goz   ...
              and right's love   can not attract to good
              'It is good and right that anyone whom the fear of God and
              love of justice cannot attract to the good ...'
                                    (Old Danish c. 1241 [*Jutland Law*],
                                                Haugen 1976:230)

(25)

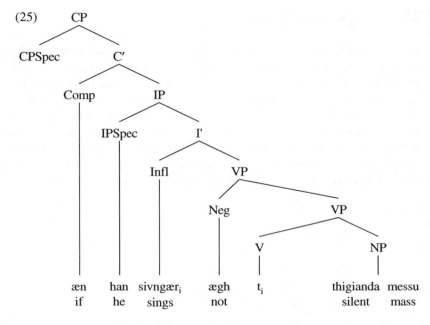

	æn	han	sivngær$_i$	ægh	t$_i$		thigianda	messu
	if	he	sings		not		silent	mass

According to Haugen (1982: 137–8), "in standard speech the mainland languages generalized -*r* into the pl., probably by 1500". Wessen (1970 I: 151) states with respect to Swedish that "in the plural ... the different person endings remained intact throughout the Old Swedish period", i.e. until the 16th century. For the 16th century, he lists the first person plural marker -*e*, the second person plural markers -*e* and -*a* and the third person plural marker -*a* as "very common", "common except for the ecclesiastical language" and "common", respectively (Wessen 1970 I: 283–4). In other words, the Early Modern Swedish of c. 1500 had the paradigm in (26), in which either [1ST] or [2ND] was no longer distinctively marked.

(26)   Early Modern Swedish
        INF *kasta* "throw"
        IND PRES

	SG	PL
1ST	kasta(-r)	kast-e
2ND	kasta(-r)	kast-e/-a
3RD	kasta(-r)	kast-a

Haugen (1976: 209) claims that the Late Old Danish of c. 1350 had a paradigm very similar to the Early Modern Swedish one, in which "distinction of persons was lost, with -*r* (from 2. and 3.p.) generalized in the pres. sg. and -*æ* (-*e*) (from -*a* of the 3.p.) in the pres. pl.". Seip (1970) gives two somewhat conflicting dates for the leveling of Norwegian person distinctions. He writes on the one hand that "already before 1300, the collapse of the person endings in the singular and the plural must have been pretty much completed" (Seip 1970: 357) and on the other hand that "at the end of the Middle Norwegian period [c. 1370–1530, B.R.], the simplification of the present tense had progressed so far that the singular and the plural were each reduced to a single form" (Seip 1970: 399). I will assume that the loss of distinctive person marking in Mainland Scandinavian can be dated reasonably well to the year 1500 or shortly earlier.

Larsson (1931: 189) states that in Swedish, "negation slowly starts to push the verb into third position during the 14th century. The development starts in the relative clauses, and the other subordinate clauses begin to participate in it at the beginning of the 15th century". But Platzack (1988) points out that none of these early cases of preverbal negation and sentential adverbs provide clear evidence for the lack of V to I raising. Sentences like (27) containing a subject gap have to be disregarded since they may involve stylistic fronting (cf. the discussion around (6) above), i.e. adjunction of the negation marker or adverb to the left of the verb in Infl.

(27)   Huar sum *ei*   *halder* kunungx dom   …
        who that not keeps   king's   verdict
        'Whoever doesn't keep the king's verdict …'
                        (Old Swedish c. 1350 [*Erikssons Landslag*],
                                        Platzack 1988, ex. (16))

Platzack argues that once possible cases of stylistic inversion and other doubtful examples are excluded, the first unambiguous V in situ sentences (cf. (28a)) show up at the beginning of the 16th century, but Falk (1993), who applies the same strict criteria as Platzack, finds such examples already in the late fourteen-hundreds (cf. (28b) and (28c)).

(28)   a.   wm annar   sywkdom *ey*   *krenker* nokon.
              if   another illness   not afflict   someone
              '… if another illness didn't afflict someone.'
                        (Early Modern Swedish c. 1515 [Månsson *Bondakonst*],
                                        Platzack 1988, ex. (28a))

b.   om thenne her œrende *ekke faa* en snar   ænda.
     if   these   errands not get an immediate end
     '... if these errands do not come to an immediate end.'
               (Early Modern Swedish 1471 [Styffe], Falk 1993:172)
c.   medhen mannen *ey betaldhe* gudhi then heder.
     since   the-man not paid   god   that honor
     '... since the man didn't pay that honor to god.'
          (Early Modern Swedish 1487 [*Buddes Bok*], Falk 1993:172)

Table 4.3 and Figure 4.3 show that according to Platzack's study, the rate of
these clear examples of V in situ grows from around 0% in 1500[13] to an average
of well over 50% in 1600, with the steepest increase in the first half of the
century. In other words, V to I raising was lost in the fifteenhundreds, shortly
after the loss of distinctive person marking around the year 1500.

Table 4.3: *The increase of V in situ in Swedish embedded clauses I (after Platzack
1988)*

Author	Born	Total S	S w/ V in situ	
		n	n	%
P. Månsson	1480	16	1	6.3
O. Petri	1493	11	0	0.0
P. Swart	1495?	25	13	52.0
B. Olai	1524	17	6	35.3
C. Carlsson	1574	13	11	84.6
A. Oxenstierna	1583	25	10	40.0
G. Oxenstierna	1587	25	18	72.0
J. Hand	1590	25	15	60.0
J. Baner	1596	25	16	64.0
P. Gyllenius	1622	14	11	78.6
A. Horn	1629	25	19	76.0
J. Ekeblad	1629	25	19	76.0
O. Hermelin	1658	25	18	72.0
S. Bark	1662	25	18	72.0
M. Stenbok	1663	25	22	88.0

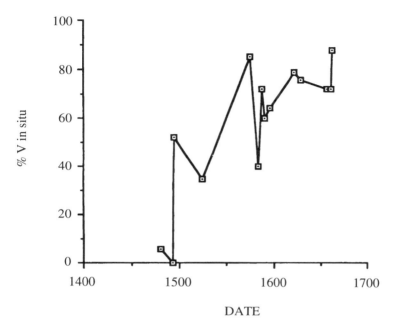

Figure 4.3: *The increase of V in situ in Swedish embedded clauses I*

A study conducted by Cecilia Falk and summarized in Table 4.4 and Figure 4.4 offers even clearer results. In Falk (1993), the proportions of V to I raising and V in situ in embedded clauses are established in two different ways. The inclusive count takes all evidence for either word order into consideration. Thus all and only embedded clauses with post-verbal negation (pro/Pro/NP^V^Neg) are taken to illustrate V to I raising and all and only embedded clauses with NP-subjects and pre-verbal negation or adverb (NP^Neg/Adv^V) are taken to illustrate V in situ. Post-verbal adverbs are excluded from the sample since they may be attached not to the (higher) VP of a finite verb which has raised, but to the (lower) VP of a non-finite verb, in which case there is no evidence whether the finite verb has raised or not. This problem does not arise in connection with sentences containing pre-verbal adverbs, and these are therefore included in the sample. Sentences with empty or pronominal subjects are barred as evidence for V in situ since in these cases, the pre-verbal position of adverbs may be due to stylistic fronting.[14] They are allowed as evidence for V to I rising since in these cases, stylistic fronting is not an issue. The exclusive count takes only comparable evidence for either word order into consideration. Thus all and only embedded sentences with NP subjects and post-verbal negation (NP^V^Neg) are assumed to involve V to I rising and all and only embedded sentences with NP subjects and pre-verbal negation (NP^Neg^V) are assumed to involve V in situ. Neither the inclusive nor the exclusive count excludes cases possibly involving CP recursion (i.e. complements of affirmed bridge-verbs) from the sample. Both counts converge in their results: V to I rising was lost in the sixteenth century, shortly after distinctive person marking had been lost. V in situ increases to over sixty percent in the first third of that century and approaches ninety percent in the last third.[15] The history of Swedish thus further corroborates the central hypothesis of this book, according to which V to I rising is triggered by and depends on the distinctive marking of the referential Infl-features.

Table 4.4: *The increase of V in situ in Swedish embedded clauses II (after Falk 1993)*

Year of Birth	Inclusive Count			Exclusive Count		
	Total S	S w/ V in situ		Total S	S w/ V in situ	
	n	n	%	n	n	%
1470	25	7	28	20	5	25
1495–1535	122	75	61	99	59	60
1536–1570	64	35	55	44	21	48
1570–1600	122	107	88	97	83	86
1601–1635	86	67	78	66	56	85
1635–1670	108	91	84	81	68	84
1671–1700	76	70	92	44	41	93
1701–1735	125	115	92	90	81	90

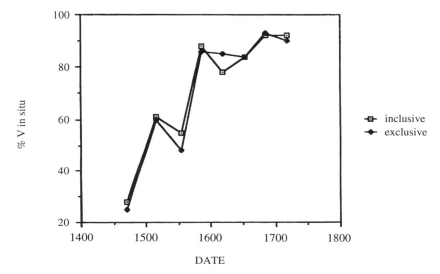

Figure 4.4: *The increase of V in situ in Swedish embedded clauses II*

The evidence regarding Danish and Norwegian is more anecdotal in nature: In Danish for example, the first clear instances of V in situ seem to appear in the 15th century, cf. (29). Here the loss of V to I movement appears to lag behind the loss of distinctive person marking by about a hundred years, but still the temporal correlation is relatively tight, especially if one takes into consideration that whatever time lag there occurred may reflect conservative tendencies in the written language rather than an actual discrepancy in the spoken language. More data would be needed to settle the issue, especially in the case of Norwegian.

(29)   Nu vel iek syæ af en annen vey ofuer land ter som mand
        now will I   seek of an other way across land if that one
        engælund ma kommæ pooæ hafuet.
        not   may come   on   sea-the
        'I will now seek another way across land if one cannot get there by
        sea.'   (Early Modern Danish c. 1475 [*Mandevilles Reise*],
                                                    Vikner 1991, ex. 2(251))

Basing our conclusions primarily on the Swedish data, we may say that like English, Mainland Scandinavian lost V to I raising shortly after it had lost the distinctive marking of (at least one of) the person features. This confirms the theory developed in this dissertation, according to which V to I raising depends on exactly this type of inflectional morphology.

4.3 Auxiliaries in the History of English and Mainland Scandinavian

4.3.1 *The Modern Contrast: English Aux^Neg versus Mainland Scandinavian Neg^Aux*

As discussed in sections 2.4.2.1–3, English, Danish, Swedish, Norwegian and Faroese main verbs must follow negation or sentential adverbs in contexts where Verb Second caused by V to C is excluded, a fact that indicates that these languages lack V to I raising. But English on the one side and Mainland Scandinavian and Faroese on the other side differ with respect to the position of auxiliaries: Whereas the English modals and finite *have* and *be* obligatorily precede negation and sentential adverbs as in (30a) and (31a), there Mainland Scandinavian and Faroese counterparts obligatorily follow these elements as in (30b–e) and (31b–e).

(30) a. I regret that you *could not* come to my party.
      b. Hun bekræftede at   hann *ikke kunne* have begået
          she confirmed that he   not could have committed
          forbrydelsen.
          crime-the
          'She confirmed that he couldn't have committed the crime.'
                              (Danish, based on Vikner 1995a, ex. 4(160a))
      c. Vilken fest sa   hon att vi *inte skulle* köpa roliga hattar till.
          which party said she that we not should buy funny hats   for
          'For which party did she say that we shouldn't buy funny
          hats?'   (Swedish, Holmberg 1986, ex. 4(84a))
      d. Men det vilja me tenkja, at her *alltid vil* finnast
          but that will we believe, that here always will exist
          Folk, som ...
          people who ...
          'But we will believe that there will always be people...'
                              (Norwegian 1858 [Aasen *Maalstriden*],
                              Haugen 1976:429)

e. Eg segði tað, at   hann *ikki skuldi* havt nakað.
    I   said it, that he   not should have anything
    'I said that he shouldn't have anything.'

    (Faroese, Lockwood 1964:157)

(31)   a. I regret that you *have not* read "Oblomov".

       b. Det var en overrakelse at   de   slet   *ikke var*   uenige.
           that was a surprise   that they at-all not were disagreed
           'It was a surprise that they weren't disagreed at all.'

           (Danish, Vikner 1995a, ex. 4(170a))

       c. Jag beklager att   Johan *inte har* köpt   boken.
           I   regret   that J.   not has bought the-book
           'I regret that J. hasn't bought the book.'   (Swedish)

       d. Bukken kom dit   den *aldri hadde* vært før.
           the-buck came (to a place) it   never had   been before
           'The buck came to a place where it had never been before.'

           (Norwegian, Seip 1971)

       e. Tað var óvæntað, at   dreingirnir als   *ikki vóru* ósamdir.
           it   was unexpected that boys-the   at-all not were disagreed
           'It was unexpected that the boys didn't disagree at all.'

           (Faroese, Vikner 1991, ex. (15b))

Mainland Scandinavian and Faroese auxiliaries follow the pattern established by the main verbs of these languages and surface inside VP. The Danish sentence in (30b) for example has the S-structure in (32).

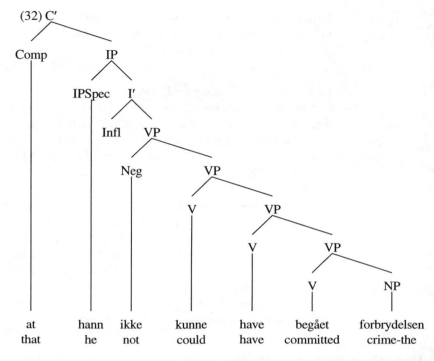

(32)

at	hann	ikke	kunne	have	begået	forbrydelsen
that	he	not	could	have	committed	crime-the

What is surprising is that English modals and finite *have* and *be*, unlike English main verbs, surface in Infl. This is indicated in (33), the S-structure of sentence (30a).

(33)

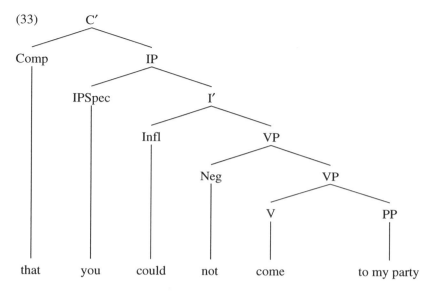

It is customary to assume that English modals are base-generated in Infl. But contrary to Chomsky (1989), Kayne (1989), Pollock (1989) and many others, I will assume that English finite *have* and *be*, too, are base-generated in their surface position, not base-generated in V and raised to Infl. As I will show immediately, a raising analysis for either (30a) or (31a) must be rejected because it cannot satisfactorily explain why Mainland Scandinavian auxiliaries are prohibited from undergoing this type of movement.

According to Pollock (1989), English (and Mainland Scandinavian) main verbs (that is, verbs that assign primary θ-roles) cannot raise to Infl because this position is θ-opaque in these languages. English auxiliaries do not assign primary θ-roles and may hence undergo V to Infl raising. They must do so overtly because as semantically empty elements, they cannot satisfy feature checking requirements at LF (cf. Chomsky 1992). According to Lasnik (1994), English main verbs cannot raise to Infl because this position is occupied by an affix which merges with the verb under adjacency rather than triggering raising (cf. note 4). English auxiliaries cooccur not with an movement-blocking affix, but with a strong inflectional feature that triggers overt raising. Lasnik suggests that this difference between English main verbs and auxiliaries is due to the affixal versus suppletive nature of their inflection. But as noted in Green (1990) for African American English and Henry (1991) for Hiberno English, the

habitual auxiliaries of these languages must remain in situ as shown in (34) from
Green (1990) although they do not assign primary θ-roles[16] and although at least
in African American English, inflection on the habitual auxiliary is suppletive
(cf. the paradigms in (35) after Green 1990 and Henry 1991).

(34)   Bob doesn't be angry.   (African American &
       'B. isn't usually angry.'   Hiberno English)

(35)   a.   African American Eng.   b.   Hiberno Eng.
            INF *be*   INF *be*
            IND PRES   IND PRES

	SG	PL		SG	PL
1ST	am	be	1ST	be	be
2ND	be	be	2ND	be	be
3RD	be	be	3RD	be-s	be

More needs also to be said about Mainland Scandinavian, where we have just
seen that modals and *have* and *be* cannot raise to Infl even in cases where they
do not assign primary θ-roles. Kayne (1989) argues that English auxiliaries raise
to Infl because English *be* shows some overt agreement and that their Danish,
Swedish and Norwegian counterparts stay in situ because none of them bears any
overt agreement. The relevant paradigms are reproduced below in (36a) and
(36b). A similar approach might hold that the English regular third person
singular marker (cf. (37a)) and the absence of any comparable marker in Danish,
Swedish or Norwegian (cf. (37b)) are responsible for the word order asymmetry
in question. Neither proposal works, since Faroese *vera* "be" with the paradigm
in (36c) and Faroese main verbs with the paradigm in (37c) have as much overt
verbal agreement as their English equivalents, yet like Mainland Scandinavian,
Faroese requires auxiliaries to follow negation and remain in their D-structural
position inside VP (cf. (30e) and (31e)). African American and Hiberno English
habitual auxiliaries pose a similar problem Kayne's proposals. Remember that in
both languages, habitual *be* may not raise to Infl (cf. (34)) although it shows
some overt agreement (cf. (35)).

(36)   a.   English *be*   b.   Swedish *war-a*
            IND. PRES   IND. PRES.

	SG	PL		SG	PL
1ST	am	are	1ST	är	är
2ND	are	are	2ND	är	är
3RD	is	are	3RD	är	är

c. Faroese *ver-a*

IND. PRES.

	SG	PL
1ST	er-i	er-u
2ND	er-t	er-u
3RD	er	er-u

(37) a. English *throw*

IND PRES

	SG	PL
1ST	throw	throw
2ND	throw	throw
3RD	throw-s	throw

b. Swedish *kasta* "throw"

IND PRES

	SG	PL
1ST	kasta-r	kasta-r
2ND	kasta-r	kasta-r
3RD	kasta-r	kasta-r

c. Faroese *kasta* "throw"

IND PRES

	SG	PL
1ST	kast-i	kasta
2ND	kasta-r	kasta
3RD	kasta-r	kasta

At first blush, Lasnik's approach fares better with the Mainland Scandinavian data than Kayne's: The fact that neither the Swedish (cf. (36b)) nor the Faroese (cf. (36c)) auxiliary paradigm is suppletive within its finite forms might suggest that like non-suppletive English main verbs, Mainland Scandinavian auxiliaries cooccur with movement-blocking affixes in Infl. But Lasnik explicitly rejects this suggestion because such an affix would have to merge with the auxiliary under adjacency and any negation marker intervening between the affix and the auxiliary should then trigger English-style *do*-support (cf. note 4). Since this prediction is not borne out by the facts (cf. (30b,c,e) and (31b,c,e)), Lasnik proposes that Mainland Scandinavian auxiliaries pattern with English auxiliaries rather than with English main verbs, i.e. they cooccur with a movement-inducing inflectional feature rather than with a movement-blocking affix in Infl. The only difference between Mainland Scandinavian and English auxiliaries is that whereas this feature is strong in English, triggering overt movement at S-structure, it is weak in Mainland Scandinavian, triggering covert movement at LF. But this difference must be stipulated (notice that the Faroese auxiliary paradigm in (36c) is as "rich" as the English auxiliary paradigm in (36a)), and Lasnik's proposal therefore does not explain the facts, it merely describes them (cf. the discussion in Chapter 1).

Given these comprehensive synchronic similarities between the inflectional systems of V in situ languages with auxiliaries in Infl (e.g. English) and V in situ languages with auxiliaries in the VP (e.g. Faroese), it is hard to see how a V to Infl raising approach to (30a) and (31a) which relates raising to the synchronic nature of the morphology (or for that matter any synchronic account) could explain the different rules of auxiliary placement in English and Mainland Scandinavian. I will now show that under the assumption that all verbal elements in the modern languages under discussion are base generated in their respective surface positions, a satisfactory diachronic explanation for these different positions can be given.

4.3.2 Historical Reanalysis in English and the Lack thereof in Mainland Scandinavian

Like their Modern English successors, Old and Middle English finite pre-modals and *have* and *be* surfaced in Infl (and therefore before negation and sentential adverbs, cf. (38)).[17] This was of course the canonical position for all Old and Middle English finite verbs (cf. Section 4.2.1), and at least originally, the order (PRE-)MODAL^Neg/ADV must have reflected the general V to I raising then in effect and not, as I claim it does today, base-generation as the head of an inflectional projection. Among the reasons for this assumption is the following. In Modern English, base-generation in Infl is associated with the lack of modals to occur in non-finite forms or to take direct objects. In Middle English, some pre-modals still occurred in non-finite forms (cf. (39a)) or took direct objects (cf. (39b)). There is hence good reason to believe that once, pre-modals were full verbs that (like other full verbs) were base-generated in V and raised to Infl. At some point, a sentence like (38a) must have had (40) instead of the modern (33) as its S-structure.[18]

(38)   a.   A blynde man *kan nat* juggen wel in hewis.
            a blind   man can not judge   well in colors
            'A blind man cannot judge colors well.'

                              (Middle English 1387 [Chaucer *Troilus*],
                                        Roberts 1993, ex. 3(11a))

b. Ofte siþæs hit ilamp,   þ[æt] englæs *beoð ofte*   hyder on
    often has it happened that angels are   often hither into
    middanearde isende.
    the-world   sent
    'Often has it happened that angels have been sent to the earth.'
                                (Middle English 12th century [HomU1 (Belf 10)],
                                            Roger Higgins class notes 1990)

(39) a. I shall *not konne* answere.
          I shall not can   answer
          'I shan't be able to answer.'
                                        (Middle English 1386 [Chaucer CT,B],
                                                    Roberts 1993, ex. 3(12a))

      b. The leeste ferthyng þat y men *shall*.
          the last   farthing that I man owe
          'The last farthing that I owe to somebody.'
                                        (Middle English c. 1425 [Hoccleve *Min.Poems*],
                                                    Lightfoot 1979, ex. (49))

(40)

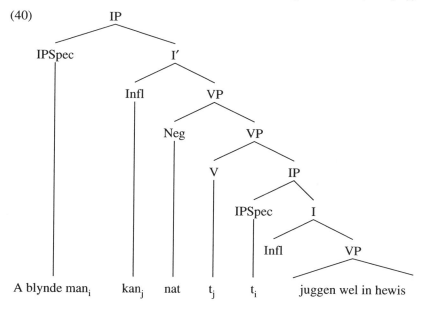

Old and Middle English pre-modals differed from regular main verbs in one important respect. As members of the Germanic class of preterit-present verbs (whose preterit had taken over the function of the present already in Proto-Germanic), they did not have the regular paradigm (1), but the irregular paradigms in (41), after Wyld (1927).

(41)   a.   Old English *cunn-an*   a.   Middle English *conn-en*
            'to be able, to know'

IND PRES			IND PRES		
	SG	PL		SG	PL
1ST	can	cunn-on	1ST	can	conn-e(n)
2ND	can-st	cunn-on	2ND	can-st	conn-e(n)
3RD	can	cunn-on	3RD	can	conn-e(n)

Note that the Old and Middle English pre-modal paradigms — unlike the regular paradigms — did not distinctively mark the referential Infl-feature [1ST], since the forms for first and third person singular were identical. In other words, in Old and Middle English the trigger for V to I raising was instantiated only in the regular verbal paradigm but not in the pre-modal paradigm. Recall from the discussion of the Yiddish paradigm in (62b) and the Yiddish example in (64) in the last chapter that if the regular paradigm of a language minimally distinctively marks the referential Infl-features [1ST] and [2ND], then all of its affixes, including those which do not distinctively mark either [1ST] or [2ND], are lexically listed and syntactically inserted in Infl where they trigger V to I raising. By the same token, all irregular paradigms of that language, including those which do not minimally distinctively mark either [1ST] or [2ND], are also lexically listed and syntactically inserted in Infl where they trigger V to I raising. This means that in Old and Middle English, V to I raising took place not only with the regular verbs which minimally distinctively marked both [1ST] and [2ND] in their paradigm, but also with the pre-modals which failed to minimally distinctively mark [1ST] in their paradigm. Although irregular verbs like the pre-modals that do not display the relevant morphology cannot be exempted from V to I raising as long as they are verbs, they can be excluded from the category verb and reanalyzed as inflectional elements. Confronted with an input in which all verbs surfaced in Infl, including some that did not exhibit the trigger morphology for V to I raising, the language learner made a minimal change to regularize the system, i.e. she assumed that those verbs which did not have the relevant morphology were not raised to Infl but directly base-generated there.

After this reanalysis of the preterit presents, which had the effect of reducing the bi-clausal structure of sentences containing a pre-modal to a mono-clausal structure as shown in (42), all elements undergoing V to I raising exhibited the trigger for this type of movement.

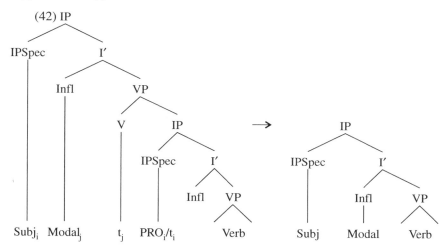

Modals had already been excluded from the category verb and reanalyzed as Infl-elements when Early Modern English lost V to I raising in the 16th century shortly after the loss of distinctive person marking. Since they were no longer verbs, their position was not affected by the loss of verb raising to Infl. Recall from the previous chapter that structurally, V to I raising corresponds to the projection of AgrSP (cf. structure (76) in Chapter 3)) and the absence of V to I raising corresponds to the failure to project AgrSP (cf. structure (74) in Chapter 3)). The second, post-reanalysis structure in (42) therefore actually collapses the two structures in (43), depending on whether AgrSP is present or not. In the V to I raising structure (43a), modals have been reanalyzed as inflectional elements and are base-generated in the appropriate inflectional head, MOOD (for modality). Finite main verbs raise to the highest inflectional head, AgrS, which contains an affix that needs to be bound, and subjects raise to the highest inflectional specifier SpecAgrSP. Both modals in MOOD and finite main verbs in AgrS surface in front of VP-adjoined adverbs and negation. This is the situation in Middle English. In the V in situ structure (43b), modals continue to be analyzed as inflectional elements and are again base-generated in MOOD.

Finite main verbs do not raise to the highest inflectional head, Tense, which contains only abstract features that do not need to be bound, and subjects surface again in the highest inflectional specifier, SpecTP. Whereas modals in MOOD surface in front of VP-adjoined adverbs and negation, finite main verbs in situ surface behind these elements. This is the situation in Modern English.

(43)

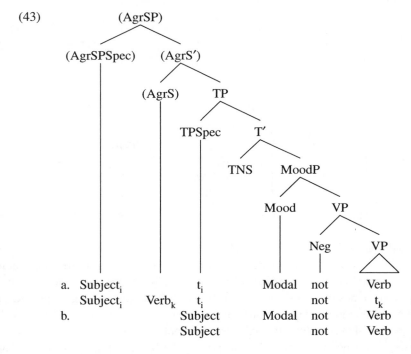

a.	Subject$_i$		t$_i$	Modal	not	Verb
	Subject$_i$	Verb$_k$	t$_i$		not	t$_k$
b.			Subject	Modal	not	Verb
			Subject		not	Verb

Roberts (1985) and (1993) proposes essentially the same reanalysis of modals from verbs to inflectional elements, but for entirely different reasons. He also observes that the morphological irregularity of the Old and Middle English pre-modals. But in his account, this state of affairs merely serves to morphologically distinguish pre-modals from regular main verbs: It does and (given Roberts's theory of V to I raising summarized in Section 3.2.3) cannot motivate the reanalysis. Instead, Roberts argues that the loss of the infinitival marker -en and the subjunctive inflection conspired together with the irregular semantic interpretation of the pre-modal past tense to actuate the change.

The two theories make different predictions with respect to the starting date of the reanalysis. Roberts's theory predicts that the reanalysis started not before (the end of) the Middle English period when the infinitival marker and the subjunctive inflection were lost. In fact, Roberts follows Lightfoot (1979) and (1991) and assumes that the pre-modal verbs were reanalyzed as inflectional elements in a cataclysmic change in the early sixteenth century. My theory predicts that the reanalysis started already during the Old English period, when the irregular preterit present paradigm was already in place. I will now show that the evidence points to an early starting date in the Old English period and thus supports my theory.

As mentioned above, the reanalysis of the modals as Infl-elements resulted in the loss of their ability to occur in non-finite forms and to take direct objects, presumably because Infl is associated with finiteness and because no primary θ-roles can be assigned from Infl. Warner (1983) points out that at least some pre-modals occurred only in finite forms from very early on. The MED states that non-finite forms of *shall* and *must* are lacking throughout Middle English and the evidence that such forms existed in Old English is doubtful according to the OED. Warner (1990: 547) writes that these gaps "seem unlikely to be merely accidental ... Ælfric interestingly seems to avoid the infinitive of *mot* ["must", B.R.] just when he has need of it in [(44), B.R.] to render the paradigm of Latin *licere* in his grammar."

(44)   *licet mihi bibere* mot ic drincan, *mihi licuit* ic moste,
                        may I drink   I   might
        ..., *si nobis liceret* gyf we moston, INFINITIVUM *licere*
                        if   we may
        beon alyfed
        to-be allowed

                                (Old English [Ælfric *Grammar*], late 9th century)

Old and Middle English pre-modals generally were not passivizable, "at least when occurring with an infinitival complement" (Plank 1984: 317), and at least one pre-modal, *must*, "was never recorded with a direct object" (Allan 1987: 140). Denison (1989) observes a curious interaction between pre-modals and impersonal verbs: "An auxiliary + impersonal verb group behaves exactly like a finite impersonal, its argument structure and Case assignment being entirely determined by the impersonal verb" (Denison 1989: 143), cf. the following minimal pair:

(45)   a.   ... ðæt nanne mon   þæs   ne tweoð þæt ...
             that no   man-ACC that-GEN not doubts that ...
             '... that nobody doubts it that ...'
                              (Old English [BO 38.3], Denison 1989, ex. (1))
       b.   ... þætte nænne mon   þæs   tweogan ne þearf Þætte ...
             that   no   man-ACC that-GEN doubt-to not needs that
             '... that nobody needs to doubt it that ...'
                              (Old English [BO 26.12], Denison 1989, ex. (6))

The fact that in (45b), the Case of the subject is fixed by the infinitival main
verb and not by the finite pre-modal is incompatible with both of the bi-clausal
un-reanalyzed structures for sentences containing pre-modals (cf. the first tree in
(42)): Neither control (in root modality) not raising (in epistemic modality)
allows Case-marking of the (highest) subject by the lower verb. In control
constructions, the higher subject is never in the Case-assignment domain of the
embedded verb and in raising constructions, the subject moves to the matrix
SpecIP precisely because it cannot get Case in the embedded clause.[19] Instead,
what seems to be required for examples like (45b) is a mono-clausal reanalyzed
structure (cf. the second tree in (42)) in which accusative Case is assigned to the
subject by the main verb in exactly the same manner as in the simpler example (45a).

Evidence of this kind suggests that the historical reanalysis in (42) was
already in progress during the old English period, a conclusion which supports
my view that this reanalysis was motivated by the (early) loss of distinctive
person marking and not by the (late) loss of infinitival and subjunctive morphology. What needs to be explained is why the reanalysis of modals as Infl-elements
was such a drawn-out process, i.e. why examples of modals as main verbs are
still attested in late Middle English (cf. (39)). The reason has to do with several
factors that were already mentioned in note 1. First, Old English was a V2
language and in matrix clauses, verb raising to Comp therefore buried the word
order evidence for V to I raising. Second, Old English was an OV language that
allowed Infl-final structures alongside Infl-medial structures. Pintzuk (1991)
estimates that roughly fifty percent of all embedded clauses containing pre-
modals were of the former type (cf. (46)). Since the highest verb and Infl are
always adjacent in these examples, there is again no word order evidence for V
to I raising: Sentence (46) is compatible both with the V to I raising analysis in
(47a) and with the V in situ analysis in (47b).[20]

(46)   ... þæt se byrnwiga   bugan *sceolde* ...
      that the mailed-warrior fall   must
    '... that the mailed warrior must fall ...'

(Old English mid 7th to early 11th century [Beowulf],
Pintzuck 1991, ex. 2(4))

(47)

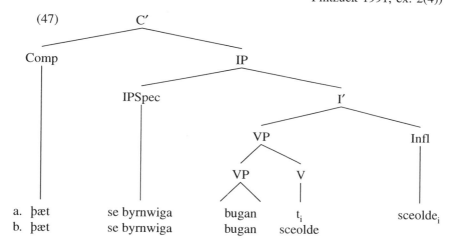

  a. þæt   se byrnwiga   bugan t_i sceolde$_i$
  b. þæt   se byrnwiga   bugan   sceolde

Even examples like (48) could in principle be analyzed as V/Infl final with V in situ plus Dutch-style verb projection raising, but Pintzuck argues convincingly that verb projection raising was at best marginal in Old English and that the majority of sentences like (48) should be analyzed as reflecting verb movement to clause-medial Infl.

(48)   ... þe ær   nan folc   ne *mehte* mid gefeohte gewinnan.
      who before no   people not could in   battle   overcome
    '... who no people could overcome in battle before.'

(Old English c.894 [Orosius], Pintzuck 1991, ex. 3(50))

There was then relatively little direct evidence from word order for V to I raising in Old English, and hence little motivation for a reanalysis of the preterit presents as Infl elements. In Middle English, V2 was lost and Infl became uniformly clause-medial. As a result of these changes, the word order of all sentences containing a negation marker or sentential adverb presented direct evidence for V to I raising and the motivation for a reanalysis of the preterit presents increased considerably. This explains why the historical reanalysis of

Old English pre-modals was a drawn-out process which proceeded quite slowly during the Old English period and accelerated considerably during the Middle English period until it was by and large completed at the beginning of the Early Modern period and, crucially, before the loss of V to I raising.

With respect to *have* and *be*, note that Old English had two paradigms for *be*: the one in (49a) with irregular singular forms and the one in (49b) with more or less regular singular forms. Again, all paradigms follow Wyld (1927).

(49)   Old English *be-on* "be"
        IND PRES

a.   SG   PL
    1ST   eom   sindon/sint
    2ND   eart   sindon/sint
    3RD   is   sindon/sint

b.   SG   PL
    1ST   bēō   bēō-ð/bio-ð
    2ND   bi-st   bēō-ð/bio-ð
    3RD   bi-ð   bēō-ð/bio-ð

In Middle English, the regular singular forms lost out against the irregular ones. Chaucer had the paradigm below.

(50)   Middle English *be-e(n)* "be"
        IND PRES

            SG PL
    1ST   am be-e(n)
    2ND   art be-e(n)
    3RD   is be-e(n)

Have underwent a similar development: The regular Old English paradigm in (51a) was replaced by the irregular Middle English paradigm in (51b).

(51)   a. Old English *hæbb-an*   b. Middle English *hav-e(n)*
            IND PRES   IND PRES

                    SG   PL   SG   PL
        1ST   hæbb-e   habb-aþ   1ST   hav-e   hav-e(n)
        2ND   hæf-st   habb-aþ   2ND   hast   hav-e(n)
        3RD   hæf-þ   habb-aþ   3RD   has   hav-e(n)

It is crucial here that whereas the singular forms of the regular Middle English in (4) can be split up into invariant stem (*cast-*) plus various affixes (*-e*, *-est*, *-eþ*), the Middle English singular forms of *be* in (50) and *have* in (51b) cannot be straightforwardly analyzed in this way. This is particularly clear in the case of *be* with the three suppletive forms *am*, *art* and *is*. These forms cannot be the result of transparent syntactic affixation and must instead be due to post-syntactic spell-out. I have argued in Chapter 3 that syntactic affixation and more specifically Lasnik's Filter, i.e. the prohibition against affixes that remain unbound at S-structure, is behind all V to I raising: Languages with distinctive marking of all referential Infl-features in their regular paradigm(s) have lexically listed inflectional affixes that are inserted under Infl at D-structure and need to be bound at S-structure via V to I raising. I have argued earlier in this chapter in connection with the pre-modals that the lexical listing and syntactic insertion of inflectional affixes is not restricted to the regular paradigms which minimally distinctively mark [1ST] and [2ND], but extends to any irregular paradigms which do not minimally distinctively mark one (or both) of the referential Infl-features. Thus the affixes of the Old and Middle English pre-modal paradigm did not minimally distinctively mark [1ST] but were nevertheless lexically listed and syntactically inserted, triggering V to I raising just like the affixes of the regular paradigm. By the same token, the affixes of the Middle English paradigms for *have* and *be* were entirely abstract (the overt inflectional material being realized through post-syntactic spell-out) and hence did not minimally distinctively mark either [1ST] or [2ND]. Nevertheless they, too, were lexically listed and syntac-tically inserted, again triggering V to I raising just like the affixes of the regular paradigm. Like the pre-modals, *have* and *be* occurred in Infl without exhibiting the trigger morphology for V to I raising. Like the pre-modals, finite *have* and *be* were therefore removed from the category verb and reanalyzed as base-generated in the appropriate inflectional head, where they continue to appear today after the loss of AgrSP and V to I raising (which did not affect the base-generation of modals and auxiliaries as inflectional heads). For pre-modals, I have assumed above that the inflectional head in question is MOOD. For finite *have* and *be*, it seems reasonable to assume that the appropriate head is ASP (for aspect). We arrive at the reanalyzed structures in (52), where (52a) represents the situation before the loss of AgrSP and V to I raising (i.e. late Middle English) and (52b) represents the situation after the loss of AgrSP and V to I raising (i.e. early Modern English). These structures should be compared with those for modals in (43).

(52)

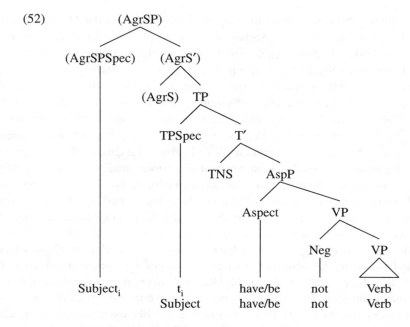

Unlike modals, Modern English *have* and *be* still have non-finite forms. The reasons for this difference are unclear to me. Note that "two- and three-year-olds generally use perfective *have* exclusively in finite forms" (Radford 1992: 38) and that problems with non-finite perfective *have* persist until much later. These facts indicate that in any event, something special needs to be said about non-finite *have* (and *be*). Non-finite *have* and *be* may be placed both in front (cf. (53a)) and after negation (cf. (53b)).

(53) a. To *have not* liked "Vertigo" is unusual.
      b. To *not have* liked "Vertigo" is unusual.

Pollock (1989) therefore assumes that non-finite *have* and *be* optionally raise to Infl. Not only is this conclusion problematic because Infl is already occupied by a non-affixal element, i.e. the infinitival marker *to*, it is also incompatible with the V to I raising theory argued for here, according to which this type of movement, if it occurs at all, is general in that it extends to all verbs. There is however evidence against Pollock's view. Akmajian, Steele and Wasow (1979) observe that only the finite, but not the non-finite forms of *have* and *be* can contract with negation.

(54)   a.   I *haven't* seen "2001" in ten years.
        b.   *To *haven't* seen "2001" is unusual.

Akmajian et al. conclude that contraction is restricted to elements in Infl (Tense in our terms), that only the finite forms of *have* and *be* are located in this position, and that the non-finite forms of *have* and *be* are located in V. The word order variation in (53) is then due to the fact that English negation may adjoin to any VP, as illustrated in (55), the S-structure of (53a), and (56), the S-structure of (53b).

(55)

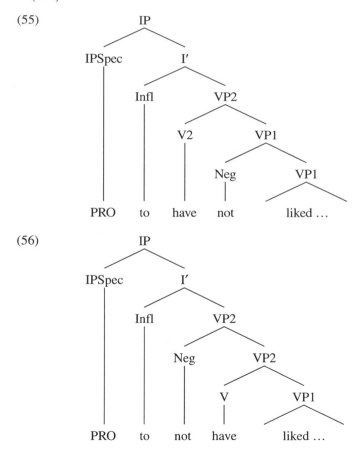

Another problem arises in connection with British English possessive *have* (cf. note 16). Possessive *have* is main verb that takes a direct object to which it assigns a primary θ-role. Above I assumed that primary θ-roles cannot be assigned from inflectional heads, and possessive *have* should therefore not occur in this position. Consequently, *do*-support is expected in questions and negative declaratives containing possessive *have*. This expectation is borne out in American English (cf. (57a), but not in British English (cf. (57b).

> (57) a. I *don't have* any money.   (American English)
>   b. I *haven't* any money.   (British English)

The British English construction in (57b) is otherwise marked as exceptional. Shawn (1985) (cited in Kroch 1990) found that during the second half of the 19th and the first third of the 20th century, British English replaced possessive *have* by *have got* (with auxiliary use of *have*) in questions and negative declaratives, but not affirmative declaratives (cf. (58)). Radford (1992) reports that British children never position possessive *have* in Infl and instead always employ American English-style *do*-support (cf. (59)).

> (58) I *haven't got* any money.

> (59) It *doesn't have* legs, does it?   (Emma 3:1; from Radford 1992)

(58) and (59) reveal that even in British English, there is a strong tendency to avoid overtly situating main verb *have* in Infl, presumably because in Modern English, *have* could only be base-generated there and Infl is not a position from which θ-roles are usually assigned. I assume that (57b) is a hold-over from the time when English was a V to I raising language. It is at least partly due to the confusion created by the fact that English has two *haves*: an auxiliary, which is generated in its finite forms in Infl, and a main verb, which should always be generated in V but is sometimes (in analogy to the auxiliary) inserted in Infl.

In a way, the explanation for the exceptional behavior of Modern English modals and finite *have* and *be* turns the traditional view upside down: Modals and finite *have* and *be* appear in Infl not because they are the only Modern English verbs that may raise to this position, but because they were the only Old and Middle English verbs that had no morphological motivation to raise there. It is not the case that the θ-theoretic properties of today's auxiliaries allow V to I raising. On the contrary, these properties only reflect the fact that the predecessors of the auxiliaries ceased to raise to Infl and were instead base-generated there.

Little needs to be said with respect to the Mainland Scandinavian counterparts of the English modals and finite *have* and *be*. Examples (60) and (61) show that in the Old Mainland Scandinavian languages, these verbs raised to Infl like all other verbs. Their paradigms in (62) and (63), although mostly irregular in the singular, could be split into stem plus affix and distinctively marked both person features in the plural, just as regular verbs did. Since they exhibited the morphological trigger for V to I raising, there was no reason to reanalyze Mainland Scandinavian "auxiliaries" and they retained their status as full verbs. Accordingly, modals continue to appear in non-finite forms (cf. (64a)) and to take direct objects (cf. (64b)).

(60) a. hafþe þu vitit   at kon(ung)i *ville   eg* lyþa.
          had   you known that the-king   would not listen
                          (Old Swedish c. 1367 [*St. Birgitta* MS KB A65],
                                                          Haugen 1976:233)

      b. de   som dem lase oc *kunde icke* forstaa   dem
          those who it   read and can   not understand it
          'Those who read it and cannot understand it'
                          (Early Modern Danish c. 1531 [Pederson *Psalms*],
                                                          Haugen 1976:343)

(61) a. när   thet *är ey* stenoghth.
          when it   is not stony
                          (Early Modern Swedish c. 1515 [Månsson *Bondakonst*],
                                                          Platzack 1988, ex. (29a))

      b. at   æinfolld tru   oc heilogh *hafi ækki* rum ...
          that simple   truth and holy   have not   room
          'That simple and holy truth has no room ...'
                          (Old Norwegian 1240–1263 [*Konungs Skuggsiá*],
                                                          Haugen 1976:238)

(62) Old Swedish *kunn-a*
      IND PRES

	SG	PL
1ST	kan	kunn-um
2ND	kan-t	kunn-in
3RD	kan	kunn-u/-a

(63) a. O. Swedish *var-a* "be" b. O. Swedish *hav-a* "have"
IND PRET   IND PRES

	SG	PL		SG	PL
1ST	vår	vār-um	1ST	hav-i(r)/-ęr	hav-um
2ND	vă-st	vār-in	2ND	hav-i(r)/-ęr	hav-in
3RD	vår	vār-u	3RD	hav-i(r)/-ęr	hav-a

(64) a. Han skal *kunne* svømme for at få jobbet.
   he must can swim for to get the-job
   'He must be able to swim in order to get the job.'
                              (Danish, Vikner 1988, ex. (24e))
   b. Det eneste han *vil* er at svare på spørgsmålet.
   the only-(thing) he wants is to answer on the-question
                              (Danish, Vikner 1988, ex. (26a))

I have argued in this section that the synchronic word order difference between English Aux^Neg on the one hand and Mainland Scandinavian and Faroese Neg^Aux on the other hand is best accounted for with reference to a diachronic difference: Old and Middle English pre-auxiliaries did not exhibit the trigger morphology for V to I raising and were therefore reanalyzed as base-generated in Infl, while their Old Mainland Scandinavian counterparts displayed the relevant morphology and were therefore treated as full verbs. The behavior of Old and Middle English pre-modals is particularly interesting: The reanalysis of the pre-modals as Infl-elements on the basis of their failure to distinctively mark the referential Infl-feature [1ST] in their paradigm lends support to my hypothesis that V to I raising depends on the Full Paradigm, i.e. the distinctive marking of all referential Infl-features. Earlier in this chapter, the loss of the Full Paradigm was shown to have been responsible for the loss of V to I raising in both English and Mainland Scandinavian. The history of the Germanic VO languages hence corroborates the theory of V to I raising developed in this book.

Notes

1. Old English was a V2 language with the inflectional heads (again summarily referred to as Infl below) in either clause-final or clause-medial position. Subject pronouns and the negation marker *ne* functioned as pre-verbal clitics. This combination of V2, Infl-final and cliticization often makes it difficult to correctly identify V to I raising in Old English. The verb of the embedded clause in (i) for example might be taken to sit in Infl (as in (ii)), but it is in fact just

as likely to be in Comp (as in (iii)). In the latter case, the sentence may or may not involve V to I raising (cf. Chapter 2), a fact that renders it useless for the present discussion.

(i)   Behreowsiendum mannum gemiltsað se Halga Gast, ac ðam he ne miltsað
       penitent   man-the pities   the Holy Ghost, but those he not pities
       næfre þe   his gyfe forseoð.
       never who his gift scorn
       'The Holy Ghost pities the penitent, but he never pities those who scorn his gift.'
                                            (Old English 990–992 [Ælfric *Homilies*], Roger Higgins, p.c.)

(ii)

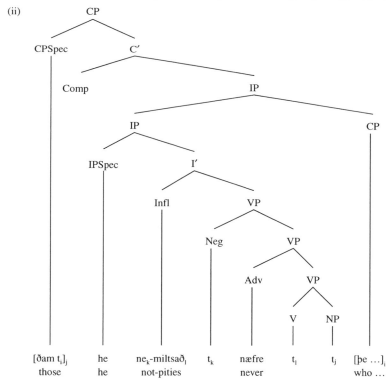

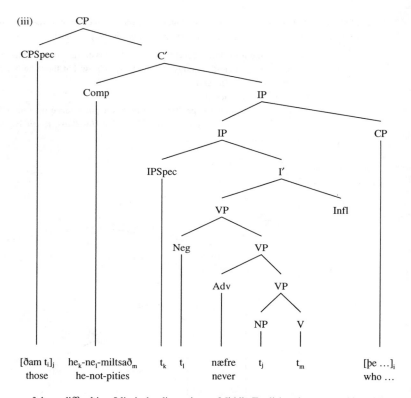

(iii)

[ðam tᵢ]ⱼ   heₖ-neₗ-miltsaðₘ   tₖ tₗ   næfre   tⱼ   tₘ   [þe ...]ᵢ
those   he-not-pities   never   who ...

Because of these difficulties, I limit the discussion to Middle English, a language which lacked V2, had clause-medial Infl and used a stationary negation marker.

2. It follows from the discussion in Section 3.4 that in (3), the phrase labeled IP is in fact not the same projection in Old and Middle English on the one hand and in Modern English on the other hand. Rather, it is AgrSP in the V to I raising languages Old and Middle English but it is TP in the V in situ language Modern English. This distinction should be kept in mind throughout this section; it will be taken up again in the next section.

3. For word order in negative declaratives (and interrogatives) underlyingly containing an auxiliary such as a modal or finite *have* or *be*, see the next section.

   In the following, I will by and large disregard a third environment for *do*-support, emphatic declaratives. Since emphasis depends not only on word order, but also on stress (cf. *I DO/*do see the problem*), it is harder to identify than interrogation and negation in historic texts which often do not provide direct clues with respect to phonological phenomena like stress.

4. Lasnik (1994) and Bobaljik (1995) propose a theory of *do*-support that is based on Lasnik's Filter but does not rely on affix-hopping. In their theory, the affix in Infl and the verb in V merge at PF under adjacency. Where adjacency is broken up by PF-visible material like *not*,

merger is impossible and the stranded affix is rescued by *do*-support. The main problem with this theory is that it has to stipulate that adverbs, which intervene between Infl and V, are not PF-visible, otherwise it would incorrectly derive (i) instead of (ii):

(i)   Pat does often eat cake. (unemphatic)

(ii)   Pat often eats cake.

5. Simple omission of the offensive affix does of course not help either (cf. (i)), and as a result aspectual *come* and *go* are not possible with third person singular subjects.

(i)   "*Mechthild go/come play soccer every Sunday."

I believe that the data in (10b,c) and (i) pose a challenge for Optimality Theory (Grimshaw 1997 inter alia), since they do not seem to be reconcilable with the idea that grammars are rankings of violable constraints and that a derivation is grammatical if there is no other equivalent derivation whose highest-ranked violated constraint is ranked lower than the highest-ranked violated constraint of the first derivation. Such a theory predicts that one of the sentences in (10b,c) and (i) is grammatical or that there is some alternative way to use aspectual *come* and *go* with a third person singular subject, but this is not the case.

6. Why ΣP blocks government of the verb by Infl is a non-trivial issue. Note in particular that ΣP does not always constitute a barrier in the sense discussed in Section 2.3 (see definitions (20) and (21)), since *not* can adjoin to Infl. That this adjunction is a syntactic rather than a phonological phenomenon is shown by further movement of the Infl-*not* complex to Comp via subject-aux inversion, cf. (i):

(i) $[_{CP}$ Which book $[_{C'}$ [did n't$_i]_k$ $[_{IP}$ you $[_{I'}$ t$_k$ $[_{\Sigma P}$ t$_i$ $[_{VP}$ read]]]]]]?

Moreover, none of the other languages discussed in this book employ *do*-support. In the other Germanic V in situ languages, *not* presumably does not head a projection in negated declaratives and is instead adjoined to VP, and if V to C movement proceeds through Infl, the projection headed by Q in questions is lexically governed by the intermediate trace of the verb. In Icelandic and Yiddish and the Romance languages other than Brazilian Portuguese, V to I raising always results in lexical government of ΣP. It would be crucial to investigate the situation in Brazilian Portuguese and other non-V2, V in situ languages, but since in this book, *do*-support is not the central topic but merely serves as a diagnostic for the loss of V to I raising in the history of English, I will leave this issue unresolved at this point.

7. More precisely, the absence of V to I raising is a necessary but not sufficient condition for *do*-support, as shown by the lack of *do*-support in the V in situ languages of Mainland Scandinavia (cf. the previous note). Many of the other, presumably English-specific factors that together with the loss of V to I raising are responsible for the emergence of *do*-support remain to be discovered.

8. Note for example that *do*-support in non-emphatic positive declaratives is found in many dialects of German and Dutch, languages that are commonly assumed to have V to I raising and that do not require *do*-support in negative declaratives or questions. In my own idiolect of German, (i) and (ii) coexist. However, it is not clear that *tu* in (i) is a truly periphrastic marker. Instead, it may have aspectual meaning.

(i)   Ich tu heut Fußball spielen.
        I   do today soccer   play

(ii)   Heut spiel ich Fußball.
        today play I   soccer
        'Today I'll play soccer.'   (German)

The pattern in (i) is particularly common in child language. Compare the Early Child Dutch
utterance in (iii) with (iv), its counterpart in the adult language.

(iii)   Hij doe huile.
        He does cry
        'He cries.'   (Jasmijn 2:5; from Jordens 1990)

(iv)   Hij huilt   (Dutch)

9.   In adducing examples from poetry (cf. (17)) and translations (cf. 18)), I abstract from the non-
     trivial problems posed by these types of sources. I will simply assume that equally striking
     examples can be found in original Early Modern English prose as well.

10. The terms "core language" and "periphery" are used in the sense of Chomsky (1986b: 147):
     "Suppose we distinguish *core language* from *periphery*, where a core language is a system
     determined by fixing values for the parameters of UG, and the periphery is whatever is added
     on in the system actually represented in the mind/brain of a speaker-hearer."

11. Alternatively, one might pursue a different approach to syntactic competition of the kind
     discussed here in which a speaker maintains several (possibly conflicting) core grammars at the
     same time, cf. the Double Base Hypothesis of Kroch (1990), Pintzuck (1991) and Santorini
     (1989).

12. Earlier stages of Faroese presumably had verbal paradigms and word order patterns that were
     (in the relevant aspects) similar to the Mainland Scandinavian ones. Since virtually no Faroese
     texts predating the late 18th century have survived, nothing more concrete can be said about the
     issue.

13. Strictly speaking, the dates refer to the birth of the authors rather than to the creation of their
     works. But since verb placement is acquired very early (cf. Section 3.3), this difference is not
     likely to be relevant.

14. As mentioned earlier, Modern Icelandic restricts stylistic fronting to sentences with a subject
     gap. Old Swedish seems to have allowed it in sentences with a pronominal subject as well.
     Platzack (1988) suggests that Old Swedish pronouns were in fact clitics that vacuously right-
     adjoined to Comp and left a subject gap behind.
         Falk notes that most of the (excluded) sentences with a null or pronominal subject and
     a pre-verbal adverb or negation marker (pro/Pro^Neg/Adv^V) presumably nevertheless represent
     V in situ, since stylistic fronting becomes increasingly uncommon after the year 1500. The
     exclusion of these sentences from the sample thus distorts the picture and the loss of V to I
     raising proceeded slightly faster and/or earlier than suggested in Table 4.4 and Figure 4.4.

15. Like Schäufele (1993) in the case of English (cf. the discussion above), Falk is concerned about
     the fact that for roughly two centuries after the loss of person agreement, V to I raising is still
     marginally possible in Swedish. Although she notes that "the change of grammars that seems

to have had the greatest influence on the embedded word order is ... the loss of agreement in person" (Falk 1993:184), she develops a theory according to which V to I rising is necessary with person agreement but possible with number agreement. Since in Swedish, the former was lost already in second half of the 15th century while the latter was lost only towards the end of the 17th century, this approach explains why V to I raising and V in situ coexisted for some time. In Section 3.2.3, I argued that Falk's proposal should be rejected because it suffers from arbitrariness and because it wrongly predicts V to I raising to be freely available in Faroese. In the present diachronic context, note that if Falk understands number agreement to involve distinct non-empty affixes in both the singular and the plural, then her theory does not explain the survival of V to I raising in Early Modern English until at least the 17th century, given that the plural marker -*en* was lost probably already in the late 15th century (cf. Roberts 1993). Clearly, we would like to have a unified account for the roughly twohundred years of coexistence of V to I raising and V in situ in both Swedish and English. Above, I suggest such an account: V to I raising remained marginally possible for some time after the loss of distinctive person marking due to the peripheral interference of (remnants of) the old word order in the input.

16. A converse problem involving British English possessive *have* is better known. Possessive *have* is a main verb which has to θ-mark its NP-argument. In American English, it occurs with *do*-support as expected (cf. (i)). In British English, it does not, surfacing instead in Infl before negation (cf. (ii)). Neither Pollock's θ-based nor Lasnik's inflection-based approach to the English auxiliary/main verb asymmetry can explain this behavior. Since the proposal I will make below faces a similar problem, I will discuss the matter there (cf. Section 4.3.2).

     (i)   I don't have any money.   (American English)

     (ii)   I haven't any money   (British English)

17. For the reasons mentioned in note 1, only Middle English examples have been chosen.

18. (40) illustrates the epistemic (or raising-verb) reading of the (pre-) modal in (38a). For the root (or control-verb) reading, replace t_i with PRO_i.

19. Lightfoot (1991) maintains that a raising analysis for examples like (45b) is possible, given that quirky (dative) Case subjects may sometimes appear in clear raising constructions in Old English.

20. In German, all complementizer-introduced embedded clauses are of the type in (46). Since German is also a V2 language, there is thus no word order evidence for V to I raising. This explains why German shows no signs of a modal reanalysis like that in (42), in spite of the fact that its modal paradigm is equivalent to the Old/Middle English one in (41) in all relevant respects. It is more mysterious why Yiddish continues to treat modals like main verbs, since the language has clause-medial Infl and inflects modals like German or Old/Middle English.

CHAPTER 5

Beyond Verb Movement in the Germanic VO Languages

5.1 Introduction

The previous chapters investigated (from both a synchronic and a diachronic point of view) the role that distinctive marking of the referential Infl-features [1ST] and [2ND] plays with respect to V to I raising in the Germanic VO languages. Below, I will extend the theory developed in Chapter 3 to other, related topics. Section 5.2 shows that Infl-referentiality also determines the V to I raising properties of the Romance languages. The case is straightforward in Italian (cf. Section 5.2.1) with V to I raising and a Full Paradigm of verbal affixes which distinctively mark [1ST] and [2ND] in both singular and plural of the present tense and most other tenses. Things are more interesting in French (Section 5.2.2) with V to I raising but arguably an incomplete paradigm of present tense affixes which do not distinctively mark [1ST] or [2ND] in either number. The situation is similar in other tenses. There is however good evidence that in Colloquial French, subject clitics (which form a Full Paradigm) have become quasi-obligatory and function in effect as agreement markers. I conclude that these clitics are base-generated in Infl and thus responsible for V to I raising in French. The inflectional paradigms of European and Brazilian Portuguese (Section 5.2.3) exhibit a crucial difference: In the former, all referential Infl-features are distinctively marked. In the latter [2ND] is never distinctively marked. As expected, European but not Brazilian Portuguese displays verb movement to the highest inflectional head. Section 5.3 argues that the principle of Infl/Agr-referentiality and affix-lexicality in (63) and (77) of Chapter 3 licenses not only V to I raising, but also *pro*-drop: As argued in Speas (1994), the highest projection of any clause must have content and hence either an overtly filled specifier or an overtly filled head. In languages without a Full Paradigm (i.e. without minimal distinctive marking of both [1ST] and [2ND]), TP is the highest inflectional projection and since its head is filled with a non-overt tense feature, its specifier must be filled with an overt subject. In languages with a Full Paradigm, AgrSP is the highest inflectional projection and since its head is filled with an overt affix and, after V to I raising, the verb, its specifier can be filled with an empty subject (*pro*). *Pro* can receive a referential interpretation if it is identified through Case and agreement by the same head (cf. Jaeggli and Hyams 1988). Given these assumptions, much of the distribution of referential null subjects in the Germanic and Romance languages follows. Section 5.4 summarizes Bobaljik's treatment of transitive expletive constructions and full-NP object shift which carries over more or less unchanged into the current approach: Languages with a Full Paradigm have agreement projections and hence extra positions to accommodate transitive expletives (SpecAgrSP) and shifted full-NP objects (SpecAgrOP).

5.2   V to I Raising in Romance

5.2.1   *Italian*

Italian distinctively marks the referential Infl-features [1ST] and [2ND] in, among other tenses, the indicative present, as shown in (1).

(1)   Italian
        INF   *parl-a[1]-re* "to speak"
                            SG   PL
        IND PRES   1ST   parl-o   parl-iamo
                    2ND   parl-i   parl-a-te
                    3RD   parl-a   parl-a-no

Given the Full Paradigm in (1), the theory developed in Chapter 3 of this book predicts that in Italian, the Infl-affixes have lexical entries, are inserted at D-structure under Infl (or Agr(S), the highest inflectional head according to the Split-Infl Hypothesis), and trigger verb movement at S-structure to Infl (or Agr(S)) in order to pass Lasnik's Filter. It is standardly assumed that this type of movement does in fact occur in Italian. The following discussion is based on Belletti (1990, 1994), to which I have little to add.

   We saw in Chapter 2 that in the Germanic VO languages, the position of sentential negation relative to the position of the finite verb indicates (at least in some environments) whether V to I raising has taken place. This is however not the case in Italian (and most other Romance languages), where the negation marker *non* is a clitic which must left-adjoin to (and hence immediately precede) the verb, thereby obscuring the position of the latter. The post-verbal occurrence of negative polarity items like *più* "anymore", *ancora* "yet" and *mai* "ever" is more revealing: It is reasonable to assume that these elements are generated at the left periphery of VP (or further to the left), that they stay in situ (or move to SpecNegP), and that their post-verbal position therefore indicates that verb movement has taken place. Belletti assigns the sentence in (2) (= Belletti 1994, ex. (13b)) the S-structure in (3), where the verb moves first to Tense, then directly across the clitic in Neg and the negative polarity item in SpecNegP to Agr; Neg finally cliticizes to Agr. Note that this analysis strongly resembles the proposal for verb movement to Comp in Mainland Scandinavian I made in Chapter 2 (direct V to Comp with independent adjunction of Infl to (the verb in) Comp, cf. the discussion of structures (22) and (27) in Chapter 2).

(2) Gianni non *scrive mai* un lavoro e   poi lo pubblica.
     G.   not writes ever a   work and then it publishes
     'Gianni doesn't ever write a work and then publish it.'   (Italian)

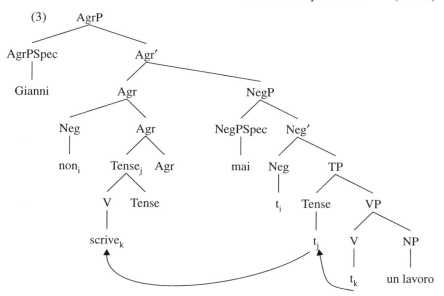

Like the position of negation, the position of adverbs is less clearly indicative of V to I raising in Italian than it is in the Germanic VO languages. Sentential or, in Belletti's terms, 'higher' adverbs are found clause-initially in the unmarked case (cf. (4a) = Belletti 1994, ex. (27a)). Sentences where the subject precedes them (cf. (4b) = Belletti 1994, ex. (27b)) or where they occur clause-finally (cf. (4c) = Belletti 1991, ex. (27c)) have the flavor of topicalization or right-dislocation, respectively. In simple tenses, sentential adverbs never follow the verb clause-medially (cf. (4d)). These judgments are captured by Belletti's assumption that Italian sentential adverbs are underlyingly adjoined to AgrP as shown in (5), in which case their position relative to that of the finite verb does not bear on the question whether the latter has moved or not.[2]

(4)   a.   *Probabilmente* Gianni *arriverà*   domani.
              probably   G.   will-arrive tomorrow.

    b.   Gianni *probabilmente arriverà*   domani.
              G.   probably   will-arrive tomorrow

    c.   Gianni *arriverà*   domani, *probabilmente.*
              G.   will-arrive tomorrow probably

    d.   *Gianni *arriverà*   *probabilmente* domani.
              G.   will-arrive probably   tomorrow
              'Gianni will probably arrive tomorrow.'   (Italian)

(5)

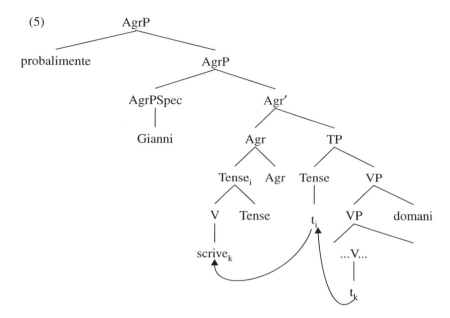

VP- (or, in Belletti's terms, 'lower') adverbs in simple tenses either directly follow the verb clause-medially (cf. (6a) = Belletti 1990, ex. I(67a)) or occur clause-finally (cf. (6b) = Belletti 1990, ex I(68a)) but never precede the verb (cf. (6c)). Belletti assumes that VP-adverbs can be both left- and right-adjoined to VP. The former option is chosen in (6a) where the post-verbal position of *completamente* therefore reflects verb movement to Agr, as shown in (7a). The latter option is chosen in (6b) where the post-verbal position of *completamente* is therefore compatible with both verb movement to Agr and V in situ, as shown in (7b). Under Belletti's assumption that clause-medial VP-adverbs are adjoined to the left of VP, the ungrammaticality of (6c) shows that V in situ is not available.

(6)   a.   Quel medico *risolverà completamente* i   tuoi problemi.
                 that doctor will-solve completely   the your problems
        b.   Quel medico *risolverà* i   tuoi problemi *completamente*.
                 that doctor will-solve the your problems completely
        c.   *Quel medico *completamente risolverà* i   tuoi problemi.
                 this doctor completely   will-solve the your problems
                 'That doctor will completely solve your problems.'   (Italian)

(7)   a.   b.

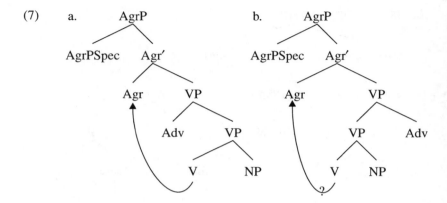

If Italian VP-adverbs can be adjoined to the right of VP, the question arises whether they are not always found in this position and whether the word order in (6a) is not due to extraposition of the object (cf. (8)) instead of movement of the verb (cf. (7a)). This is in fact the analysis Galves (1990) proposes for the parallel case in Brazilian Portuguese where, as we will see in Section 5.2.3, there is reason to believe that the finite verb does not move at all (or at least does not move to the highest inflectional head). It is also reminiscent of the analysis I proposed in Section 2.4.2.1 for English sentences in which a main verb precedes an adverb and a prepositional phrase (cf. the structure in (61) in Section 2.4.2.1 and the discussion there).

(8)

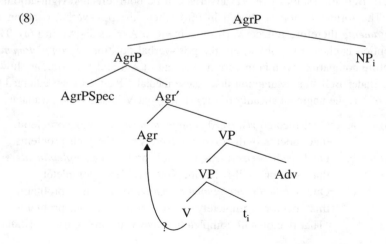

Complex tenses however provide evidence that VP-adverbs cannot be uniformly right-adjoined to VP in Italian and that (6a) involves verb movement. In complex tenses, VP adverbs may not only appear in the positions attested in simple tenses (compare (9a) = Belletti 1990, ex. I(79b) with (6a) and (9b) = Belletti 1990, ex. I(80a) with (6b)), but also between the auxiliary and the main verb (cf. (9c) based on Belletti 1990, ex. I(82)). The latter word order requires the adverb to be generated at the left periphery of VP (or even further to the left). If verbs did not move in simple tenses, we would expect them to be able to follow VP-adverbs when the latter are left-adjoined to VP, an option that must be available in the light of (9c). Since the order ADV^V is in fact ungrammatical in this context (cf. (6c)), we must conclude that Italian finite verbs obligatorily raise out of VP.

> (9)   a.   Quel dottore *ha* risolto *completamente* i   tuoi problemi.
>   that   doctor   has solved completely   the your problems
>   b.   Quel dottore *ha* risolto i   tuoi problemi *completamente*.
>   that   doctor   has solved the your problems completely
>   c.   Quel dottore *ha completamente* risolto i   tuoi problemi.
>   that   doctor   has completely   solved the your problems
>   'That doctor has completely solved your problems.'

>   (Italian)

The arguments based on the distribution of negative polarity items and VP-adverbs for finite verb raising in Italian also go through with respect to Italian infinitivals such as the complements of control verbs (cf. (10) with the infinitival marker *di*) or modals (cf. (11) without *di*). To see this, compare (10a) (= Belletti 1990, ex. I(89)) and (11a) (based on Belletti 1990, ex. I(98b)) with (2), (10b) (= Belletti 1990, ex. I(102a)) and (11b) (based on Belletti 1990, ex. I(102b)) with (6a,c), and (10c) and (11c) (based on Belletti 1990, ex. I(104a)) with (9c). I will not go into details since the data are self-explanatory given the discussion above.

> (10)   a.   Gianni ha deciso di non *tornare mai*.
>   G.   has decided to not return   ever
>   'John has decided to never come back.'
>   b.   Quel   medico sostine di *risolvere completamente* (*risolvere*)
>   Which doctor   claims to solve   completely
>   i tuoi problemi.
>   your   problems

    c.   Quel medico sostine di *aver completamente* risolto i tuoi
        that doctor claims to have completely   solved your
        problemi.
        problems

(11)   a.   Gianni potrebbe non *tornare mai*.
        G.   could   not return ever
        'John could never return.'
    b.   Quei medici potrebbero *risolvere   completamente*
        those doctors could   completely solve
        (*risolvere*) i-tuoi problemi.
        solve   your problems
    c.   Quei medici potrebbero *aver completamente* risolto i tuoi
        those doctors could   have completely   solved your
        problemi.
        problems   (Italian)

Belletti points out that the distribution of floating quantifiers provides additional support for the claim that the verb moves to the highest inflectional head in Italian finite and infinitival clauses. Following Sportiche (1988), she assumes that when a quantified subject moves to its S-structural position (i.e. AgrPSpec), the quantifier may be left behind in the D-structural subject position (i.e. SpecVP) or in an intermediate specifier through which the subject has moved (e.g. SpecTP), thus giving rise to a 'floated' quantifier (cf. the discussion of quantifier floating in English in Section 2.4.2.1). The fact that in Italian, floated quantifiers obligatorily follow the highest finite (cf. (12) = Belletti 1990, ex. I(83a) and I(84a)) or non-finite verb (cf. (13) = Belletti 1990, ex. I(104ab)) then proves that the verb must move to the highest inflectional head as shown in (14). If the verb moved only to an intermediate inflectional head (e.g. Tense), we would expect a floated quantifier located in the specifier of that projection (e.g. SpecTP) to be able to precede the verb, contrary to fact (cf. (12b,13b)).

(12)   a.   Gli invitati *salutarono tutti* Maria.
        the guests greeted   all M.
    b.   *Gli invitati *tutti salutarono* Maria.
        the guests all greeted   M.

(13)   a.   Quei medici potrebbero *risolvere tutti* il   difficile problema
            those doctors could   solve   all   the difficult problems
            di quel paziente.
            of that patient

       b.   *Quei medici potrebbero *tutti risolvere* il   difficile problema
            Those doctors could   all   solve   the difficult problems
            di quel paziente.
            of that patient   (Italian)

(14)   AgrP

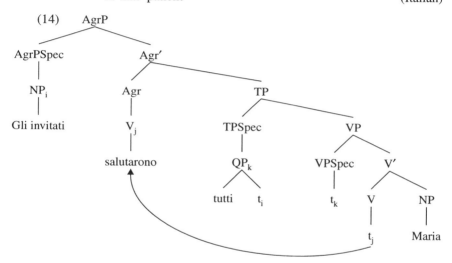

The theory developed in this book appears to be compatible with the facts in Italian, where the verb raises to the highest inflectional head because all referential inflectional features are distinctively marked in the regular verbal paradigms.

5.2.2   *French*

Unlike their Italian counterparts, French finite and infinitival verbs occupy different positions in the clause. While finite main verbs obligatorily precede VP-adverbs (cf. (15) based on Pollock 1989, ex. (3bd)) and the negation marker *pas* (cf. (16) based on Pollock 1989, ex. (2b)), infinitival main verbs only optionally precede VP-adverbs (cf. (17) based on Pollock 1989, ex. (27a) and (24a)) and obligatorily follow *pas* (cf. (18) = Pollock 1989, ex. (16dc)). Infinitival auxiliaries on the other hand may precede *pas* (cf. (19) = Pollock

1989, ex. (15ba)), although this is a marked option which is absent in colloquial speech.

(15) a. Marie *embrasse souvent* Jean.
          M.   embraces often   J.
      b. *Marie *souvent embrasse* Jean.
          M.   often   embraces J.

(16) a. Marie n'*aime   pas* Jean.
          M.   NEG/likes not J.
      b. *Marie ne   *pas aime* Jean.
          M.   NEG not likes J.
          'Mary doesn't like John.'

(17) a. *Parler à peine* l'italien est une disgrace.
          to-talk hardly Italian is a   disgrace
      b. *A-peine parler* l'italien est une disgrace.
          hardly   to-talk Italian is a   disgrace
          'To hardly speak Italian is a disgrace.'

(18) a. *Ne *posséder pas* de voiture rend   la vie difficile.
          NEG to-own   not a car   renders the life difficult
      b. Ne *pas posséder* de voiture rend   la vie difficile.
          NEG not to-own   a car   renders the life difficult

(19) a. (?)N'*être   pas* heureux est une condition   pour écrire
          NEG/to-be not happy   is a   prerequisite for   writing
          des-romanes.
          novels
      b. Ne *pas être* heureux est une condition   pour écrire
          NEG not to-be happy   is a   prerequisite for   writing
          des-romanes.
          novels   (French)

These data can be at least partially captured if we adopt a clause structure that is very similar to the one proposed by Belletti (1990) for Italian and in which *pas* is the stationary specifier of NegP, *ne* is the head of NegP and cliticizes to Agr, adverbs are left-adjoined to VP and finite verbs move to the highest inflectional head above NegP while infinitival verbs may only move to an intermediate head between NegP and VP (compare (20) with (3) and (7a)). This proposal is essentially identical with the one made in Pollock (1989), where the order of AgrP and TP is inverted.

(20)

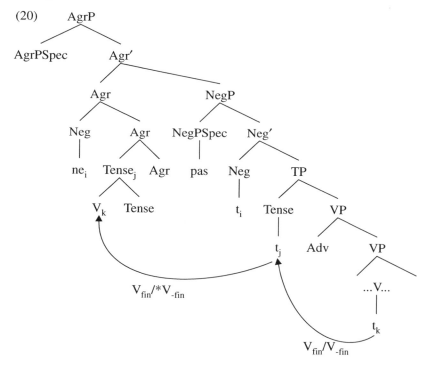

As pointed out by Pollock, the claim that in French, finite verbs must move to the highest inflectional head while non-finite verbs move only optionally to an intermediate inflectional head is supported by the distribution of floating quantifiers in this language. As in Italian, floating quantifiers must follow the verb in finite clauses (compare (21) = Sportiche 1988, ex. (4b) with (12)) and (21a) has essentially the same S-structure as (12a), namely (14) with the verb in the highest inflectional head. Unlike Italian, French permits floating quantifiers not only to follow but also to precede the verb in non-finite clauses (compare (22) = Pollock 1989, ex. (28a) & (25a) with (13)). Under the assumption that French infinitivals move only optionally to an intermediate inflectional head (e.g. Tense), this variability can be explained as follows. When the verb moves to Tense, it precedes a quantifier stranded in the D-structural subject position (SpecVP) as shown in (23a), the S-structure of (22a). When the verb stays in

situ, it follows a quantifier in the same position, as shown in (23b), the S-structure of (22b).

(21)   a.   Les enfants *verront tous* ce film.
            the children will-see all   this movie
       b.   *Les enfants *tous verront* ce film.
            the children all   will-see this movie

(22)   a.   On imagine mal   les députés   *démissionner tous* en
            one imagines badly the representatives resign   all   at
            même temps.
            same time
       b.   On imagine mal   les députés   *tous démissionner* en
            one imagines badly the representatives all   resign   at
            même temps.
            same time
            'It is hard to imagine the representatives all resigning at the
            same time.'   (French)

(23)   a.   b.

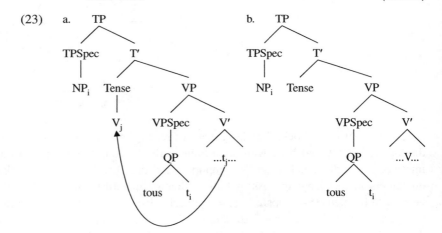

Does French V to I raising conform to the theory developed in Chapter 3,
i.e. is it triggered by the (minimal) distinctive marking of the referential Infl-
features [1ST] and [2ND]? At first glance, this does not seem to be the case. (24)
illustrates central portions of the paradigm for the most common and most
productive class of regular verbs (i.e. the verbs of the *-er* conjugation) with the
pronunciation of the endings listed in square brackets.

(24)   French

INF *mang-er* [*-e*] "to eat"

a.   PRES

	SG		PL	
1ST	mang-e	[−Ø]	mang-e	[−Ø]
			mang-ons	[−õ]
2ND	mang-es	[−Ø]	mang-ez	[−e]
3RD	mang-e	[−Ø]	mang-ent	[−Ø]

b.   IMPERF

	SG		PL	
1ST	mang-eais	[−ɛ]	mang-eait	[−ɛ]
			mang-i-ons	[−õ]
2ND	mang-eais	[−ɛ]	mang-i-ez	[−e]
3RD	mang-eait	[−ɛ]	mang-eaint	[−ɛ]

c.   FUT

	SG		PL	
1ST	mang-er-ai	[−ɛ]	mang-er-a	[−a]
			mang-er-ons	[−õ]
2ND	mang-er-as	[−a]	mang-er-ez	[−e]
3RD	mang-er-a	[−a]	mang-er-ont	[−õ]

In the singular of all tenses, the forms for second person are identical with the forms for third person and [2ND] is therefore not distinctively marked. In the plural of the present tense, the form for second person is identical with the infinitive and hence again not distinctively marked. In the plural of the imperfective and future tenses, the forms for second person are distinct from the infinitive, but this distinction is contributed by tense affixes. The agreement affix itself is identical with the infinitival affix and [2ND] is therefore again arguably not distinctively marked. In the singular of the present and imperfective tenses, the forms for first person are identical with the forms for second and third person and [1ST] is therefore not distinctively marked. In the singular of the future tense, the form for first person is distinct from the forms for second and third person, but once the tense affix is factored out, the agreement affix is identical with the infinitival affix and [1ST] is therefore again arguably not distinctively marked. Moreover, in colloquial speech the impersonal forms *on mange/mangeait/mangera* often replace the personal forms *nous mangons/mangions/mangerons* as the forms for the first person plural. In all three tenses, one of the two first person plural forms is identical with the third person plural (cf. the impersonal form of the present and imperfective tenses and the personal form in the future tense) and

[1ST] is therefore once more probably not distinctively marked. There is then reason to believe that neither [1ST] nor [2ND] are minimally distinctively marked in spoken French. Since colloquial speech in general lacks liaison, there is little motivation to hypothesize that the verbal affixes distinctively mark the person features in the underlying representation and are leveled only in Phonetic Form.

It thus appears that Colloquial French lacks a Complete Paradigm with minimal distinctive marking of both [1ST] and [2ND] despite the fact that it has V to I raising. French would then constitute a serious counter-example against the theory of V to I raising argued for in this book. I however think that this conclusion is premature because it disregards the role that subject clitics play in this language. French has two series of subject pronouns which are often called 'weak' or 'atonic' (cf. (25a)) and 'strong' or 'tonic' (cf. (25b)). Atonic pronouns ('clitics' for short) appear attached to the immediate left of the finite verbal complex in declarative clauses. Tonic pronouns ('pronouns' for short) have the same distribution as full NP subjects.

(25) a. French subject clitics   b. French subject pronouns

	SG	PL		SG	PL
1ST	je	on (nous)	1ST	moi	nous
2ND	tu	vous	2ND	toi	vous
3RD MASC	il	ils	3RD MASC	lui	eux
FEM	elle	elles	FEM	elle	"
IMP	ce/ça	ces	IMP	ça	—

Roberge (1990) points out that in Canadian and Northern African French, the clitics can redundantly appear in the presence of a pronoun or full NP-subject ('clitic doubling') as shown in (26) (= Kaiser and Meisel 1991, ex. (10cb)) without adding emphasis on the subject or requiring an intonational break between pronominal or NP-subject and clitic (i.e. without the properties of left dislocation).

(26) a. Lui il   mange.
           He 3SG eats
           'He is eating.'
      b. Jean il   mange.
           J.   3SG eats.
           'John is eating.'   (French)

According to Sankoff (1982), the clitic doubling illustrated in (26) is in fact more widespread among speakers in France (over 80% of all sentences with NP-subject) than in Canada (ca. 55%). Barnes (1986) finds clitic doubling with 66% of all NP-subjects "where a [left] dislocation would not have violated a pragmatic or syntactic constraint." Kaiser and Meisel (1991) present similar numbers for NP-subjects (65% clitic doubling) and add that clitic doubling is obligatory with pronouns; overall, clitics are found in almost 95% of all finite clauses. It is highly unlikely that this phenomenon can be reduced to left dislocation, especially since it does not require emphasis or an intonational break. Let us instead assume that the subject surfaces in its canonical position in SpecIP and that the clitic is not an argument of the verb, but rather a reflection of subject-verb agreement. The latter idea is by no means new: It can be traced back to at least the late 19th century, where it was already well established among traditional French grammarians (see Kaiser and Meisel for references). Since French clitics (now understood as agreement markers) distinctively mark the referential Infl-features [1ST] and [2ND], the Principle of Infl/Agr-referentiality and Affix-Lexicality in (63) and (77) of Chapter 3 predicts that they have lexical entries and are (at D-structure) adjoined to Agr where they trigger S-structural verb movement because they have to be bound at this level. According to this analysis, a sentence like (26b) has the structure in (27), similar to what has been proposed by Rizzi (1986b) and Brandi and Cordin (1989) for Northern Italian dialects, by Jaeggli (1981), Roberge (1990) and Kaiser and Meisel (1991) for French and by Benedicto (1994) for Puerto Rican Spanish.

(27)

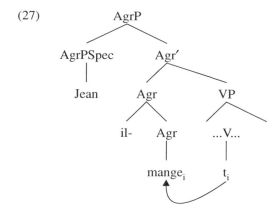

What about the inflectional suffixes on the verb? I propose that since these do not form a Full Paradigm, they do not have lexical entries, are not present during syntax and are introduced in Phonetic Form by spell-out rules as discussed in

Chapter 3. This means that in syntax, the verb bears abstract agreement features which are then spelled out at PF in the form of the suffixes. After substitution into Agr at S-structure, the verb is in a spec-head configuration with the subject which allows checking of these abstract features. According to this view, French inflectional morphology is a mixed system: Part of it (i.e. the clitics) is lexical and hence syntactically relevant and part of it (i.e. the suffixes) is PF-introduced and hence syntactically irrelevant.

I think that this way of looking at things may ultimately explain why French infinitival main verbs do not raise to the highest inflectional head whereas their Italian (and possibly Icelandic, cf. Section 2.4.2.4) counterparts do. In Italian, the verbal suffixes (including the infinitival marker -re) have lexical entries because they are part of a Full Paradigm. Inserted under the highest inflectional head, finite and infinitival affixes alike trigger V to I raising.[3] In French, the verbal suffixes (including the infinitival marker -er) do not have lexical entries because they are part of an incomplete paradigm. Introduced post-syntactically via spell-out, they do not affect the position of the verb. In finite clauses, clitics are generated adjoined to Agr and these clitics trigger verb movement via Lasnik's Filter. In non-finite clauses, no overt clitics occur and I crucially assume that there are no empty clitics either. A possible reason for this assumption is suggested in Benedicto (1994), according to which clitics are generated as a last resort strategy to overtly mark a distinction that has otherwise been lost from the paradigm. Empty clitics would be incompatible with this function and they do therefore not exist. It then seems reasonable to assume that in French infinitivals, Agr contains no (overt or covert) morphological material at all that could trigger verb movement to this position.[4]

Support for this analysis comes from the history of French. Roberts (1993) points out that infinitivals did in fact raised across *pas* and negative polarity items like *jamais* "ever", *plus* "more" and *point* "at all" in Old and Early Middle French (compare (28) (from de Kok (1985: 335)) with (18a)), i.e. earlier stages of the language when the pronunciation of the verbal suffixes still approximated the orthography in (24) which hence constituted a Full Paradigm.

(28)   Pour ce, me chière filles,   est-il bon de ne se   *haster point.*
        for that my dear daughters is it good to not oneself hurry at all
        'It is therefore good, my dear daughters, not to hurry oneself at
        all.'   (Middle French [*La Tour*] 1372)

Infinitival raising was lost as a result of the leveling of the verbal suffixes and their replacement under Infl by the clitics in Middle French (ca. 1300–1600). De Kok (1985) cites (29) as the last example:

(29)   C'est pourquoi le devine Platon ... advertit justement ceux qui
    this-is why   the divine Plato   advised exactly   those who
    aiment une bonne renommée ... de ne se *commettre jamais*
    like   a   good   reputation   to NEG REFL mingle   ever
    avec une Poëte.
    with a   poet
    '...to never mingle with a poet.'

(Late Middle French [*Colletet*] 1658)

De Kok (1985:335) notes that this change can be relatively closely dated because it was noticed by the 17th century grammarian de Vaugelas who writes:

'It must be noted that with infinitives *pas* and *point* are much more graceful when put in front instead of after them, for example, to say *pour ne pas tomber dans le inconvénients* ["in order not to encounter inconveniences"] ... is much more elegant than *pour ne tomber pas...*'

(de Vaugelas 1647, *Remarque*)

De Kok (1985:335) writes that this testimony is supported by the fact that "since first half of the 17th century there are abundant examples with preposition of the adverb of negation".

It thus seems that French progressed from an earlier stage (resembling Italian) with lexical finite and infinitival verbal suffixes triggering V to I raising in finite and infinitival clauses to a modern stage with lexical finite clitics triggering V to I raising in finite clauses only and non-lexical finite and infinitival verbal suffixes not affecting the verb-syntax. Unlike the languages discussed so far in this dissertation, in which inflectional morphology is either always lexical or always post-syntactic, French thus uses both lexical and post-syntactic inflectional morphology. Since nothing in the theory disallows such mixed systems, French fills an important gap and thus supports the view of inflectional morphology argued for in this book.

5.2.3   *European and Brazilian Portuguese*

The inflectional paradigms of European (cf. (30a) from Hundertmark-Santos Martins 1982) and Brazilian Portuguese (cf. (30b) from Bianchi and Figueiredo-

Silva 1993) differ in that the referential Infl-feature [2ND] is minimally distinctively marked only in the former, but not in the latter. The distinctively marked
'direct' second person plural *vós comprais* "y'all sell" was lost in both dialects,
leaving only the 'indirect' second person plural *vocês compram* which is
indistinguishable from the third person plural. Unlike European Portuguese,
Brazilian Portuguese also lost the distinctively marked 'direct' second singular *tu
falas* "you speak" around the beginning of this century (cf. Duarte 1993), leaving
only the 'indirect' second singular *você fala* which is indistinguishable from the
third person singular. In addition, Brazilian Portuguese (like French, cf. (24))
replaced the personal first person plural *nos falamos* "we speak" with the
impersonal *a gente fala*.

(30)	a.	European Portuguese *compr-ar* "to sell"		b.	Brazilian Portuguese *fal-ar* "to speak"	
		IND PRES			IND PRES	
		SG	PL		SG	PL
		1ST compr-o	compr-amos		1ST fal-o	fal-a
		2ND compr-as	compr-am		2ND fal-a	fal-am
		3RD compr-a	compr-am		3RD fal-a	fal-am

If V to I raising depends on minimal the distinctive marking of all referential
Infl-features as claimed in this book, we predict that European Portuguese has
verb movement to the highest inflectional head whereas Brazilian Portuguese
does not have this type of movement. These actually seem to be just the right
predictions: It has been argued in the literature that European Portuguese has V
to I (Rouveret 1989) while Brazilian Portuguese has either V in situ (Galves
1989, 1990) or verb movement to an intermediate, but crucially not the highest
inflectional head (Bianchi and Figueiredo Silva 1993 and Mendes 1993; but see
Figueiredo Silva 1991 for a dissenting view).

Whether there are substantial differences between European and Brazilian
Portuguese with respect to the type of evidence adduced in sections 5.2.1 and 5.2.2
in support of V to I raising in Italian and French (i.e. negative polarity items, adverbs
and floating quantifiers) is unclear. Sentence (31) (based on Figueiredo Silva 1992,
ex. (20a)), which is entirely parallel to the Italian example in (2), seems to be
grammatical in both European and Brazilian Portuguese, and it is tempting to assign
the same S-structure to the Italian (cf. (3)) and European and Brazilian Portuguese
examples (cf. (32)) and to conclude that just like Italian, both European and Brazilian
Portuguese have verb movement to the highest inflectional head.

(31) Maria nao *fala*   *nunca* disso.
      M.   NEG speaks never of-this
      'Maria never speaks about this.' (Eu. & Br. Portuguese)

(32)

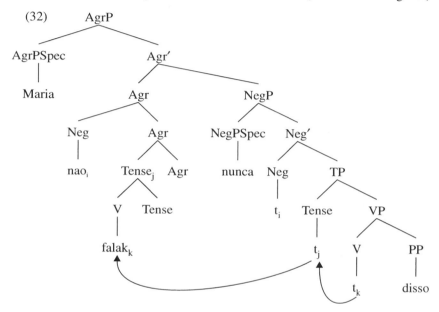

However, the negative clitic *nao* need not be present in sentences containing negative polarity items and if *nao* is absent, the negative polarity item obligatorily precedes the verb as in (33) (based on Figueiredo Silva 1992, ex. (23)), which has the same interpretation as (31).

(33) Maria *nunca fala*   disso.
      M.   never speaks of-this (Portuguese)

There is no straightforward way to explain (33) on the basis of the structure in (32). *Nunca* otherwise does not behave like a clitic and it is therefore presumably not adjoined to Agr. Adjunction to X' (in this case Agr') is probably excluded in general. Since the clause-initial subject does not seem to be topicalized or left-dislocated, adjunction to AgrP is not an option either. But as long as the position of *nunca* in (33) is not determined, it seems premature to draw any conclusions regarding the position of *nunca* and (more importantly) the verb in (31).

Bianchi and Figueiredo Silva (1993:13) point out that unlike Italian (cf. (4b)), Brazilian Portuguese (cf. (34) = Bianchi and Figueiredo Silva 1993, ex. (20)) freely allows "the order Subject-Adverb-Verb ... even when the subject is neither dislocated nor topicalized". The adverb therefore cannot be AgrP-adjoined, and if (as suggested above) adjunction to Agr′ is not available, the verb cannot have moved to the highest inflectional head. Interestingly, (34) is bad in European Portuguese (Pilar Barbosa, p.c.) where adverbs "normally follow the verb they relate to" (Hundertmark Santos-Martin 1982), a fact which is at least compatible with (if not evidence for) the view that the verb always moves to the highest inflectional head in this dialect.

(34)   Ninguém *provavelmente telefonu.*
         nobody   probably   called   (Brazilian Portuguese)

Galves (1990) observes that in Brazilian Portuguese, only adverbs that can occur VP-finally allow the order Subject-Verb-Adverb-Object and argues that this order is always due to right-adjunction of the adverb to VP in combination with extraposition of the object as illustrated in (35). If this analysis is correct, post-verbal adverbs do not indicate that the verb leaves VP in Brazilian Portuguese (cf. the discussion of the highly similar English facts in Section 2.4.2.1).

(35)

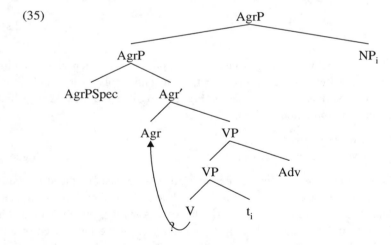

If the distribution of negative polarity items and in particular the grammaticality of (31) in European and Brazilian Portuguese seems to suggest that both dialects have V to I raising, then the distribution of floating quantifiers and in particular the grammaticality of (36) seems to suggest exactly the opposite, i.e. that both European and Brazilian Portuguese lack movement to the highest inflectional head. A pre-verbal floating quantifier is out in Italian (cf. (12b)) and French (cf. (21b)) finite clauses, but according to Figueiredo Silva (1990), it is the most natural order in Brazilian Portuguese and Pilar Barbosa (p.c.) confirms that the same is also true for European Portuguese (cf. (36) = Figueiredo Silva 1992, ex. (5b)).

(36)　　Os caras *todos receberam* uma carta.
　　　　 the boys all　　received　 a　 letter　　　(E. & B. Portuguese)

If the above discussion of French and Italian floating quantifiers is on the right track, the floating quantifier in (36) is located either in SpecVP or in the specifier of one of the lower inflectional projections and the verb following it has moved either not at all or to the head of one of the lower inflectional projections. (36) could thus have an S-structure that is similar to (23b), the S-structure of the French non-finite example in (22b). Alternatively, it could have the S-structure in (37). In either case, the verb has not moved to the highest inflectional head.

(37)

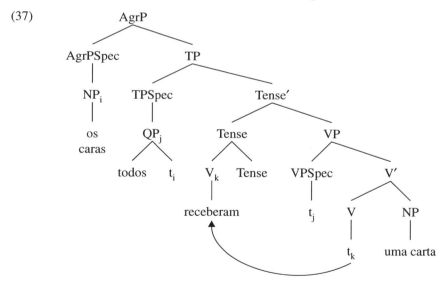

Figueiredo Silva (1990) however argues that the order in (36) is not due to quantifier floating, but instead to free permutability of the quantifier and the NP it modifies. She observes that in French complex tenses, floating quantifiers are able to surface in a specifier between the finite auxiliary and the participial main verb. If non-finite verbs such as participles do not move at all, the quantifier can remain in SpecVP, the D-structural subject position. If participles move to the head of an inflectional projection (call it PrtP) below the base position of the auxiliary, the quantifier can remain in the specifier of this inflectional projection if it is an intermediate subject position. The second, more complex derivation is illustrated in (39) for the grammatical French example in (38) taken from Sportiche (1988).

(38)   Les enfants   ont   *tous vu*   ce   film.
         the   children   have   all   seen this movie   (French)

(39)

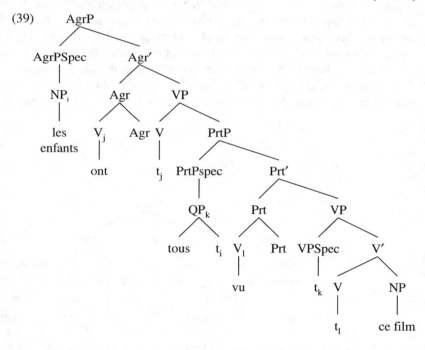

From the fact that in Portuguese complex tenses, a quantifier between the auxiliary and the main verb is less than perfect (cf. (40a) from Figueiredo Silva 1990). Figueiredo Silva concludes that Portuguese does not have quantifier floating and that sentence (36) has the S-structure in (41) instead of (37) which, unlike the latter, is ambiguous with respect to verb movement. It is however not

entirely clear how strong this argument is, since Italian also disprefers the order
Aux^Q^V in complex tenses (cf. (40b) from Belletti 1990) yet in simplex tenses,
it allows the order V^Q which is standardly analyzed as resulting from quantifier
floating (cf. (12a) with the S-structure in (14)).

> (40)   a.   ?Os caras tinham *todos recebido* uma carta.
>   the boys have   all   received a   letter   (Portuguese)
>   b. (?)Gli invitati hanno *tutti salutato* Maria.
>   the guests have   all   greeted M.   (Italian)

(41)

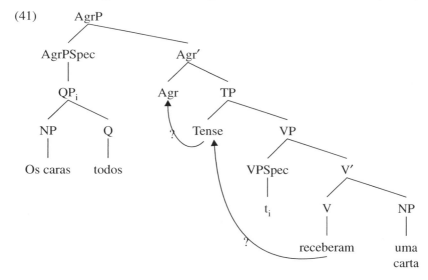

So far, no clear picture has emerged with respect to V to I raising or V in situ
in Brazilian and European Portuguese from the behavior of negative polarity
items, adverbs and quantifier floating. Clearer (albeit indirect) evidence in
support of the conclusion that the verb raises to the highest inflectional head in
European but not in Brazilian Portuguese comes from the different distribution
of null objects in the two dialects. In Section 5.2.4, I argue that this conclusion
is also supported by cliticization strategies European and Brazilian Portuguese,
although here the data are again extremely complex across the Romance
languages and I cannot attempt to fully explain them at this point.

European Portuguese allows null objects that refer to a specific, pragmatically salient inanimate antecedent in declarative matrix clauses (cf. (42a)) and those

embedded clauses which permit extraction (cf. (42b)). Empty objects of this type ,
are however excluded from extraction islands such as complex NPs (cf. (42c)),
sentential subjects (cf. (42d)) or adjuncts (cf. (42e)); they are also unavailable in
matrix wh-questions (cf. (42f)).[5] In the following examples (taken from Raposo
1986), the gap is intended to refer to a specific object that has been made salient
(mentioned, pointed out, etc.) earlier in the discourse.

(42) a. o   Manel guardou e no cofre de sala de jantar.
          the M.   kept   (it) in safe of dining room
          'Manuel kept it in the safe of the dining room.'

      b. eu disse ao António que perdise ao Manel que guardasse e
          I told the A.   that asked the M.   that keep   (it)
          no cofre da sala de jantar.
          in safe of dining room
          'I told Anthony to ask Manuel to keep it in the safe of the
          dining room.'

      c. *eu informei a polícia da possibilidade de o Manel ter
          I informed the police of possibility   of the M.   had
          guardado e no cofre da sala de jantar.
          kept   (it) in safe of dining room
          'I informed the police of the possibility that Manuel had kept it
          in the safe of the dining room.'

      d. *Que a IBM venda a particulares   surpreende-me.
          That the IBM sells to private individuals surprises   me .
          'That IBM sells it to private individuals surprises me.'

      e. *O pirate partiu para as Caraíbas depois de ter guardado
          the pirate left   for the Caribbean after to have guarded
          e cuidadosamente no cofre.
          (it) carefully   in safe
          'The pirate left for the Caribbean after he had carefully guarded
          it in the safe.'

      f. *Quando é que o Manel vai oferecer e ao António?
          when   is that the Manuel goes to-offer (it) the Anthony
          'When is Manuel going to offer it to Anthony?'

                                                        (European Portuguese)

The ungrammaticality of empty objects in islands and direct wh-questions
suggests that the construction involves A'-movement of an empty, discourse-

identified operator to the matrix SpecCP as proposed by Huang (1984) for analogous cases in Chinese. This analysis was adopted for European Portuguese by Raposo (1986). Example (42a) receives the S-structure in (43) and (42c–f) are excluded since operator movement must obey the relevant locality restrictions and the matrix SpecCP must be available as a landing site.

(43)

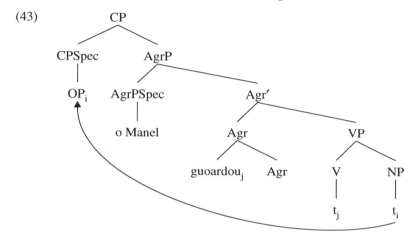

Unlike their European Portuguese counterparts, Brazilian Portuguese inanimate referential null objects are not sensitive to islands effects[6] (compare (44a) = Farrell 1990, ex. (27b) with (42c) and (44b) Galves 1989, ex. (9) with (42d)) and they are available even in direct questions where there is no empty SpecCP available as a landing site for operator movement (compare (44c) = Galves 1989, ex. (11) with (42f)). Overt A′-movement on the other hand is just as sensitive to island effects in Brazilian Portuguese as it is in European Portuguese (cf. (45) = Farrell 1990, ex. (27a)), so it is not simply the case that operator movement is freer in the new world dialect than in the old world dialect.

(44)   a.   Eu vou beber a   cerveja antes   de brigar com a   pessoa
I   go   drink the beer   before to fight   with the person
que deixou *e* fora da geladeira.
who left   (it) out of refrigerator
'I'm going to drink the beer_i before fighting with the person
who left it_i outside the refrigerator.'

    b. Que a IBM venda a particulares   surpreende-me
        That the IBM sells to private individuals surprises me.
        'That IBM sells it to private individuals surprises me.'
    c.   Para qual dos filhos   o Manel ofereceu *e*?
        to   which of his-children the M.   offered (it)
        'To which if his children has Manuel offered it?'
                                              (Brazilian Portuguese)

(45) *O que_i eu briguei com a pessoa que deixou t_i fora da geladeira?
      what I fought with the person who left   out of refrigerator
      '$What_i$ did I fight with the person who left t_i outside the refrigerator?'
                                              (Brazilian Portuguese)

Farrell (1990) and Bianchi and Figueiredo Silva (1993) conclude that Brazilian Portuguese inanimate referential null objects are *pro*s instead of operator bound variables. This solution is suspect for a variety of reasons. First, note that Brazilian Portuguese would constitute a unique case where referential *pro* is restricted to 'third' person. Otherwise, referential *pro* occurs either in all persons (e.g. Spanish, cf. note 16 in Chapter 3) or only in first and second person (e.g. Modern Hebrew and Finnish, cf. (37) and (38) in Chapter 3). The language-specific restriction of referential *pro* to first and second person is probably due to the fact that only in the these persons does the verbal inflection bear a person feature (i.e. [1ST] or [2ND]) that positively establishes the reference of the missing argument (cf. the discussion in Section 3.3). The converse restriction of referential *pro* to third person cannot be explained along similar lines. Second, as noted by Farrell, Brazilian Portuguese object *pro* would violate the identification requirement for empty categories since it is identified neither via operator-binding nor via verb-agreement. Third, if the different distribution of empty objects in European and Brazilian Portuguese is due to the availability of object *pro* in the latter but not the former, we have to essentially stipulate this difference because it is not reflected anywhere else in the grammar.

    Galves (1989) makes a proposal that does not encounter these problems. She assumes that both European and Brazilian Portuguese inanimate null objects involve an operator-variable relation. But while the subject raises to the specifier of the highest inflectional head (AgrPSpec) in European Portuguese, the subject (as well as the verb) remains in situ inside VP in Brazilian Portuguese. In European Portuguese, SpecCP is the only position to which the empty operator can (and must) raise, as shown in (43), and this position is therefore unavailable for wh-movement (cf. the ungrammatical (42f)). In Brazilian Portuguese on the other hand, the empty SpecTP is an additional position to which the empty operator can raise, (cf. the discussion of IP-internal topicalization in Yiddish in Section 2.4.2.5) and this short operator movement leaves SpecCP open for wh-movement as shown in (46), the S-structure of the grammatical (44c). Crucially, this structure involves V in situ.

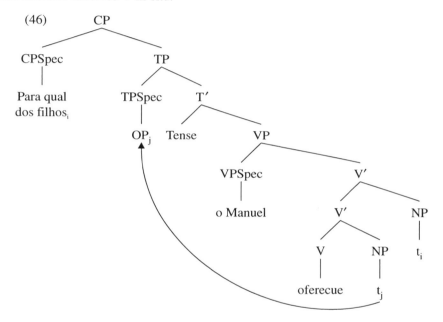

In sentences like (42d), where the empty object is contained in an island, the operator must move out of the island to SpecCP in European Portuguese, resulting in the ungrammatical S-structure in (47). But in the corresponding Brazilian Portuguese sentences like (44b), the operator never leaves the island and moves instead to the embedded SpecTP, resulting in a grammatical S-structure in (48). Again, this structure crucially involves V in situ..

(47)

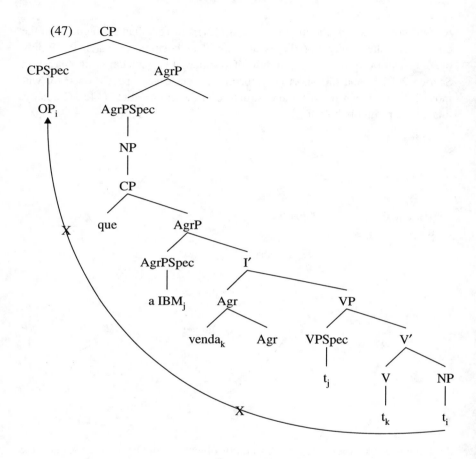

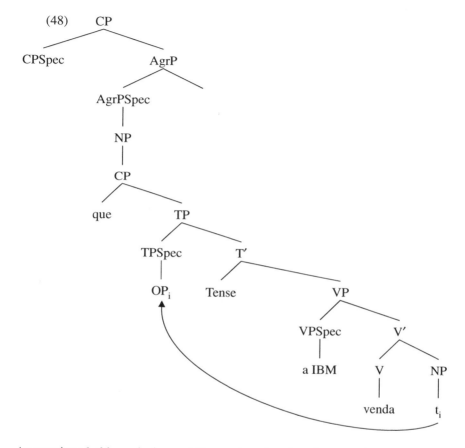

As mentioned, this analysis crucially requires that there be no verb movement (to the head of the highest inflectional projection) in this language. Conversely, this analysis is at least compatible with the view (arguably supported by enclisis in simple root clauses, cf. Section 5.2.4) that the verb moves to the highest inflectional category in European Portuguese. The lack of V to I raising in Brazilian Portuguese (where [2ND] is never distinctively marked) and its presence in European Portuguese (where [1ST] and [2ND] are both distinctively marked in the singular of the indicative present) are correctly predicted by a theory such as the one argued for here in which this type of movement depends on the minimal distinctive marking of all referential Infl features. We will see in Section 5.3 that Brazilian and European Portuguese moreover differ as predicted with respect to another syntactic phenomenon that I will argue is dependent on the minimal distinctive marking of all referential Infl features (and the projection of AgrP from an agreement affix), i.e. referential *pro*, which is vanishing from Brazilian Portuguese but continues to be present in European Portuguese.

Galves (1990) interprets the Portuguese V to I raising facts in terms that are very similar to mine. She argues that "Agr in B[razilian] P[ortuguese] is an empty category at D-structure which is morphologically realized only in phonological structure" and that "in E[uropean] P[ortuguese], however, Agr functions as a lexical pronoun". This difference is "related to the morphological richness of Agr (for example, we might say that a regular paradigm is lexically inserted at D-structure)." Although it is unclear in what sense the European Portuguese paradigm in (30a) but not the Brazilian Portuguese paradigm in (30b) is regular (note that neither (30a) nor (30b) has unique forms for all person/number combinations and that both are 'morphologically uniform' in having overt affixes throughout the paradigm), the affinity between the two theories is obvious. The fact that data from different language families independently motivated similar approaches to inflectional morphology only supports the claim that inflectional morphology operates in the way Galves and I claim: inflectional morphology is inserted either at D-structure (if subject-verb agreement is 'rich') or at PF (if subject-verb agreement is 'poor'). Only in the first case is V to I raising triggered by Lasnik's Filter.

5.2.4   *Object Clitics in Romance: Evidence for Verb Movement?*

In this section, I discuss cliticization facts from Italian, French and European and Brazilian Portuguese and argue that for the most part, they are indeed compatible with (if not evidence for) what was said above about verb movement in these languages. Cliticization in Romance is however a notoriously difficult phenomenon, and I do not attempt to explain all of the facts. The account I adopt below leaves a number of problems unsolved. For this reason, the discussion below should be regarded as preliminary and suggestive rather than definitive and conclusive.

In infinitival clauses, object clitics appear encliticized to the verb in Italian (cf. (49a) = Kayne 1991, ex. (3)) but procliticized to the verb in French (cf. (49b) = Kayne 1991, ex. (1)).

(49)   a.   *Parlargli*   sarebbe un errore.
                to-speak-him would-be a   mistake
                'To talk to him would be a mistake.'   (Italian)

       b.   *Lui parler*   serait   une erreur.
                him to-speak would-be a   mistake
                'To talk to him would be a mistake.'   (French)

Kayne (1991) suggests that this contrast between enclisis in Italian infinitives and proclisis in French infinitives is due to a difference in verb movement rather than to a difference in clitic-placement: in structures exhibiting enclisis, the verb has moved further to the left than in structures exhibiting proclisis. If this is the right way of looking at things, we should be able to use cliticization as a test for verb movement.

Concretely, Kayne (1991) proposes that in infinitivals, Tense is empty and the infinitival marker is generated as the head (INF) of a separate inflectional projection (InfP) between TP and VP. In Italian, clitics are generated adjoined to the empty Tense and adjunction of the verb+INF complex to Tense' (skipping Tense) results in enclisis as shown in (50). In French, clitics are generated adjoined to INF and verb movement to this head (but not higher) results in proclisis as shown in (51).

(50)

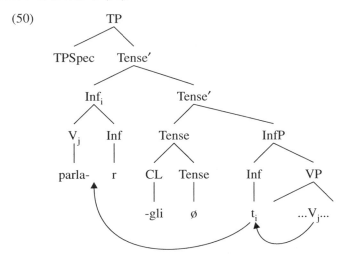

(51)

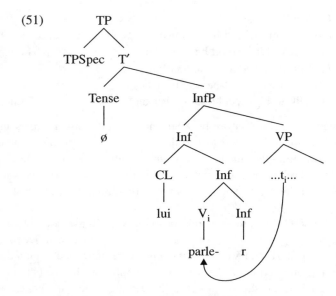

Kayne's analysis is unsatisfactory in at least two respects. First, it relies on different adjunction sites for clitics in Italian and French, a difference that is not independently motivated. Second, it relies on head-adjunction of the verbal complex to a non-minimal projection (i.e. T′), a process that presumably violates Structure Preservation. We can however preserve the basic insight of Kayne's analysis while avoiding the two problems just mentioned if we assume that clitics are in fact generated adjoined to AgrO in both languages and that in Italian, the infinitival verb left-adjoins to the AgrO complex (i.e. outside the clitic) on its way to the highest inflectional head, resulting in enclisis as shown in (52a), whereas in French, the infinitival verb either does not move at all or moves only to an inflectional head below AgrO, resulting in proclisis as shown in (52b) which illustrates the former option.[7]

(52) a.   b.

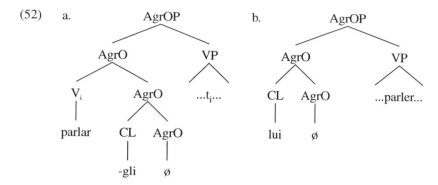

In finite clauses, Italian (cf. (53a) = Bianchi and Figueiredo Silva 1993, ex. (1b)) and French (cf. (53b) based on Rouveret 1989, ex. (7)) both exhibit proclisis.

(53)   a.   Gianni *lo ha* comprato ieri.
             G.   it has bought   yesterday
             'John bought it yesterday.'   (Italian)
       b.   Maria *le lui a* donné hier.
             M.   it him has given yesterday
             'Mary gave it to him yesterday.'   (French)

Given (our version of) Kayne's theory of clitic placement and our earlier assumption that Italian and French finite verbs move to the highest inflectional head, the consistent proclisis displayed in Italian and French finite clauses might come as a surprise. The problem disappears if we assume that in both Italian and French, the finite verb left-adjoins to AgrO itself (i.e. inside the clitic) on its way to the highest inflectional head, resulting in proclisis as shown in (54).

(54)

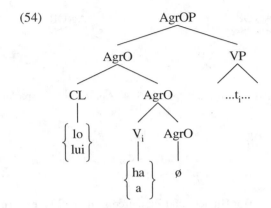

Why should there be this difference between infinitival and finite verbs, i.e. why should infinitival verbs adjoin to the AgrO complex (i.e. outside the clitic) but finite verbs to AgrO itself (i.e. inside the clitic)? I would like to suggest that this difference is due to the different nature of AgrO and therefore the different reasons for verb movement to AgrO in infinitival and finite clauses. Concretely, I assume that infinitival AgrO does not contain any features that need to be checked and verb movement to AgrO takes place only as part or verb movement to AgrS. Finite AgrO on the other hand does contain features that need to be checked and verb movement to AgrO takes place not only as part of verb movement to AgrS, but also in order to check these features. Under the not unreasonable assumption that head movement that targets a head solely to escape a Head Movement Constraint violation adjoins to the outermost layer of the targeted head whereas head movement that targets a head (also) for feature checking purposes adjoins to innermost layer of the targeted head (where it enters into a sisterhood relationship with the features that need to be checked), the observed difference between clitic placement in Italian and French infinitival clauses on the one hand and clitic placement in Italian and French finite clauses on the other hand follows.

Is there any independent evidence supporting the claim that Italian and French infinitival AgrO does not contain features that need to be checked and the converse claim that Italian and French finite AgrO does contain such features? Fortunately, I believe that this question can be answered affirmatively. Both Italian and French infinitival clauses never contain overt object agreement, suggesting that infinitival AgrO does not contain any features that need to be checked. On the other hand, both Italian and French finite clauses sometimes contain overt object agreement, suggesting that finite AgrO contains features that need to be checked. In both languages, this overt agreement in finite clauses takes the form of participle agreement. In Italian, the participles shows up with the neutral -*o* inflection when the direct object is a full NP (cf. (55a) = McKee and Emiliani 1992, ex. (1a)) but agrees with the direct object in gender and number when the latter is a clitic (cf. (55b) = McKee and Emiliani 1992, ex. (3a)). In fact, Italian participle agreement with full NP objects was still common in the last century (cf. (55c) = Belletti 1990, fn. 27. ex. (ic)) and has survived in some dialects (cf. (55d) = Belletti 1990, fn. 27 ex. (iia)). Moreover, children acquiring the modern standard dialect go through a stage that resembles these earlier and regional variants (cf. (55e) = Borer and Wexler 1992, ex. (3a)). See Borer and Wexler 1992, and McKee and Emiliani 1992, for discussion).

(55)   a.   La bambina ha rotto   una bicicletta.
             the girl   has broken-Ø a   bicycle-F

        b.   Il   puffo li   ha mangiati.
             the smurf them-M has eaten-M,PL
             'The smurf has eaten them.'   (Standard Italian)

        c.   Lucia aveva avute   due buone ragioni.
             L.   had   had-F,PL two good   reasons-F
                            (19th century Italian [*Manzoni*])

        d.   a'   vinnute l-ova.
             has-3SG sold-F,PL the-eggs-F
             'He has sold the eggs.'   (Salentino Italian)

        e.   La signora ha chiusa   la porta.
             the lady   has closed-F,SG the door-F   (Child Italian [1;10])

As shown in (56a, b), Standard French duplicates the Standard Italian contrast in (55a, b). In fact, the past participle agrees even with a full NP direct object whenever the latter precedes it, which is the case in complement questions (cf. (56c)), imperatives and relative clauses.

(56)   a.   Elle m'a   écrit   une lettre.
             she me-has written-Ø a   letter-F
             'She wrote me a letter.'

        b.   Cette lettre, je l'ai   écrite   hier.
             this   letter-F I it-have written-F,SG yesterday
             'I wrote this letter yesterday.'

    c.   Combien de lettres   avez-vous écrites?
        how many of letters-F,PL have you   written-F,PL
        'How many letters did you write?'   (French)

Let us now turn to European and Brazilian Portuguese and begin our discussion of clitic placement in these dialects with the observation that in infinitivals, European Portuguese echoes Italian by displaying enclisis (compare (57a) = Rouveret 1989, ex. (4)) with (49a)) whereas Brazilian Portuguese echoes French by displaying proclisis (compare (57b) = Mendes 1993, ex. (16a) with (49b)).

    (57)   a.   A Ana espera *ver* *-te*   esta tarde.
               the A. wants to-see-you this afternoon.
                                      (European Portuguese)
        b.   Ela quer *me ver.*
               she wants me to-see
               'She wants to see me.'   (Brazilian Portuguese)

The European Portuguese example in (57a) has the same structure as the Italian example in (49a), i.e. it has the structure in (52a): Due to the featureless nature of infinitival AgrO (reflected in the lack of any overt object agreement in European Portuguese infinitives), the infinitival verb left-adjoins to the AgrO complex (i.e. outside the clitic) on its way to the highest inflectional head, resulting in enclisis. Infinitival verb movement to the highest inflectional head takes place in both languages for the same reason: V to I raising is triggered by a minimally distinctive paradigm of verbal affixes (including the infinitival marker)[8] which are inserted under and attract the verb to the highest inflectional head. The Brazilian Portuguese example in (57b) on the other hand does not have the same structure as the French example in (49b), i.e. it does not have the structure in (52b). I have argued in Section 3.4 that only V to I raising languages but not V in situ languages project AgrP and in Section 5.4, I will argue that this covers both AgrSP and AgrOP. Hence object clitics can be adjoined to AgrO in the V to I raising language French but must be adjoined to another inflectional head or the verb in the V in situ language Brazilian Portuguese.

    In finite clauses that are affirmative, unembedded and do not contain a quantified subject ('simple root clauses', cf. (58a) = Rouveret 1989, ex. (6a)), European Portuguese exhibits enclisis but Brazilian Portuguese exhibits proclisis (cf. (58b) = Galves 1989, fn. 26 ex. (iv)).

(58) a.   A Maria *deu-lhe*   esse livro ontem.
           the M.   gave-him this book yesterday.

                                        (European Portuguese)

      b.   O Pedro *me chamou* ontem.
           the P.   me called   yesterday
           'Peter called me yesterday.'   (Brazilian Portuguese)

Why does the V to I raising language European Portuguese display enclisis in simple root clauses whereas the V to I raising languages Italian and French display proclisis in the same environment? The answer to this question involves the different properties of AgrO in the two sets of languages. Above, we saw that Italian and French finite clauses sometimes have overt object agreement on participles (cf. (55) and (56)), and I argued that this reflects the presence of features in AgrO that are in need of checking. I further argued that feature checking takes the form of adjunction of the verb to AgrO itself, i.e. inside the AgrO-adjoined clitic, resulting in proclisis (cf. (54)). European Portuguese finite clauses, unlike their Italian and French counterparts, never have overt object agreement and past participles surface only with the neutral *-o* inflection (cf. Hundertmark-Santos Martins 1982, and Bianchi and Figueiredo Silva 1993). It hence seems reasonable to assume that European Portuguese non-agreeing finite AgrO, like Italian and European Portuguese non-agreeing infinitival AgrO, does not have any features that need to be checked and verb movement to the highest inflectional head satisfies the Head Movement Constraint by adjoining the verb to the complex AgrO, i.e. outside the clitic, resulting in enclisis (cf. (52a)).

   Proclisis in Brazilian Portuguese finite clauses (cf. (58b)) can be explained along the same lines as proclisis in Brazilian Portuguese infinitivals (cf. (57b)). Again, AgrOP is not projected and the clitic is adjoined to some other inflectional head or to the verb in situ.

   In general, then, clitic placement in the Romance languages is compatible with what we said about verb movement in these languages and in the case of the two Portuguese dialects, it may in fact provide us with much needed evidence that the verb moves to the highest inflectional head in European Portuguese but stays in situ in Brazilian Portuguese.[9] However, at least two major problems remain for this theory of clitic placement in Romance. First, in European Portuguese, object clitics procliticize to the verb in embedded finite clauses (cf. (59) = Rouveret 1989, ex. (2)) and other finite clauses that aren't simple root declaratives. The logic of the argument above seems to suggest that

in these clauses, the verb does not move to the highest inflectional head, but this
is an unacceptable conclusion. I do not know what is responsible for the position
of the clitic in (59).

(59)   Eles perguntaram que   livro a   Maria *lhe deu* ontem.
        They asked   which book the M.   him gave yesterday
        'They asked which book Mary gave to him yesterday.'
                                                        (European Portuguese)

Second, in Italian (cf. (53a)), French (cf. (53b)) and European Portuguese
(cf. (60a) = Mendes 1993, ex. (15b)) complex tenses, the clitic appears on the
auxiliary. In Brazilian Portuguese complex tenses, on the other hand, the clitic
appears on the participle (cf. (60b) = Mendes 1993, ex. (15a)).

(60)   a.   Tinha-me repetidamente visto.
             had-me   repeatedly   seen   (European Portuguese)
        b.   Ela tinha repetidamente me visto.
             she had   repeatedly   me seen
             'She had seen me repeatedly.'   (Brazilian Portuguese)

It is desirable to link this difference to the fact that the verb moves to the
highest inflectional head in Italian, French and European Portuguese but stays in
situ in Brazilian Portuguese. Unfortunately, it is not clear to me how to establish
this link. Although much further work is needed to sort out these and other
problems that arise in connection with clitic placement in the Romance languages, I hope to have shown that a theory such as the one developed in this book
which predicts that verbs raise to the highest inflectional head in Italian, French
and European Portuguese but not in Brazilian Portuguese derives considerable
support from the clitic placement facts.

5.3 Pro-Drop

In Section 3.4, terminology originating within the standard theory of *pro*-drop
allowed us to develop a new theory of V to I raising (cf. (60,61): "An NP/Infl is
referential (if and) only if it has the specification of person."). It is natural to ask
whether the converse is also true, i.e. whether the new theory of V to I raising
also allows us to better understand null subject phenomena. In this section, I will
argue that this is indeed the case and that the Principle of Agr Referentiality and

Lexicality in (77) of Section 3.4 licenses not only V to I raising, but also *pro*-drop. My argument is based on the theory of *pro*-drop developed in Speas (1994) which is in turn based on the theory of V to I raising developed in Rohrbacher (1994). Certain changes that the latter theory has undergone since its inception (and in particular the elimination of radically empty Agr, cf. Section 3.4) require corresponding changes in Speas's theory which I will detail below.

As is well known, languages typically allow null subjects if they have morphologically 'rich' or 'strong' subject-verb agreement (e.g. Spanish in (61a) = Speas 1994, ex. (3a)) or no overt subject-verb agreement at all (e.g. Japanese in (61b) = Speas 1994, ex. (5)), but not if they have morphologically 'poor' or 'weak' subject-verb agreement (e.g. English in (61c)).[10]

(61)   a.   Habl -o /-as /-a   Espanol.
            speak-1SG/-2SG/-3SG Spanish
            'I/you/(s)he speaks Spanish.'   (Spanish)
       b.   Sasimi -o   tabe-ru.
            sashimi-ACC eat -PRES
            I/you/she eats sashimi.   (Japanese)
       c.   *(I/you/(s)he) speak-Ø/-s Spanish.   (English)

In the standard theory of *pro*-drop, the cross-linguistic distribution of null subjects is governed by two independent principles according to which *pro* must be both licensed (cf. (62a)) and identified (cf. (62b)).

(62)   a.   *Licensing of pro:*
            pro is Case-marked by X^0_y.   (Rizzi 1986a: 524)
       b.   *Identification of pro:*
            Let X be the licensing head of an occurrence of *pro*:
            then *pro* has the grammatical specification of the features on X
            coindexed with it.   (Rizzi 1986a: 520)

Of these two principles, the first is largely stipulative in nature: for no apparent reason, Infl happens to bear the y-subscript and thus license empty subjects in some languages (e.g. Spanish) but not in others (e.g. English). The second principle is more explanatory in nature: due the amount of overt agreement, Infl can recover the content of licensed empty subjects in some languages but not in others. The theory developed in Speas (1994) constitutes an improvement over the standard theory of *pro*-drop since it replaces the stipulatory licensing principle in (62a) with the independently motivated Principle of Economy of

Projection in (63a) requiring the head or the specifier of each projection to have phonological or semantic content.

(63)   a.   Project XP only if XP has content.   (Speas 1994:186)
       b.   A node X has content if and only if X dominates a distinct phonological matrix or a distinct semantic matrix.

(Speas 1994:187)

Speas adopts the theory developed in Rohrbacher (1994) according to which AgrS is underlyingly filled with an agreement affix in languages with 'rich' agreement morphology but underlyingly empty in languages with 'poor' agreement morphology. At the same time, Speas revises this theory by assuming that AgrS(P) is altogether absent (rather than underlyingly empty) in languages with no agreement morphology whatsoever (cf. Section 3.4 and Bobaljik 1995) and that agreement is strong in exactly those languages whose agreement paradigm is morphologically uniform (rather than minimally distinctive for the features [1ST] and [2ND]). Her version of morphological uniformity in (64) should be compared with the original version of this concept in Jaeggli and Safir (1989).

(64)   An inflectional Paradigm P in a language L is morphologically uniform for feature F iff P has only derived inflectional forms expressing F.   (Speas 1994:197)

Spanish has 'rich' (i.e. morphologically uniform) agreement and AgrS is hence underlyingly filled with an agreement affix. Due to the presence of this distinct phonologically matrix in its head, AgrSP satisfies the Principle of Economy of Projection regardless of whether its specifier is empty (cf. (65a)) or filled (cf. (65b)). *Pro*-drop is possible in Spanish because SpecAgrSP can be empty.

(65)   a.   AgrSP   b.   AgrSP

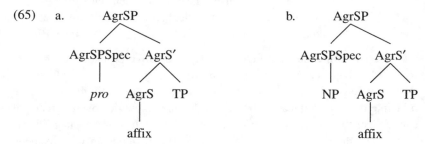

English has 'poor' (i.e. morphologically non-uniform) agreement and AgrS is hence underlyingly empty. Due to the absence of a distinct phonological (or semantic) matrix in its head, AgrSP violates the Principle of Economy of Projection if its specifier is empty (cf. (66a)) and satisfies it only if its specifier is filled (cf. (66b)). *Pro*-drop is impossible in English because SpecAgrSP must be filled.

(66)   a.

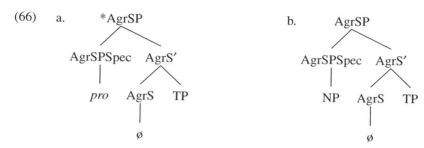

Japanese does not have any agreement morphology and AgrSP is therefore absent in this language. This leaves TP as the highest inflectional projection. Universally, Tense is underlyingly filled with the appropriate tense specification. Due to the presence of this independent semantic matrix in its head, TP satisfies the Principle of Economy of Projection regardless of whether its specifier is empty (cf. (67a)) or filled (cf. (67b)). *Pro*-drop is possible in Japanese because SpecTP can be empty.

(67)   a.

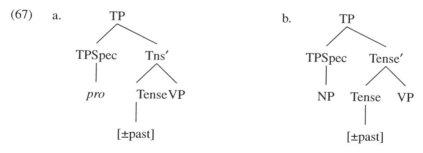

I would like to adopt the basic idea behind Speas's theory of *pro*-drop. However, regarding its details, a number of revisions are in order. Recall for example that in Section 3.4, I have adopted the Bare Phrase Structure theory of Chomsky (1995) according to which no projection has an underlyingly empty head and as a consequence, I have argued that English and the other V in situ languages have structures without an AgrSP like those in (67) rather than structures with an empty-headed AgrSP like those in (66). In other words, English has the structure that Speas assigns to Japanese, and this structure therefore cannot license null subjects, contrary to what is assumed by Speas. We derive the desired result by reformulating the Principle of Economy of Projection in the following way:

(68)   A projection XP is licensed only if its specifier SpecXP or its head X has phonological content.

Whereas in Speas's original formulation, both the phonological content and the semantic content of a phrase are relevant, in our reformulation, only the phonological content but not the semantic content of a phrase is relevant. As a result, due to the absence of a distinct phonological matrix in its head, TP violates the Principle of Economy of Projection if its specifier is empty (cf. (67a)) and satisfies it only if its specifier is filled (cf. (67b)). *Pro*-drop is impossible in English because SpecTP must be filled. If this explanation of the ungrammaticality of *pro*-drop in English is on the right track, then either Japanese does not have the structure in (67) or empty subjects in this language are not of the *pro* variety. Since Japanese empty subjects are discourse identified, it is not unreasonable to assume that they are of the Topic Drop variety (cf. note 10 and the discussion of Yiddish below), in which case they fall outside the scope of this study. In any event, it is unclear whether it is feasible or even desirable to develop a unified theory for null subjects in languages with 'rich' agreement like Spanish and languages with no agreement like Japanese and I will not attempt to do so here. In the rest of this section, the focus of the discussion will be on Spanish- and English-type languages with 'rich' and 'poor' agreement.

Whereas Speas defines 'strong' agreement in terms of morphological uniformity, I have defined it in this book in terms of minimal distinctive marking of [1ST] and [2ND]. The latter choice is clearly the right one with respect to V to I raising: the V to I raising language Icelandic and the V in situ language Faroese both have paradigms that are morphologically uniform,[11] but whereas Icelandic has a paradigm that distinctively marks both [1ST] and [2ND] in the plural, Faroese has a paradigm that never distinctively marks [2ND] (cf. (69)). Only minimal distinctive marking but not morphological uniformity can therefore capture the difference between Icelandic and Faroese regarding V to I raising.

(69)   a.   Icelandic   b.   Faroese
            segj-a "say"   *nevna-a* "name"
            IND PRES   IND PRES

	SG	PL		SG	PL
1ST	seg-i	segj-um	1ST	nevn-i	nevna-a
2ND	seg-ir	seg-ið	2ND	nevn-ir	nevna-a
3RD	seg-ir	segj-a	3RD	nevn-ir	nevna-a

There is evidence suggesting that the definition of 'strong' agreement argued for in this book (i.e. in terms of distinctive marking rather than morphological uniformity) is the right one not only with respect to the licensing of V to I raising, but also with respect to the licensing of *pro*-drop. Consider the European and Brazilian Portuguese paradigms in (70).

(70)   a.   European Portuguese   b.   Brazilian Portuguese
            compr-ar "to sell"   *fal-ar* "to speak"
            IND PRES   IND PRES

	SG	PL		SG	PL
1ST	compr-o	compr-amos	1ST	fal-o	fal-a
2ND	compr-as	compr-am	2ND	fal-a	fal-am
3RD	compr-a	compr-am	3RD	fal-a	fal-am

Both of these paradigms are morphologically uniform since all combinations of person and number are represented by derived forms.[12] If morphological uniformity sufficed to 'license' *pro* as argued by Speas, we would expect *pro* to be equally licensed in both European and Brazilian Portuguese. Null subjects are however much more common in European than in Brazilian Portuguese (see Valian & Eisenberg (1995) for an overview of the literature). Moreover, the problem in Brazilian Portuguese seems to be one of licensing proper and not just one of identification, since null subjects have receded not only in the ambiguously marked (indirect) second person singular, but also in the unambiguously marked first person singular. This is graphically shown in figures 5.1 and 5.2 from Duarte (1993) who investigated seven Brazilian Portuguese texts written between 1845 and 1992.

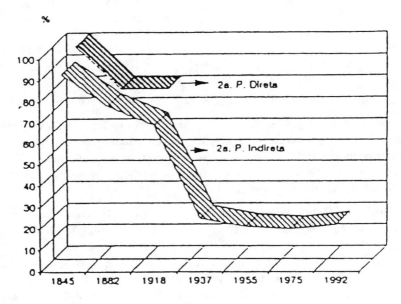

Figure 5.1: *Null Subjects with Direct and Indirect 2nd Person (Duarte 1993: 113)*

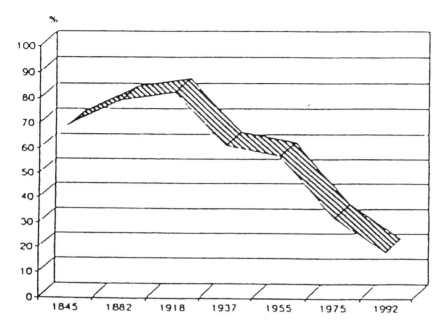

Figure 5.2: *Null Subjects with 1nd Person (Duarte 1993: 115)*

Duarte found that the distinctive direct second person was last used in a text from 1918. In later texts, only the non-distinctive indirect second person appeared. For us, this means that around that time, Brazilian Portuguese went from a complete paradigm licensing both V to I raising and *pro*-drop to an incomplete paradigm licensing neither V to I raising nor *pro*-drop. Immediately thereafter, empty second person pronouns indeed plunged from 69% in 1918 to 25% in 1937 and first person pronouns started a slower, but equally steady decline from ca. 80% in 1918 to well under 20% in 1992. In the spoken language, the numbers are even lower than that, sometimes by as much as ten percentage points. In other words, whereas European Portuguese fits the bill of a typical *pro*-drop language, Brazilian Portuguese appears to be rapidly loosing *pro*-drop, and this loss seems to be the direct consequence of the loss of minimal distinctive marking of [2ND]. The Brazilian Portuguese data prove two different points: They prove that the strength of agreement is involved in the licensing of *pro*-drop, as proposed in Speas (1994) contra standard theories of *pro*-drop, and that strength of agreement should be defined in terms of minimal distinctive marking of [1ST] and [2ND], as proposed here contra Speas (1994).

We have arrived at the following unified theory of V to I raising and *pro*-drop. In languages where [1ST] and [2ND] are minimally distinctively marked, AgrSP is projected and AgrS is filled by a phonologically concrete, affixal agreement marker. Because this marker is affixal, it attracts the verb (via Lasnik's Filter) and thus triggers V to I raising, and because it is phonologically concrete, it allows SpecAgrSP to be empty (via Economy of Projection) and thus licenses *pro*-drop. In language where [1ST] or [2ND] is not minimally distinctively marked, AgrSP is not projected and Tense is filled by a phonologically abstract, non-affixal tense marker. Because this marker is non-affixal, it does not attract the verb and thus triggers V in situ, and because it is phonologically abstract, it requires SpecTP to be filled and thus does not license *pro*-drop.

This theory predicts that *pro* is licensed in all (and only in) V to I raising languages. Referential *pro* is ungrammatical in the V to I raising language Icelandic (cf. (71a)), but the grammaticality of expletive *pro* in Icelandic impersonal passives and existential clauses (cf. (71b,c)) suggests that *pro* is as predicted licensed but cannot be identified in this language.[13] Both referential (cf. (72a) and expletive (cf. (72b,c) *pro* are ungrammatical in the V in situ language Swedish (and in Mainland Scandinavian in general), suggesting that *pro* is as predicted not licensed in this language.

(71) a. *Dansar.
          dance-3SG
          'S/he dances.'

      b. Í gær   var (*það) dansað á   skipinu.
          yesterday was   it   danced on ship-the
          'Yesterday, there was dancing on the ship.'

      c. Í dag hafa (*það) komið margir málvísindamenn hingað.
          today have it   come many linguists   here
          'Today many linguists have come here.'
                              (Icelandic, Holmberg & Platzack 1995:99,100)

(72) a. *Dansar.
          dance-PRES
          'S/he dances.'

b. Igår   dansades   *(det) på skeppet.
    yesterday was-danced   it   on ship-the
    'Yesterday, there was dancing on the ship.'

c. Idag har *(det) kommit många lingvister hit.
    today have it   come   many linguists here
    'Today many linguists have come here.'

(Swedish, Holmberg & Platzack 1995:99,100)

One might expect the unambiguous agreement in the Icelandic first singular and first, second and third plural (cf. (69a)) to be able to identify the content of referential *pro*. However, in addition to its content, the function of referential *pro* must be identified, too. Let us assume that it is indeed agreement which identifies the content of referential *pro* and that it is Case which identifies its function. Thus agreement identifies the missing argument as referring to the speaker(s), hearer(s) or other(s) and Case identifies it as functioning as the subject or the object. Let us further assume that these two forms of identification must be carried out by the same element, as already implicitly assumed in Rizzi (1986a) (cf. (62)) and explicitly proposed for the first time in Jaeggli and Hyams (1988):

(73) **Identification by Agreement**
      Agr can identify an empty category as (thematic) pro iff the category containing Agr Case-governs the empty category.

(Jaeggli and Hyams 1988)

In Icelandic, a V2 language in which *pro* is licensed and nominative Case is assigned by [+F] in Comp (cf. Section 2.3) but agreement is contained in AgrS, *pro* cannot be identified in accordance with (73) and referential *pro* is therefore ruled out. This is shown in (74), the S-structure of (71a). Note that even after verb movement to Comp, $AgrS_i$ is not contained in Comp as required by (73), given the standard definition of containment in terms of domination by every segment.

(74)

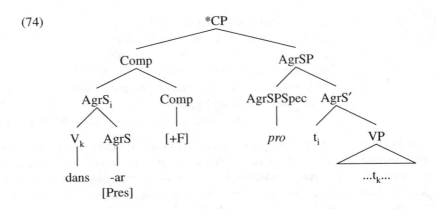

In general, a V2 language in which *pro* is licensed and Comp assigns nominative Case will be able to identify *pro* (and hence allow referential *pro*) only if Comp also contains agreement, i.e. only if the language has complementizer agreement. This prediction was already made by Hyams and Jaeggli (1988) and is confirmed by the facts. With the exception of Yiddish, which I will discuss below, the (standard) V2–dialects without complementizer agreement all rule out referential *pro* and only the (non-standard) V2–dialects with complementizer agreement allow referential *pro*. Thus German and Dutch, like Icelandic, lack complementizer agreement and rule out referential *pro* but Bavarian (cf. (75a) from Bayer 1984), West Flemish (cf. (75b) from Haegeman 1992) and Frisian (cf. (75c) from Platzack 1992; see also Hoekstra and Marácz 1989) have complementizer agreement and allow referential *pro*. The S-structure of (75a) is given in (76) which should be compared with (74).

(75)   a.   obts   (ihr) nach Minga   kummts.
               whether-2PL you to   Munich come
               'whether you come to Munich.'   (Bavarian)
     b.   Kpeinzen dank   (ik) goan kommen.
               I-think   that-1SG I   go   come
               'I think that I will come.'   (West Flemish)
     c.   Hy tinkt datst   (do) jûn   komst.
               he thinks that-2SG you tonight come-2SG
               'He thinks that you'll come tonight.'   (Frisian)

(76)

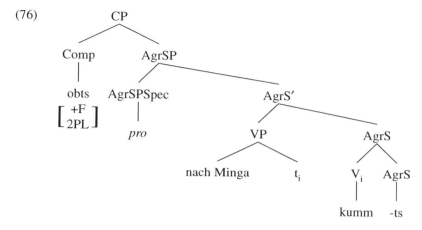

V2 languages in which *pro* is licensed and nominative Case is assigned by AgrS rather than Comp should not be restricted in this way, i.e. they should allow referential *pro* even in the absence of complementizer agreement. At first glance, Yiddish seems to disconfirm this prediction. The Full Paradigm in (77) with minimal distinctive marking of [1ST] and [2ND] in the singular should license *pro*. In Section 2.4.2.5, I argued for a Uniform IP Analysis of V2 in this language according to which in matrix and embedded clauses alike, the finite verb moves to Infl and SpecIP is occupied by the subject or a topic. If this is indeed the correct analysis for V2 in Yiddish, then there is every reason to assume that nominative Case is assigned by AgrS rather than Comp, and AgrS should be able to identify *pro* in accordance with (73) even though the language does not have complementizer agreement. It thus comes as a surprise that Yiddish apparently does not allow referential *pro*. Yiddish referential null subjects are often reported to show the distribution of Topic Drop rather than *pro*-drop, i.e. they are restricted to the utterance-initial position, thus being permitted in matrix clauses without topicalization (cf. (78a)) but being barred from questions (cf. (78b)), matrix clauses with topicalization (cf. (78c)), and embedded clauses (cf. (78d)).

(77)   Yiddish *kuk-n* "look"
        IND PRES

	SG	PL
1ST	kuk-Ø	kuk-n
2ND	kuk-st	kuk-t
3RD	kuk-t	kuk-n

(78)   a.   Horevet iber di koykhes.
              works over the strength
              'She is working too hard.'
        b.   Vu   bist *(du), Rokhl?
              where are   you Rachel
        c.   Aza   shayle kenst *(du) mir oykh paskenen.
              a-such question can   you me also answer
              'Such a question you can also answer for me.'
        d.   Vorem Gitl iz take   gerekht, vos   *(zi) zogt, az *(du)
              because G. is indeed right   when she says that you
              tselozt Steren.
              spoil   Stere

                                          (Yiddish, Prince 1994: 2 & 4)

Recall from note 10 that this is exactly the distribution of referential null subject topics in the non-*pro*-drop language English and that this distribution differs sharply from the distribution of referential null subjects *pros* in the *pro*-drop language Italian. A closer look at the pragmatic restrictions on the distribution of null subjects in Yiddish shows that it would however be premature to conclude from the data in (78) that Yiddish has only Topic Drop but not *pro*-drop. Referential *pro*-drop does in fact occur in the language (as does of course Topic Drop), but due to (among other things) massive homophony within the verbal agreement paradigm (cf. (77)), it is more restricted in its distribution than referential *pro*-drop in e.g. Italian. The following discussion is heavily based on Prince's (1994) thorough analysis of null subjects in Peretz Hirschbein's play "Grine Felder".

Prince's analysis is couched in terms of Centering Theory, a (partial) "theory of local discourse coherence" that models "attentional states in discourse" (Prince 1994:8, Joshi and Weinstein 1981, Grosz, Joshi and Weinstein 1986). According to Centering Theory, each utterance implicitly or explicitly evokes a set of discourse entities that are exhaustively ranked on the basis of their formal properties. Just how this ranking is established is a non-trivial issue which I will not address here. Based on this ranking, a number of Discourse Centers can be defined of which the Preferred Center (c.f. (79a)) involves the coherence between an utterance and the following utterance and the Backward-Looking Center (cf. (79b)) involves the coherence between an utterance and the preceding utterance.

(79)   *Centering Theory (Joshi & Weinstein 1981, Grosz, Joshi & Weinstein 1986)*
   a.   *Preferred Center (Cp) of Utterance U_i*
        The highest-ranked discourse entity evoked by U_i.
        The Cp of U_i is predicted to be the topic of the next utterance, U_{i+1}.
   b.   *Backward-Looking Center (Cb) of Utterance U_i*
        The highest-ranked discourse entity evoked by the previous utterance, U_{i-1}, which is also evoked by U_1.

The relative coherence of a discourse can be established in part by comparing the Backward-Looking Center of an utterance with the Preferred Center of that utterance and the Backward-Looking Center of the previous utterance. Such a comparison defines the four transition types summarized in Table 5.1.

Table 5.1: *Centering transitions (Prince 1994)*

	$Cb\,(U_i) = Cb\,(U_{i-1})$	$Cb\,(U_i) \neq Cb\,(U_{i-1})$
$Cb\,(U_i) = Cp\,(U_i)$	Continue	Smooth-Shift
$Cb\,(U_i) \neq Cp\,(U_i)$	Retain	Rough-Shift

Very loosely speaking, these four types of transitions fall into two classes. In the type of transition that is most coherent (or easiest to process), i.e. "Continue", the most prominent discourse entity evoked by the current utterance (and expected topic of the next utterance) has already been continuously foregrounded in both of the previous two utterances. In the types of transitions that are less coherent (or harder to process), i.e. "Retain", "Smooth-Shift", and "Rough-Shift", the most prominent discourse entity evoked by the current utterance (and expected topic of the next utterance) has not already been continuously foregrounded in both of the previous two utterances.[14]

Using Centering Theory to analyze referential null subjects in main-clause-initial position (i.e. in the sole environment where Topic Drop is possible) in Hirschberg's play "Grine Felder", Prince (1994) found two significant differences between second person singular and all other person and number combinations. First, null subjects that did not translate into second person singular pronouns were almost always the Backward-Looking Center of their clause. Null subjects that translated into second person singular pronouns on the other hand were quite often not the Backward-Looking Center of their clause. Second, null subjects that did not translate into second person singular pronouns occurred almost always in Continue Transitions and virtually never in Retain, Smooth-Shift or Rough-Shift Transitions. Null subjects that translate into second person singular pronouns on the other hand were just as likely to occur in Retain, Smooth-Shift or Rough-Shift Transitions as in Continue Transitions. The latter difference is visible both when all person and number combinations and all transition types are separated (cf. Table 5.2) and, more strikingly, when all person and number combinations other than second person singular and all transition types other than Continue are collapsed (cf. Table 5.3).[15]

Table 5.2: *Main-Clause-Initial Null Subjects, all person and number combinations and all transition types separated (Prince 1994)*

	Continue	Retain	Smooth-Shift	Rough-Shift
1SG	1/128 (1%)	0/58 (0%)	0/40 (0%)	0/67 (0%)
2SG	37/50 (74%)	13/18 (71%)	20/22 (90%)	27/37 (70%)
3SG	18/65 (28%)	0/9 (0%)	1/22 (5%)	1/18 (6%)
1PL	0/5 (0%)	0/1 (0%)	0/2 (0%)	0/0 (0%)
2PL	2/21 (10%)	0/3 (0%)	1/5 (20%)	0/10 (0%)
3PL	12/19 (63%)	0/0 (0%)	0/1 (0%)	0/0 (0%)

Table 5.3: *Main-Clause-Initial Null Subjects, all person and number combinations other than 2SG and all transition types other than Continue collapsed (Prince 1994)*

	Continue	Other
2SG	37/50 (74%)	60/77 (76%)
Other	33/238 (14%)	3/236 (1%)

The different pragmatic distribution of non-second singular null subjects and second singular null subjects is exemplified in the example in (80) with the Centering analysis in Table 5.4. (80c,e) contain non-second singular null subjects while (80d) contains a second singular null subject. The non-second singular null subjects in (80c,e) are the Backward-Looking Centers of their clauses and occur in Continue transitions while the second singular null subject in (80d) is not the Backward-Looking Center of its clause and occurs in a transition other than Continue.[16]

(80)   (a) Az zi_i vet   zayn dayn$_j$ vayb, (b) vet zi_i dir$_j$ krikhn unter   di
      if   she will be   your wife   will she you crawl   under the
      negl. (c) e_i Iz efsher   nokh a mol azoy shtark vi ikh_k. (d) e_j Host
      nails   is perhaps again once   as   strong as I$^{\cdot}$ have
      gezen ire$_i$ hent$_{i'}$? (e) $e_{i'}$ Zaynen efsher   nokh a mol azoy grob
      seen   her hands   are   perhaps again once as   thick
      vi mayne$_{k'}$.
      as mine
      'If she's your wife, she'll drive you crazy. She's perhaps twice as
      strong as I. Have you seen her hands? They're perhaps twice as
      thick as mine.'   (Prince 1994:14)

Table 5.4: *Centering analysis of (80) (Prince 1994)*

Clause	Preferred Center	Backward-Looking Center	Transition
(80a)	i	i	Continue
(80b)	i	i	Continue
(80c)	i	i	Continue
(80d)	j	i′	Retain
(80e)	i′	i′	Continue

What emerges from this discussion is that second singular null subjects are pragmatically freer than non-second singular subjects: unlike the latter, the former do not have to be properly foregrounded by the discourse. One way to explain this difference is to say that second singular subjects are in fact always properly foregrounded since they refer to a necessary participant in the discourse. But this explanation raises the question why the same is not also true for first singular subject which also refer to a necessary participant in the discourse. Another way to explain the difference between second singular and non-second singular null subjects is to say that while the latter are due exclusively to Topic Drop, the former are due at least in part to *pro*-drop. This explanation is supported below by the fact (not mentioned by Prince) that second singular and non-second singular null subjects have not only different pragmatic distributions, but also different syntactic distributions.

Why is referential *pro*-drop in Yiddish possible only in the second singular but not in any other person-number combination? The answer to this question, which was essentially already suggested in Prince (1994), involves identification rather than licensing. Although the Yiddish paradigm in (77) minimally distinctively marks both [1ST] and [2ND] and hence licenses *pro*, it has an unambiguous overt marker only in the second singular, the first singular and the stem, the third singular and the second plural, and the first and third plural being homophonous with each other, respectively. Apparently, Yiddish requires an unambiguous overt marker to identify *pro*, and referential *pro* is therefore restricted to the second singular, the only person-number combination with such a marker. Note that this requirement is language specific. In the Italian indicative present, the third singular lacks an overt marker beyond the theme vowel (cf. (1) and note 1), yet referential *pro* is possible in this case. In the Italian subjunctive present (cf. (81) = Cardinaletti 1997, ex. (66a)), all three singular forms are identical, yet referential *pro* is possible in the first and third person. The impossibility of referential *pro* in the second person nevertheless shows that in this language, too, homophony affects identification of *pro*, albeit differently than in Yiddish. Finally, in the Italian subjunctive past (cf. (81b) = Cardinaletti 1997, ex. (67a)), first and second singular forms are identical, yet referential *pro* is again possible in the first person but not in the second person, with the same ramifications as before.

(81) a. Che possa   riuscirci   non è chiaro.
          that can-SG.SUBJ.PRES manage-it not is clear
          'It isn't clear that I/*you/he can manage it.'
      b. Che potessi   riuscirci   non è chiaro.
          that can-1/2SG.SUBJ.PAST manage-it not is clear
          'It isn't clear that I/??you could manage it.'

If Yiddish second singular person null subjects are instances of *pro*, why do they
have the distribution of Topic Drop, i.e. why are they possible in matrix declaratives without topicalization (cf. (80d)) but not in questions, matrix clauses with
topicalization or embedded clauses (cf. (78b–d))? Consider the relevant structures
in (82), keeping in mind that according to the Uniform IP Hypothesis, V2 in
Yiddish is IP-internal and SpecIP can host a wh-element or topic phrase.

(82)

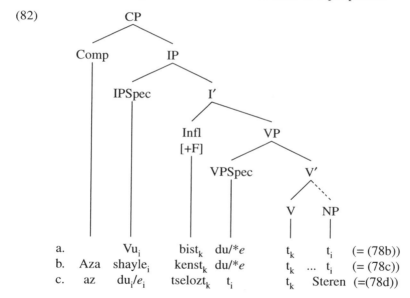

Let us adopt a proposal by Holmberg and Platzack (1995) and assume that all
noun phrases need either abstract or morphological Case in order to be licensed.
Let us further assume that in Yiddish, abstract nominative Case is assigned by
Infl (or AgrS) to SpecIP (or SpecAgrSP). This immediately explains why *pro* is
impossible in questions (cf. (82a)) and matrix clauses with topicalization
(cf. (82b)): here the subject cannot receive abstract Case since SpecIP is

occupied by the question or topic phrase. It thus needs the morphological Case which appears on overt pronouns but not on *pro*. The assumptions at the beginning of this paragraph do not explain why *pro* is allegedly impossible in embedded clauses (cf. (82c)): here SpecIP and hence abstract Case should be available for *pro*. It however turns out that contrary to generally held beliefs, second singular null subjects are in fact possible in embedded clauses, as predicted by a theory that treats them as the result of *pro*-drop rather than Topic Drop.[17] This is shown by the following example. Note that replacing the second-singular with a non-second singular null subject would as expected result in ungrammaticality.

(83)   Ikh vil   zikh itst batsien tsu dayn arbet vos host   mir
          I   want REFL now refer   to your paper that have-2SG me
          tsugeshikt a kopie.
          to-sent   a copy
          'Now, I want to refer to your paper which you sent me a copy of.'
                                  (Yiddish, Santorini 1989: 63)

The theory developed in this section thus successfully deals with the problems apparently posed by Yiddish, and a similar approach might also be on the right track with respect to Old French, a V2 language without inflected complement-izers and with referential *pro* in matrix and embedded verb second clauses (cf. Adams 1987 and Roberts 1993). Examples are given in (84) (= Roberts 1993, ex. 2(76c) and 2(29b)).

(84) a. Si   chaï   *e* en grant povreté.
          thus fell-1SG (I) into great poverty
          'Thus I fell into great poverty.'   (Old French [*Perceval*])
    b. Or voi   ge bien plains es   *e*   de mautalant.
          now see-1SG I   well full   are-2SG (you) of bad intentions
          'And now I see clearly that you are full of bad intentions.'
                                  (Old French [*Charroi*])

If Old French V2 involves verb movement to Comp triggered the generation of the Case-assigning tense operator [+F] in this head, these examples are highly problematic. Roberts (1993) however argues that Old French V2 reflects verb movement to Agr, and if an analysis along these lines is indeed feasible, it solves the problem at hand.

    In this section, I have argued that the theory of Morphology-Driven Syntax developed in this book which links the syntactic projection of AgrS(P) to the morphological marking of the agreement features explains not only why the verb moves to the highest inflectional head in some languages but not in other (V to I raising), but also why the subject can be omitted in some languages but not in others (*pro*-drop): minimal distinctive marking of the person features [1ST] and [2ND] results in the separate lexical listing of the agreement paradigm and the separate syntactic insertion of the agreement affixes under AgrS where they attract the verb and license a phonologically empty specifier. In the next and last section of this chapter, I will briefly show that in addition, this theory is compatible with Bobaljik's (1995) explanation for the distribution of NP object shift and transitive expletive constructions.

5.4 NP Object Shift and Transitive Expletive Constructions

In this book, I have discussed a split that runs through the Germanic VO languages and separates Icelandic and Yiddish, which have V to I raising and *pro*-drop, from Mainland Scandinavian and English, which do not. Bobaljik (1995) discusses a number of other syntactic phenomena whose distributions observe the same split: Icelandic and Yiddish have object shift of full NPs (cf. (85a) and Section 2.4.2.4) and expletive subjects in active transitive sentences (cf. (86a)) while Mainland Scandinavian and English do not (cf. (85b) and Section 2.4.2.2 and (86b)).[18]

(85)   a.   Jólasveinarnir borðuðu bjúgun ekki.
        b.   *Tomtarna   åt korvarna   inte.
             Christmastrolls-the ate sausages-the not
             'The Christmas trolls didn't eat the sausages.'
             (Icelandic (85a) & Swedish (85b), Bobaljik 1995, ex. I(3ab))

(86)   a.   Það hafa margir jólasveinar   borðað búding.
             there have many christmastrolls eaten pudding
             'Many christmas trolls have eaten pudding.'
             (Icelandic, Bobaljik 1995, ex. I(5a))
        b.   *Det åt mångar tomtar   korvarna.
             there ate many christmastrolls sausages-the
             'Many Christmas Trolls ate the sausages.'
             (Swedish, Bobaljik 1995, ex. I(5b))

As is evident in Table 5.5 below, Bobaljik considers not only the Germanic VO languages (i.e. English, Yiddish and the Scandinavian languages), but also the Germanic OV languages (i.e. Frisian, Dutch, Afrikaans and German). I will not do so here, for three reasons. First, whereas NP object shift and transitive expletive constructions always cooccur in the Germanic VO languages, this is not the case in the Germanic OV languages. Thus Afrikaans has NP object shift but does not have transitive expletive constructions. Second, I am not convinced that it is correct to identify, as Bobaljik does, the "scrambling" that affects the position of objects in the Germanic OV languages with NP object shift in e.g. Icelandic. Thus scrambling occurs in the absence of main verb movement but (NP) object shift does not (Holmberg's Generalization, cf. sections 2.4.2.2 and 2.4.2.4), to mention but one of the many differences between the two processes. Third, my primary interest in this section is to correlate NP object shift and transitive expletive constructions with V to I raising, and the latter process cannot be detected in OV languages due to the underlying adjacency of V and Infl (cf. Section 2.4.1). Note further that Bobaljik discusses two dialects of Faroese, Faroese I with NP object shift but without transitive expletive constructions and Faroese II without either process. Again, Faroese I is problematic because NP object shift and transitive expletive constructions do not cooccur, and for this reason I will consider only Faroese II.

Table 5.5: *V to I raising, NP object shift and transitive expletive constructions (after Bobaljik 1995:30)*

	NP Object Shift	Trans. Expl.
Afrikaans	yes	no
Dutch	yes	yes
Faroese I	no	yes
Frisian	yes	yes
German	yes	yes
Icelandic	yes	yes
Yiddish	yes	yes
Danish	no	no
English	no	no
Faroese II	no	no
Norwegian	no	no
Swedish	no	no

Bobaljik (1995) offers a simple and elegant theory for the similar distribution of NP object shift and transitive expletive constructions. He assumes that shifted objects have moved to a specifier outside VP and that (transitive) subjects are base-generated in a specifier outside VP above the surface position of objects. With respect to the second point, I will make the less controversial assumption that (transitive) subjects must move to a Case-position outside VP above the surface position of objects, although nothing hinges on this choice of assumptions. Bobaljik further proposes that in Icelandic (and other languages with NP object shift and transitive expletive constructions), the agreement phrases AgrSP and AgrOP are projected in addition to the tense phrase TP, as shown in (87). As a result, a specifier (i.e. SpecAgrOP) is available outside VP which can accommodate a shifted object, thus allowing NP object shift (cf. (87a), the S-structure of (85a), with the irrelevant CP-level omitted for reasons of space), and two subject Case-positions (i.e. SpecAgrSP and SpecTP) are available outside VP which together can accommodate both an expletive and a thematic transitive subject, thus allowing transitive expletive constructions (cf. (87b), the S-structure of (86a)).

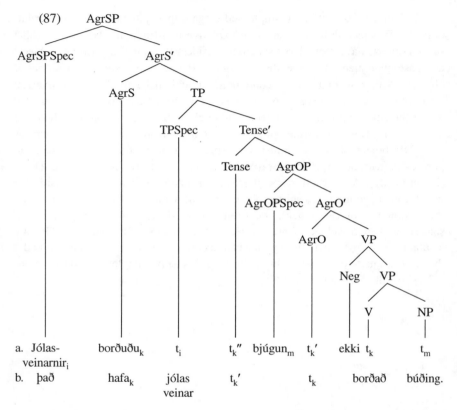

(87)

a. Jólas-   borðuðu$_k$ t$_i$ t$_k''$ bjúgun$_m$ t$_k'$ ekki t$_k$ t$_m$
   veinarnir$_i$
b. það   hafa$_k$ jólas   t$_k'$ t$_k$ borðað   búðing.
                               veinar

In Swedish (and other languages without NP object shift and transitive expletive constructions), only TP is projected but AgrSP and AgrOP are not. As a result, no specifier position is available outside VP to accommodate a shifted object and NP objects must therefore stay in situ (cf. (88a), the S-structure of the grammatical alternative to the ungrammatical NP object shift example in (85b)), and only one subject Case-position (i.e. SpecTP) is available outside VP which must host the thematic (transitive) subject, leaving no room for an expletive subject (cf. (88b), the S-structure of the grammatical alternative to the ungrammatical transitive expletive construction in (86b)).

(88)

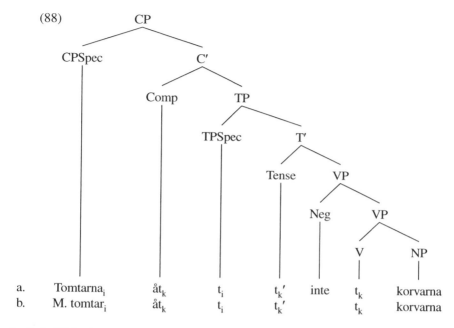

a.	Tomtarna$_i$	åt$_k$	t$_i$	t$_k'$	inte	t$_k$	korvarna
b.	M. tomtar$_i$	åt$_k$	t$_i$	t$_k'$		t$_k$	korvarna

In Bobaljik's theory, the (non-)projection of agreement phrases in a language is tied to properties of the inflectional morphology of that language (cf. (89)), but the particular morphology does not determine the syntactic representation "but is rather a reflex of the syntactic representation" (Bobaljik 1995: 253).[19]

(89) *The morphological grounding statement*
   If tense morphology blocks the appearance of agreement morphology, then the language is not a Free Agr language, i.e. it does not have Agr phrases.   (Bobaljik 1995: 263)

However, we can adopt Bobaljik's theory while tying it causally to the theory of inflectional morphology developed in Section 3.4. There I have argued that if and only if the referential Infl features [1ST] and [2ND] are minimally distinctively marked, all subject agreement affixes (including those that do not distinctively mark the relevant feature) are listed in the lexicon and project AgrSP in the syntax. Now I propose to extend this approach to object agreement affixes and AgrOP, treating subject and object agreement as parts of a single system, essentially in the spirit of the Minimalist Program. If and only if the referential Infl features [1ST] and [2ND] are minimally distinctively marked, all subject and object agreement affixes (including those that do not distinctively mark the relevant feature) are listed in the lexicon and project AgrSP and AgrOP in the syntax, respectively. In the case of Icelandic, this means that because the plural present tense subject agreement affixes minimally distinctively mark both [1ST] and [2ND], the second singular present tense subject agreement affix which is identical with the third singular present tense subject agreement affix and hence does not distinctively mark [2ND] and the object agreement affixes which are phonologically zero and hence distinctively mark neither [1ST] nor [2ND] are lexically listed alongside the plural present tense subject agreement affixes which minimally distinctively mark both [1ST] and [2ND] and all of these affixes project agreement phrases in the syntax. In Section 3.4 and elsewhere in this book, I have shown that the head of AgrSP attracts the verb (V to I raising). In Section 5.4, I have demonstrated that the specifier of AgrSP can remain empty (*pro*-drop). In this section, a third consequence of the projection of AgrSP has come to light: the specifier of AgrSP constitutes a second A-position for transitive subjects (transitive expletive constructions). Similarly, the specifier of AgrOP constitutes an A-position for objects (NP object shift). Each of the four syntactic phenomena discussed in this book is present in those languages in which the minimal distinctive marking of the person features triggers the projection of both agreement phrases, and all of them are absent in those languages in which at least one of the person features isn't minimally distinctively marked and, as a consequence, neither of the agreement phrases is projected.

In this section, I have argued that my theory of V to I raising and *pro*-drop can be unified with Bobaljik's theory of NP object shift and transitive expletive constructions. The result is a theory with considerable empirical coverage. How far this coverage can be extended even further is a question for future research. In the next and last chapter, I would like to briefly address some issues that arise in this connection.

Notes

1. This vowel belongs neither to the stem nor, strictly speaking, to the inflectional affix. Rather, it is a 'theme vowel' which defines a conjugational class and shows up only in certain forms (cf. the third singular and the second and third plural).

2. In complex tenses, sentential adverbs surface not only in the same positions as in simple tenses (compare (i-iii) = Belletti 1994, ex. (34a–c) with (4a–c)), but also clause-medially after the auxiliary (compare (iv) = Belletti 1994, ex. (35) with (4d)).

(i)   *Probabilmente* Gianni *ha* sbagliato molte volte.
      probably   G.   has erred   many times

(ii) Gianni *probabilmente ha* sbagliato molte volte.
      G.   probably   has erred   many times

(iii) Gianni *ha* sbagliato molte volte, *probabilmente*.
      G.   has erred   many times probably

(iv) Gianni *ha probabilmente* sbagliato molte volte.
      G.   has probably   erred   many times.   (Italian)

Belletti proposes that in (iv), the auxiliary has moved to a second, radically empty agreement head above the minimal clause structure as shown in (v), an option that is not available for verbs with semantic content (i.e. main verbs).

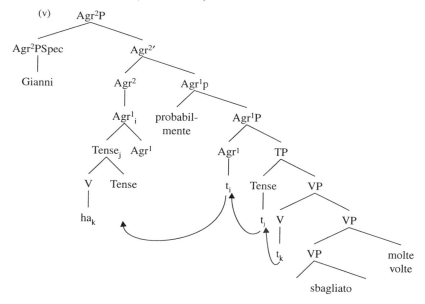

It is hard to see how such optional head-movement to a radically empty position can be reconciled with the Principle of Economy of Derivation proposed in Chomsky (1989) or the Bare Phrase Structure Model developed in Chomsky (1995) and briefly discussed in Section 3.4. Note that like English *have* and *be* (cf. Section 4.3.2), Italian *avere* and *essere* have irregular paradigms (most of) whose forms cannot be straightforwardly divided into stem and affix (cf. (vi)). It is therefore tempting to develop an analysis according to which Italian auxiliaries are (like their English counterparts) generated directly under an inflectional head instead of being (like Italian main verbs) generated inside VP and moved to an inflectional head. Such an analysis can be expected to account for the availability of (iv), although I will not pursue this issue here.

	(vi)	a.	Italian *essere* "be"			b.	Italian *avere* "have"	
			IND PRES				IND PRES	
			SG	PL			SG	PL
			1ST sono	siamo			1ST ho	abbiamo
			2ND sei	siete			2ND hai	avete
			3RD è	sono			3RD ha	hanno

3. Under the split-Infl hypothesis, this entails that like the (finite) agreement affixes, the infinitival marker -*re* is generated under Agr (instead of Tense), a non-standard assumption given that -*re* is usually analyzed as a tense marker. At least in Italian, the infinitival marker -*re* can be viewed as a default agreement marker, since no other agreement morphology appears in Italian infinitives. See however note 8 for a different situation in European Portuguese.

4. This theory does not explain why French infinitivals, unlike their English counterparts, optionally raise to Tense (cf. (17b) and (20)). In general, the explanation for such 'short' verb movement is beyond the scope of this work (and see Iatridou 1990 for arguments against short movement). My theory also does not explain why French gerunds obligatorily raise to Agr (cf. (i) = Pollock 1989, ex. (112b)).

> (i)   Ne travaillant pas, Pierre a   échoué.
> Not working   NEG, P.   has flunked

Since clitics do not occur on gerunds any more than they do on infinitivals, the word order in (i) is unexpected.

5. European and Brazilian Portuguese allow extraction from embedded wh-questions (cf. (i) = Farrell 1990, ex. (29b)) and it is therefore not surprising that empty referential objects are found in the same environment (cf. (ii) = Raposo 1986, ex. (20)).

> (i)   o   livro que eu queria saber   quem perguntou se você já   leu.
> the book that I   wanted to-know who asked   if you   already read

> (ii) Eu sei   en que   cofre o   Mane guardou *e*.
> I   know in which safe the M.   kept   (it)
> 'I know in which safe Manuel kept it.'   (Portuguese)

6. Animate referential null objects on the other hand seem to obey island constraints (compare (i) from Bianchi and Figueiredo Silva 1990 with (44a)). It is not easy to see how this difference could be explained.

> (i)   *O José conhece a   mulher que beijou *e*.
> the J.   knows   the woman who kissed (him)
> 'John knows the woman who kissed him.'   (Brazilian Portuguese)

7. This analysis of proclisis in French infinitives forces us to revise the analysis of the (optionally) pre-adverbial position of French infinitival main verbs outlined in Section 5.2.2. See Iatridou (1990) for arguments against short verb movement to an inflectional head above adverbs but below negation in French infinitives. Since I have nothing to say about short verb movement in general, I will leave this issue unaddressed.

8. See note 3. Unlike the Italian infinitival marker -*re*, the European Portuguese infinitival marker -*r* cannot be viewed as a default agreement marker since it can cooccur with non-default agreement, as in the following example from Quicole (1982):

> (i)   Convém   comprarmos una ratoeira.
>   convenient to-buy-1PL   a   mousetrap
>   'It is convenient for us to buy a mousetrap.'

9. Rouveret (1989) argues on the basis of a different clitic theory that enclisis in European Portuguese simple finite clauses is a reflex of verb movement. Galves (1989) points out that by the same token, proclisis in Brazilian Portuguese simple finite clauses is a reflex of V in situ. The theory sketched here leads to similar conclusions.

10. English does allow null subjects in certain registers, cf. the following example from the diary of Virginia Woolf (cited after Rizzi 1994).

> (i)   A very sensible day yesterday. *e* Saw no-one.

Null subjects of this variety are excluded from questions (cf. (iia)) and embedded clauses (cf. (iib)). Null subjects of the variety found in *pro*-drop languages are not restricted in this way (cf. the Italian examples from Rizzi 1982 in (iii)).

> (ii)   a.   *Why should *e* see anybody?
>   b.   *I'm glad that *e* saw no-one.
>
> (iii) a.   Quante   pietre-*pro* hai   preso?
>   how-many stones   have-2SG taken
>   'How many stones did you take?'
>   b.   Gianni mi ha chiesto se-*pro*   pensavo   che tu   avessi
>   G.   me has asked whether thought-1SG that you had
>   contattato nessuno.
>   contacted anybody
>   'John asked me whether I thought that you had contacted anybody.'

The different distribution of null subjects in English and Italian suggests that they represent different types of empty categories. I will assume with much of the literature that the former are empty topics ("Topic Drop", cf. the discussion of null subjects in Yiddish below) whereas the latter are empty pronouns ("*pro*-drop"). Only *pro*-drop is of immediate interest in this section.

11. If Roberts (1993) is right and the Faroese plural forms represent the bare stem (cf. Section 3.2.3), making the Faroese paradigm non-uniform, then the Icelandic third plural from which the Faroese plural forms are derived also represents the bare stem, making the Icelandic paradigm non-uniform as well. Even in this scenario, then, a V to I raising theory based on morphological uniformity makes the wrong predictions.

12. It may be more accurate to analyze the final vowel of the European Portuguese 3RD singular and the Brazilian Portuguese 2ND singular, 3RD singular and 1ST plural as a stem-final theme vowel and not as an affix (cf. note 1). If this is correct, neither European nor Brazilian Portuguese has a morphologically uniform paradigm, and if *pro* is licensed by morphologically uniform agreement, it should be impossible in both languages, contrary to fact.

13. In addition to expletive *pro* in impersonal passive and existential clauses in which V2 is independently satisfied, Icelandic also requires quasi-argumental null subjects in weather-verb clauses in which V2 is independently satisfied (cf. (i) = Platzack 1993, ex. (14a)). By contrast, German requires expletive *pro* in impersonal passives (cf. (iia)) and existentials (cf. (iib)) but does not allow quasi-argumental null subjects (cf. (iic)) in weather-verb clauses. Vikner (1995a:118) argues that "Faroese has no empty expletives", and that is in fact what the theory developed in this section predicts since *pro* is not licensed in this language due to the lack of minimal distinctive marking of [2ND]. Faroese nevertheless allows (but does not require) quasi-argumental null subjects (cf. (iii) = Vikner 1995a, ex. 3(74)).

(i)   Í gær   rigndi (*það) hérna allan daginn.
yesterday rained it   here all   day
'Yesterday it rained here all day.'   (Icelandic)

(ii) a.   Gestern wurde (*es) auf dem Schiff getanzt.
yesterday was   it on the ship danced
'Yesterday there was dancing on the ship.'

     b.   Heute sind (*es) hier viele Linguisten hergekommen.
today are   it here many linguists   come
'Today have many linguists have come here.'

     c.   Gestern   regnete *(es) hier den ganzen Tag.
Yesterday rained   (it) here the whole day
'Yesterday it rained here the whole day.'   (German)

(iii)   I gjár   regnaði (tað).
yesterday rains   it
'Yesterday it rained.'   (Faroese)

The complex distribution of quasi-argumental null subjects poses a problem for any theory which classifies them as instances of *pro*, and it is in fact quite possible that these null subjects are not of the *pro* variety. For this reason, I will not attempt to explain the distribution of quasi-argumental null subjects in this section.

14. Of these latter three transitions, Rough-Shift is less coherent (or harder to process) that Retain or Smooth-Shift. I will ignore this difference since is not reflected in the data we are about to discuss.

15. Each cell in both tables compares the number of null subjects in a particular environment with the sum of null subjects and overt subject pronouns in that environment. Overt subject NPs are excluded from this count. If they were included, the percentage of null subjects in first and second person would remain the same but the percentage of null subjects in third person would be greatly reduced, bringing it closer to that in the other non-second singular cases. I am not aware of any frequency counts of Topic Drop, but I suspect that Topic Drop is less frequent than *pro*-drop even in the pragmatic environments where it is licensed. If this turns out to be the case, then the fact that second singular null subjects are more frequent than non-second singular null subjects even in Continue Transitions is in and of itself another argument to treat the former as cases of *pro*-drop and the latter as cases of Topic Drop.

16. Prince implicitly assumes that for the purposes of Centering Theory, the indices i and i′ are indistinguishable.

17. Recall from note 10 that *pro*-drop is possible in embedded clauses but Topic Drop is not.

18. In addition, Icelandic and Yiddish show Diesing Effects (cf. Diesing 1992) but Mainland Scandinavian and English do not. Thus definite and indefinite subjects appear in different positions in Icelandic (cf. (i,ii)), but they appear in the same position in English (cf. the translations of (i,ii)).

(i) Í gær klaruðu (þessar mys) sennilega (?*þessar mys) ostinn.
yesterday finished (these mice) probably (these mice) cheese-the
'These mice probably finished the cheese yesterday.'

(ii) Í gær klaruðu (?margar mys) sennilega (margar mys) ostinn.
yesterday finished (many mice) probably (many mice) cheese-the
'Many mice probably finished the cheese yesterday.'

(Icelandic, Bobaljik 1995, ex. I(4))

Bobaljik (1995) relates the distribution of Diesing Effects to the distribution of transitive expletive constructions (cf. the discussion below): like the latter, Diesing Effects depend on the availability of a second subject position. In my terms, Icelandic and Yiddish project both AgrSP and TP, with the specifier of AgrSP hosting definite subjects and the specifier of TP hosting indefinite subjects. In the second of the two cases, an empty A-specifier (that of AgrSP) is available to host an expletive. English and mainland Scandinavian on the other hand project only TP, with the specifier of TP hosting definite and indefinite subjects alike. In either case, no empty A-specifier is available to host an expletive.

19. As discussed in Section 3.3, Bobaljik (1995) also proposes a second, entirely different theory of NP object shift and transitive expletive constructions according to which the particular morphology does determine the syntactic representation (cf. also Bobaljik and Jonas 1996). This theory is based on Chomsky's (1993) theory of Shortest Move (cf. (82) and (83) of Chapter 2) and Bures's (1993) assumption that while all languages project AgrSP, TP and AgrOP, only some license SpecTP as a landing site for A-movement. When SpecTP is licensed as a landing site for A-movement, the subject can move to SpecTP (and ultimately SpecAgrSP) across a shifted object in SpecAgrOP if movement of AgrO to Tense has made the two specifiers equidistant from the base position of the subject in SpecVP. When SpecTP is not licensed as a landing site for A-movement, the subject cannot move to SpecAgrSP across a shifted object in SpecAgrOP because although movement of AgrO to Tense makes SpecTP and SpecAgrOP equidistant and movement of Tense to AgrS makes SpecAgrSP and SpecTP equidistant, these head movements still leave SpecAgrSP and SpecAgrOP in different minimal domains and direct movement to the former across the latter hence violates Shortest Move. As a result, NP object shift (and, for similar reasons, transitive expletive constructions) are possible in language which license SpecTP but impossible in languages which do not.

Bobaljik suggests that whether a language licenses or does not license SpecTP as a landing site for A-movement depends on whether that language has separate or fused AgrS and Tense nodes. The latter question is decided by the inflectional morphology of the language:

(ii)   *Evidence for Fusion*

"If the appearance of Tense morphology blocks the appearance of Agreement morphology, then Tense and Agreement Vocabulary Items are in complementary distribution, and T and Agr must be fused."   (Bobaljik 1995: 48)

In, Icelandic, where tense morphology cooccurs with agreement morphology, AgrS and Tense nodes are separate at the point of lexical insertion. With Tense staying in situ until verb movement carries it along, the n-feature of Tense is checked by SpecTP, making this position a possible landing site for A-movement. Raising of the subject across the object can therefore escape a violation of Shortest Move by utilizing this position as shown in (iii) (= (46a) in Bobaljik and Jonas 1996).

(iii)

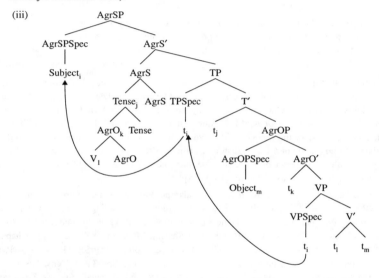

In Swedish, where tense morphology does not cooccur with agreement morphology, AgrS and Tense are fused by adjunction of the latter to the former before lexical insertion takes place. With Tense moving out of its projection prior to verb movement, the n-feature of Tense is not checked by SpecTP, excluding this position as a landing site for A-movement. Raising of the subject across the object can therefore not make use of this position (cf. (iv) = (46b) in Bobaljik and Jonas 1996), and Bobaljik (1995) and Bobaljik and Jonas (1996) assume that a violation of Shortest move ensues.

(iv)

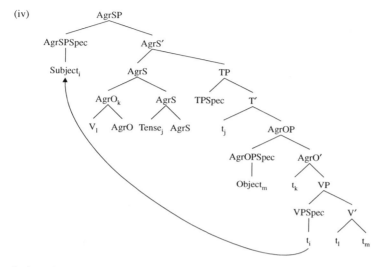

A closer look at (iv) however reveals that this assumption is wrong. Direct movement of the verb in AgrO to AgrS would put SpecAgrSP and SpecAgrOP in the minimal domain of $(AgrO_k, t_k)$ and make them equidistant from SpecVP according to the definitions in (82) and (83) of Chapter 2, and direct movement of the subject from its base position across the shifted object to its surface position would therefore satisfy Shortest Move. In other words, NP object shift should be grammatical in Swedish if it involves structures like (iv). For this reason, the alternative theory developed in Bobaljik (1995) and Bobaljik and Jonas (1996) must be rejected.

CHAPTER 6

Conclusions

In this book, I have argued that whether a language has minimal distinctive marking of the person features determines whether the language in question has V to I raising, *pro*-drop, NP object shift and transitive expletive constructions. More generally, I have defended the view that all syntactic parameters are set on the basis of language-specific overt morpho-phonological properties of functional categories. In the introduction (cf. Chapter 1), I have argued that this surface-oriented approach to crosslinguistic variation is necessary to avoid vicious circles in which syntactic phenomena are acquired on the basis of abstract functional features which are in turn acquired on the basis of the aforementioned syntactic phenomena. This book focused on the inflectional system, a part of the functional system where Morphology Driven Syntax seems especially promising. It has not addressed in detail the complementizer system, a part of the functional system where Morphology Driven Syntax seems to face greater challenges. Let us briefly consider the Verb Second (V2) phenomenon as an illustration of what is the issue here. As discussed in Section 2.3, all Germanic languages except English consistently place finite matrix main verbs in second position after the first phrasal element (cf. (1a)), a reflection of the fact that these languages have main verb movement to Comp (cf. (2a)). English on the other hand does not always position finite matrix main verbs in this way (cf. (1b)), a reflection of the fact that this language does not have main verb movement to Comp (cf. (2b)).

(1)   a.   Dieses   Buch mag ich.
             This-ACC book like I-NOM.   (German)
      b.   This book I like.

(2)   a.   b.

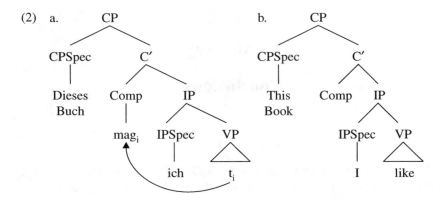

If Morphology-Driven Syntax is on the right track, then the fact that German finite matrix main verbs move to Comp whereas their English counterparts fail to do so must be related to concrete (phonetically perceptible) differences in the complementizer systems of these two languages. Of course there are obvious differences between the two systems: English *that* and *if* translate into German *daß* and *ob*, etc. But these differences are arbitrary and it would be entirely stipulative to hold them responsible for the (un-) availability of Comp as a landing site for finite main verbs (see also note 23 in Chapter 3). Whether this problem and others like it can be successfully addressed by Morphology-Driven Syntax is unclear at this point, and if it turns out to be in fact impossible to do so, the circularity problem that arises within the currently favored (abstract) lexicalist approach to parametrization will have to be rethought. But at least as far as the wide range of data discussed in this book is concerned, I hope to have shown that Morphology-Driven Syntax can offer a principled and insightful explanation that adds to our knowledge of how seemingly independent syntactic phenomena are related to each other and to morphology.

Bibliography

Abrahams, W. and E. Reuland, eds. (1991) *Issues in Germanic Syntax*. Berlin: Mouton.

Adams, M. (1987) "From Old French to the Theory of Pro-Drop". *Natural Language and Linguistic Theory* 5: 1–32.

Åfarli, T. (1991) "The Phrase Structure of Clauses". In H. Sigurðsson, þ. Indriðason & E. Rögnvadsson (eds.) *Papers from the 12th Scandinavian Congress of Linguistics*. Reykjavik: Linguistic Institute 14–25.

Akmajian, A. and F. Heny (1981) *An Introduction to the Principles of Transformational Syntax*. Cambridge: MIT Press.

Akmajian, A., S. Steele and T. Wasow (1979) "The Category Aux in Universal Grammar". *Linguistic Inquiry* 10: 1–64.

Allan, W. (1987) "Lightfoot noch einmal". *Diachronica* 4: 123–157.

Anderson, S. (1992) *A-Morphous Morphology*. Cambridge University Press.

Anderson, S. (1993) "Wackernagel's Revenge: Clitics, Morphology, and the Syntax of Second Position". *Language* 69: 68–98.

Authier, J.-M. (1992) "Iterated CPs and Embedded Topicalization". *Linguistic Inquiry* 23: 329–336.

Avrutin, S. and B. Rohrbacher (1997) "Null Subjects in Russian Inverted Constructions". *Formal Approaches to Slavic Linguistics* 4: 32–53.

Bach, E. (1962) "The Order of Elements in a Transformational Grammar of German". *Language* 38: 263–269.

Bailyn, J. (1995) A configurational approach to Russian "free" word order. Unpublished Ph. D. dissertation, Cornell University.

Baker, M. (1985) "The Mirror Principle and Morphosyntactic Explanation". *Linguistic Inquiry* 16: 373–416.

Baker, M. (1988) *Incorporation. A Theory of Grammatical Function Changing*. Chicago: University of Chicago Press.

Barnes, B. (1986) "An Empirical Study of the Syntax and Pragmatics of Left Dislocation in Spoken French". In Jaeggli & Silva-Corvalan 207–223.

Barnes, M. (1987) "Some Remarks on Subordinate-Clause Word Order in Faroese". *Scripta Islandica* 38: 3–35.

Barnes, M. (1989) Faroese Syntax — Achievements, Goals and Problems. Unpublished ms., University College London. In *Proceedings of the 7th International Conference of Nordic and General Linguistics.*

Bayer, L. (1984) "Comp in Bavarian Syntax". *The Linguistic Review* 3: 209–274.

Beard, R. (1991) Lexeme-Morpheme Base Morphology. A General Theory of Inflection and Word Formation. Ms., Bucknell University.

Belletti, A. (1990) *Generalized Verb Movement: Aspects of Verb Syntax.* Torino: Rosenberg & Sellier.

Belletti, A. (1994) "V Positions: Evidence from Italian". In D. Lightfoot & N. Hornstein (eds.) *Verb Movement.* Cambridge: Cambridge University Press 19–40.

Benedicto, E. (1994) "Agr, ƒ-features, V-movement: Identifying *pro*". *University of Massachusetts Occasional Papers in Linguistics* 17:1–18.

Benmamoun, E. (1991) "Negation and Verb Movement". *NELS* 21: 17–31.

Besten, H. den (1983) "On the Interaction of Root Transformations and Lexical Deletive Rules". In W. Abraham (ed.) *On the Formal Syntax of the Westgermania.* Amsterdam: Benjamins.

Bianchi, V. and M. Figueiredo Silva (1993) "On the Properties of Agr-Object in Italian and in Brazilian Portuguese". Talk given at the 23RD Linguistic Symposium on Romance Languages, University of Northern Illinois at Dekalb.

Bobaljik, J. (1995) Morphosyntax: The Syntax of Verbal Inflection. Unpublished Ph. D. dissertation, MIT.

Bobaljik, J. and D. Jonas (1996) "Subject Positions and the Roles of TP". *Linguistic Inquiry* 27: 195–236

Bolinger, D. (1971) *The Phrasal Verb in English.* Cambridge: Harvard University Press.

Borer, H. (1984) *Parametric Syntax.* Dordrecht: Foris.

Borer, H. (1989) "Anaphoric Agr". In O. Jaeggli & K. Safir (eds.) *The Null Subject Parameter.* Dordrecht: Kluwer 69–109.

Borer, H. (1995) "The Ups and Downs of Hebrew Verb Movement". *Natural Language & Linguistic Theory* 13: 527–606.

Borer, H. and K. Wexler (1992) "Bi-Unique Relations and the Maturation of Grammatical Principles". *Natural Language & Linguistic Theory* 10: 147–189.

Bouchard, D. (1983) *On the Content of Empty Categories.* Dordrecht: Foris.

Brandi, L. and P. Cordin (1989) "Two Italian Dialects and the Null Subject Parameter". In O. Jaeggli & K. Safir (eds.) *The Null Subject Parameter.* Dordrecht: Kluwer 111–142.

Branigan, P. and C. Collins (1993) "Verb Movement and the Quotative Construction in English". *MIT Working Papers in Linguistics* 18: 1–13.

Branigan, P. and C. Collins (1997) "Quotative Inversion". *Natural Language and Linguistic Theory* 15: 1–41.

Brown, R. (1973) *A First Language: The Early Stages.* Cambridge: Harvard University Press.

Bures, A. (1993) "There is an Argument for a Cycle at LF, here". *CLS* 28, Vol. 2: 14–35.

Bybee, J. (1985) *Morphology. A Study of the Relation between Meaning and Form.* Amsterdam: John Benjamins.

Cardinaletti, A. and I. Roberts (1991) "Clause Structure and X-Second". Unpublished ms., Università di Venezia & University of Wales.

Chomsky, N. (1981) *Lectures on Government and Binding.* Dordrecht: Foris

Chomsky, N. (1986a) *Barriers.* Cambridge: MIT Press.

Chomsky, N. (1986b) *Knowledge of Language. Its Nature, Origin, and Use.* New York: Praeger.

Chomsky, N. (1989) "Some Notes on Economy of Derivation and Representation". *MIT Working Papers in Linguistics* 10: 43–74. Reprinted in N. Chomsky (1995) *The Minimalist Program.* Cambridge: MIT Press 129–166.

Chomsky, N. (1992) *A Minimalist Program for Linguistic Theory.* MIT Occasional Papers in Linguistics 1. Reprinted in N. Chomsky (1995) *The Minimalist Program.* Cambridge: MIT Press 167–217.

Chomsky, N. (1995) "Categories and Transformations". In N. Chomsky *The Minimalist Program.* Cambridge: MIT Press 219–394.

Clahsen, H. and M. Penke (1992) "The Acquisition of Agreement Morphology and its Syntactic Consequences: New Evidence on German Child Language from the Simone-Corpus". In Meisel (ed.) 181–223.

Denison, D. (1989) "Auxiliary and Impersonal in Old English". *Folia Linguistica Historica* 9: 139–166.

Deprez, V. (1990) "Two Ways of Moving the Verb in French". Unpublished Ms., Rutgers University

Diesing, M. (1990) "Verb Movement and the Subject Position in Yiddish". *Natural Language & Linguistic Theory* 8: 41–79.

Diesing, M. and E. Jelinek (1993) "The Syntax and Semantics of Object Shift". *Working Papers in Scandinavian Syntax* 51.

Di Sciullo, A.-M. and E. Williams (1987) *On the Definition of Word*. Cambridge: MIT Press.

Duarte, M. (1993) "Do pronome nulo ao pronome pleno: a trajetória do sujeito no português do Brasil". In I. Roberts & M. Kato (eds) *Portugues Brasileiro: Uma Viagem Diachronica*. Campinas: Editora da Unicamp 107–128.

Ellegård, A. (1953) *The auxiliary DO: The Establishment and Regulation of its Use in English*. Stockholm: Almqvist & Wiksell.

Emmonds, J. (1976) *A Transformational Approach to English Syntax*. New York: Academic Press.

Falk, C. (1993) Non-Referential Subjects in the History of Swedish. Unpublished Ph. D. thesis. Lund University.

Farrell, P. (1990) "Null Objects in Brazilian Portuguese". *Natural Language and Linguistic Theory* 8: 325–346.

Figueiredo Silva, M. (1992) "About Verb Movement in Brazilian Portuguese". *Proceedings of 3rd Leiden Conference of Junior Linguists* 123–134.

Galves, C. (1989) "L'objet nul et la structure de la proposition en portugais du Brésil". *Revue des Languages Romanes* 93: 305–336.

Galves, C. (1990) "V Movement, Levels of Representation and the Structure of S". Talk given at GLOW 13, London.

Geilfuß, J. (1990) "Jiddisch als SOV-Sprache". *Zeitschrift für Sprachwissenschaft* 9: 170–183.

Gleason, H. (1965) *Linguistics and English Grammar*. New York:

Green, L. (1990) Auxiliaries and Aspectual Markers in Black English. Unpublished ms., U Mass Amherst.

Grewendorf, G. (1988) *Aspekte der deutschen Syntax. Eine Rektions-Bindungs Analyse*. Tübingen: Narr.

Grimshaw, J. (1997) "Projection, Heads, and Optimality". *Linguistic Inquiry* 28: 373–422.

Grosz, B., Joshi, A. and S. Weinstein (1986) "Towards a Computational Theory of Discourse Interpretation". Unpublished ms., University of Pennsylvania.

Haan, G. de and F. Weerman (1986) "Finitness and Verb Fronting in Frisian". In H. Haider & M. Prinzhorn (eds.) *Verb Second Phenomena in Germanic Languages*. Dordrecht: Foris 77–110.

Haegeman, L. (1992) *Theory and Description in Generative Grammar. A Case Study in West Flemish*. Cambridge: Cambridge University Press.

Haider, H. (1993) *Deutsche Syntax — generativ. Vorstudien zur Theorie einer projektiven Grammatik*. Tübingen: Narr.

Haugen, E. (1976) *The Scandinavian Languages. An Introduction to their History*. London: Faber and Faber.

Haugen, E. (1982) *Scandinavian Language Structure. A Comparative Historical Survey*. Minneapolis: University of Minnesota Press.

Henry, A. (1991) Verb Raising and Hiberno English DO BE. Unpublished ms., University of Ulster at Jordanstown.

Hoekstra, J. and L. Marács (1989) "The Position of Inflection in West-Germanic". *Working Papers in Scandinavian Syntax* 44: 75–88.

Höhle, T. (1991) Projektionsstufen bei V-Projektionen. Unpublished ms., University of Tübingen.

Holmberg, A. (1986) Word Order and Syntactic Features. Unpublished Ph. D. thesis, University of Stockholm.

Holmberg, A. and C. Platzack (1991) "On the Role of Inflection in Scandinavian Syntax". In Abraham & Reuland 93–118.

Holmberg, A. and C. Platzack (1995) *The Role of Inflection in Scandinavian Syntax*. New York: Oxford University Press.

Hornstein, N. (1990) "Verb Raising in Icelandic Infinitives". *NELS* 20: 215–229.

Hornstein, N. (1991) "Expletives: A Comparative Study of English and Icelandic". *Working Papers in Scandinavian Syntax* 47: 1–88.

Huang, C.-T. J. (1984) "On the Distribution and Reference of Empty Pronouns". *Linguistic Inquiry* 15: 531–575

Hundertmark-Santos Martin, M. (1982) *Portugiesische Grammatik*. Tübingen: Max Niemeyer Verlag.

Iatridou, S. (1990) "About Agr(P)". *Linguistic Inquiry* 21: 551–577.

Iatridou, S. and A. Kroch (1992) "The Licensing of CP-recursion and its Relevance to the Germanic Verb-Second Phenomenon". *Working Papers in Scandinavian Syntax* 50: 1–24.

Jackendoff, R. (1972) *Semantic Interpretation In Generative Grammar*. Cambridge: MIT Press.

Jaeggli, O. (1981) *Topics in Romance Syntax*. Dordrecht: Foris.

Jaeggli, O. and N. Hyams (1988) "Morphological Uniformity and the Setting, of the Null Subject Parameter". *NELS* 18: 238–253.

Jaeggli, O. & N. Hyams (1993) "On the Independence and Interdependence of Syntactic and Morphological Properties: English Aspectual *Come* and *Go*". *Natural Language & Linguistic Theory* 11: 313–346.

Jaeggli, O. and K. Safir (1989) "The Null Subject Parameter and Parametric Theory". In O. Jaeggli & K. Safir (eds.) *The Null Subject Parameter*. Dordrecht: Kluwer 1–44.

Jaeggli, O. and C. Silva-Corvalán, eds. (1986) *Studies in Romance Linguistics*. Dordrecht: Foris.

Jensen, J. and M. Stong Jensen (1984) "Morphology is in the Lexicon!" *Linguistic Inquiry* 15: 474–498.

Johnson, K. (1991) "Object Positions". *Natural Language & Linguistic Theory* 9: 577–636.

Johnson, K. (1992a) "Head Movement, Word Order and Inflection". Unpublished ms., University of California at Irvine.

Johnson, K. (1992b) "On the Typology of the V^Adverb^NP Word Order". Unpublished ms., University of Wisconsin at Madison.

Jonas, D. and J. Bobaljik (1993) "Specs for Subjects: The Role of TP in Icelandic". MIT Working Papers in Linguistics 18.

Jónsson, J. (1991a) "Stylistic Fronting in Icelandic". *Working Papers in Scandinavian Syntax* 48: 1–44.

Jónsson, J. (1991b) "On Verb Movement in Icelandic". Unpublished ms., University of Massachusetts at Amherst.

Jordens, P. (1990) "The Acquisition of Verb Placement in Dutch and German". *Linguistics* 28: 1407–1448

Joshi, A. and S. Weinstein (1981) "Control of Inference: Role of Some Aspects of Discourse Structure-Centering". *Proceedings of the International Joint Conference on Artificial Intelligence* 385–387.

Kaiser, G. and J. Meisel (1991) "Subjekte und Null-Subjekte im Französischen". In S. Olsen & G. Fanselow (eds.) *Det, Comp und Infl. Zur Syntax funktionaler Kategorien und grammatischer Funktionen*. Tübingen: Niemeyer 110–136.

Kayne, R. (1982) "Predicates and Arguments, Verbs and Nouns". GLOW-talk.

Kayne, R. (1984) "Principles of Particle Constructions". In J. Guéron et al. (eds.) *Grammatical Representation*. Dordrecht: Foris.

Kayne, R. (1989) "Notes on English Agreement". *CIEFL Bulletin*. Hyderabad.

Kayne, R. (1991) "Romance Clitics, Verb Movement, and PRO". *Linguistic Inquiry* 22: 647–686.

Kayne, R. (1994) *The Antisymmetry of Syntax*. Cambridge: MIT Press.

Kok, A. de (1985) *La place du pronom personnel régime conjoint en français. Une étude diachronique*. Amsterdam: Rodopi.

Kosmeijer, W. (1991) "Verb Second, Nominative Case and Scope". In Abrahams & Reuland 197–221.

Krenn, E. (1940) *Föroyische Sprachlehre*. Heidelberg: Carl Winter's Universitätsbuchhandlung.

Kroch, A. (1990) "Reflexes of Grammar in Patterns of Language Change". *Language Variation and Change* 1: 199–244.

Laka, I. (1990) *Negation in Syntax: On the Nature of Functional Categories and Projections*. Unpublished Ph.D. dissertation, MIT.

Larsson, C. (1931) "Ordföljdsstudies över det finita verbet i de Nordiska Fornspråken". *Uppsala Universitets Årsskrift*.

Lasnik, H. (1981) "Restricting the Theory of Transformations: a Case Study". In N. Hornstein & D. Lightfoot (eds.) *Explanation in Linguistics: The Logical Problem of Language Acquisition*. London: Longman.

Lasnik, H. (1994) "Verbal Morphology: Syntactic Structures Meets the Minimalist Program". Ms., University of Connecticut.

Lee, W. and Z. Lee (1959) *Czech*. Sevenoaks: Hodder & Stroughton.

Lehtinen, M. (1964) *Basic Course in Finnish*. The Hague: Mouton.

Lewis, C. (1967) *Turkish Grammar*. Oxford: Clarendon Press.

Lieber, R. (1992) *Deconstructing Morphology. Word Formation in Syntactic Theory*. Chicago: University of Chicago Press.

Lightfoot, D. (1979) *Principles of Diachronic Synatx*. Cambridge: Cambridge University Press.

Lightfoot, D. (1991) *How to Set Parameters: Arguments from Language Change*. Cambridge: MIT Press.

Lockwood, W. (1964) *An Introduction to Modern Faroese*. Copenhagen: Munksgaard.

Lockwood, W. (1983) *Die Färöischen Sigurdlieder nach Sandoyarbók*. Tórshavn: Foroya Fróðskaparferlag.

Magnússon, F. (1990) *Kjarnafærsla og það-insskot í aukasetningum í íslensku*. Reykjavík: Málvísindastofnun Hákóla Íslands.

Maling, J. (1990) "Inversion in Embedded Clauses in Modern Icelandic". In Maling and Zaenen (1990), 71–91.

Maling, J. and A. Zaenen, eds. (1990) *Modern Icelandic Syntax*. (Syntax and Semantics 24). San Diego: Academic Press.

Manzini, R. (1994) "Locality, Minimalism, and Parasitic Gaps". *Linguistic Inquiry* 25: 481–508.

McKee, C. and M. Emiliani (1992) "Il Clitico: C'è ma non si Vede". *Natural Language & Linguistic Theory* 10: 415–437.

Meisel, J., ed. (1992) *The Acquisition of Verb Placement. Functional Categories and V2 Phenomena in Language Acquisition* Dordrecht: Kluwer

Meisel, J. (1993) "Getting FAT. Finiteness, Agreement and Tense in Early Grammars". In J. Meisel (ed.) *Bilingual First Language Acquisition. French and German Grammatical Development*. Amsterdam: John Benjamins.

Mendes, L. (1993) "The Structure of IP, Word Order and the Position of Clitics". Talk given at the 23rd Linguistic Symposium on Romance Languages, University of Northern Illinois at Dekalb.

Mitchel, E. (1991) "Evidence from Finnish for Pollock's Theory of IP". *Linguistic Inquiry* 22: 373–379.

MED *Middle English Dictionary* H. Kurath and S. Kuhn, eds., (1954–). Ann Arbor: University of Michigan Press.

Neeleman, A. (1996) Review of Rohrbacher (1994). *GLOT International* 2.3: 10–12.

Nichols, J. (1992) *Linguistic Diversity in Space and Time*. Chicago: University of Chicago Press.

OED *Oxford English Dictionary*. (1971) Oxford: Oxford University Press.

O'Neil, W. (1979) "The Evolution of the Germanic Inflectional Systems: A Study in the Causes of Language Change". *Orbis* 27: 248–286.

Orešnik, J. (1972) "On the Epenthesis Rule in Modern Icelandic". *Arkiv för nordisk filologi* 87: 1–32.

Ottóson, K. (1989) "VP-Specifier Subjects and the CP/IP Distinction In Icelandic and Mainland Scandinavian". *Working Papers in Scandinavian Syntax* 44: 89–100.

Ouhalla, J. (1990) "Sentential Negation, Relativised Minimality and the Aspectual Status of Auxiliaries". *The Linguistic Review* 7: 183–231.

Ouhalla, J. (1991) *Functional Categories and Parametric Variation*. London and New York: Routledge.

Pesetsky, D. (1989) "Language-Particular Processes and the Earliness Principle". Unpublished ms., MIT.

Perkins, R. (1980) The Evolution of Culture and Grammar. Unpublished Ph. D. dissertation, SUNY Buffalo.

Pierce, A. (1992) *Language Acquisition and Syntactic Theory. A Comparative Analysis of French and English Child Grammars*. Dordrecht: Kluwer Academic Publishers.

Pintzuk, S. (1991) Phrase Structure in Competition: Variation and Change in Old English Word Order. Unpublished Ph. D. thesis, University of Pennsylvania.

Plank, F. (1984) "The Modals Story Retold". *Studies in Language* 8: 305–364.

Platzack, C. (1984) "The Position of the Finite Verb in Icelandic". In W. de Geest & Y. Putseys (eds.) *Sentential Complementation*. Dordrecht: Foris 195–204.

Platzack, C. (1986a) "The Structure of Infinitive Clauses in Danish and Swedish". In Ö. Dahl & A. Holmberg (eds.) *Scandinavian Syntax*. (distributed by the Institute of Linguistics, University of Stockholm), 123–137.

Platzack, C. (1986b) "Comp, Infl and Germanic Word Order". In L. Hellan & C. Christensen (eds.) *Topics in Scandinavian Syntax*. Dordrecht: Reidel 185–234.

Platzack, C. (1988) "The Emergence of a Word Order Difference in Scandinavian Subordinate Clauses". *McGill Working Papers in Linguistics*, Special Issue on Comparative Germanic Syntax, 215–238.

Platzack, C. (1993) "Complementizer Agreement and Argument Clitics". *Working Papers in Scandinavian Syntax* 50: 25–54.

Platzack, C. and A. Holmberg (1989) "The Role of Agr and Finitness in Germanic VO Languages". *Working Papers in Scandinavian Syntax* 43: 51–76

Poeppel, D. and K. Wexler (1993). "The Full Competence Hypothesis of Clause Structure in Early German". *Language* 69, 1–33.

Pollock, J.-Y. (1989) "Verb Movement, Universal Grammar, and the Structure of IP". *Linguistic Inquiry* 20: 365–424.

Prince, E. (1994) "Subject-Prodrop in Yiddish". *Working Papers of the IBM Institute for Logic and Linguistics* 6: 159–174.

Quicole, A. (1982) *The Structure of Complementation*. Ghent: E. Story — Scientia P.V.B.A.

Radford, A. (1992) "The Acquisition of the Morphology of Finite Verbs in English". In Meisel (ed.) 23–62.

Raposo, E. (1986) "On the Null Object in European Portuguese". In Jaeggli & Silva Corvalán 373–390.

Reinholtz, C. (1989) "V-2 in Mainland Scandinavian: Finite Verb Movement to Agr". *Working Papers in Scandinavian Syntax* 44: 101–117.

Reuland, E, (1990) "Head Movement and the Relation between Morphology and Syntax". *Yearbook of Morphology* 3: 129–161.

Rizzi, L. (1986a) "Null Objects in Italian and the Theory of *pro*". *Linguistic Inquiry* 17: 501–557.

Rizzi, L. (1986b) "On the Status of Subject Clitics in Romance". In Jaeggli & Silva-Corvalan 391–419.

Rizzi, L. (1990a) *Relativized Minimality*. Cambridge: MIT Press.

Rizzi, L. (1990b) "Speculations on Verb Second". In J. Mascaro & M. Nespor (eds.) *Grammar in Progress. GLOW Essays for Henk van Riemsdijk*. Dordrecht: Foris 375–386.

Rizzi, L. (1991) "Residual Verb Second and the *Wh*-Criterion. " *University of Geneva Technical Reports in Formal and Computational Linguistics* 2

Roberge, Y. (1990) *The Syntactic Recoverability of Null Arguments*. Kingston & Montreal: McGill-Queens University Press.

Roberts, I. (1985) "Agreement Parameters and the Development of English Modal Auxiliaries". *Natural Language and Linguistic Theory* 3: 21–58.

Roberts, I. (1993) *Verbs in Diachronic Syntax. A Comparative History of English and French*. Dordrecht: Kluwer.

Rögnvaldsson, E. (1984) "Icelandic Word Order and *það* Insertation". *Working Papers in Scandinavian Syntax* 8.

Rögnvaldsson, E. and H. Thráinsson (1990) "On Icelandic Word Order once more". In Maling & Zaenen.

Rohrbacher, B. (1991) The Role of Morphology in Verb Movement and DO-Support. Unpublished ms., U Mass Amherst.

Rohrbacher, B. (1993) "V-to-Agr Raising in Faroese". In L. Stvan et al. (eds.) *FLSM III. Papers from the Third Annual Meeting of the Formal Linguistics Society of Midamerica*. (distributed by the Indiana University Linguistics Club, Bloomington), 281–296.

Rohrbacher, B. (1994a) The Germanic VO Languages and the Full Paradigm: A Theory of V to I Raising. Unpublished Ph.D. dissertation, University of Massachusetts at Amherst.

Rohrbacher, B. (1994b) "*English verbs move never". *The Penn Review of Linguistics* 18: 145–159.

Rohrbacher, B. and A. Vainikka (1995) "Verbs and Subjects before Age 2: The Earliest Stages in Germanic L1 Acquisition". *Proceedings of the Northeastern Linguistic Society* 25, 55–69.

Rouveret, A. (1989) "Cliticisation et Temps en portugais européen". *Revue de Langues Romanes* 93: 337–371.

Sabel, J. (1994) Restrukturierung und Lokalität. Universelle Beschränkungen für Wortstellungsvariationen. Unpublished Ph.D. dissertation. Universität Frankfurt.

Sandqvist, C. (1981) "Några karakteristiska drag i Heðin Brú språk". *Bókatíðindi* 1: 19–32.

Sankoff, G. (1982) "Usage linguistique et grammaticalisation: les clitiques sujets en français". In N. Dittmar & B. Schlieben-Lange (eds.) *Die Soziolinguistik in romanischsprachigen Ländern*. Tübingen: Narr 81–85.

Santorini, B. (1989) The Generalization of the Verb-Second Constraint in the History of Yiddish. Unpublished Ph. D. thesis, University of Philadelphia.

Santorini, B. (1994) "Some Similarities and Differences between Icelandic and Yiddish". In D. Lightfoot & N. Hornstein (eds.) *Verb Movement*. Cambridge: Cambridge University Press 87–106.

Schäufele, S. (1993) "The History of VP-Adverbials, V-Agr Merger, and Loss of Subject-Agreement Marking in English: A Case Study in Corpus-Based Diachronic Syntactic Research". Unpublished ms., University of Illinois at Urbana Champaign.

Seip, D. (1971) *Norwegische Sprachgeschichte*. Berlin: de Gruyter.

Shawn, N. (1985) "To Have and Have Got". Talk given at NWAVE 14, Georgetown University.

Shlonsky, U. (1989) "The Hierarchical Representation of Subject Verb Agreement". Unpublished ms., University of Haifa.

Siewierska, A. and D. Bakker (1994) "The distribution of subject and object agreement and word order type". *Eurotyp Working Papers* 6.83–126.

Sigurjónsdóttir, S. (1989) "The Structure of Icelandic Infinitive Clauses and the Status of the Infinitival Marker *að*". Unpublished ms., UCLA.

Sigurðsson, H. (1990) "V1 Declaratives and Verb Raising in Icelandic". In Maling & Zaenen 41–69.

Speas, M. (1994) "Null arguments in a theory of economy of projections". In E. Benedicto and J. Runner (eds.) *Functional Projections. University of Massachusetts Occasional Papers* 17:179–208.

Spencer, A. (1991) *Morphological Theory. An Introduction to Word Structure in Generative Grammar.* Oxford: Blackwell.

Sportiche, D. (1988) "A Theory of Floating Quantifiers and its Corollaries for Constituent Structure". *Linguistic Inquiry* 19: 425–449.

Stechow, A. von and W. Sternefeld (1988) *Bausteine Syntaktischen Wissens.* Opladen: Westdeutscher Verlag.

Taraldsen, T. (1986) "On Verb Second and the Functional Content of Syntactic Categories". In H. Haider & M. Prinzhorn (eds.) *Verb Second Phenomena in Germanic Languages.* Dordrecht: Foris 7–25.

Thomas, E. (1969) *The Syntax of Spoken Brazilian Portuguese.* Nashville: Vanderbilt University Press.

Thomson, C. (1987) *Icelandic Inflections.* Helmut Buske Verlag, Hamburg.

Thráinsson, H. (1985) "V1, V2, V3 in Icelandic". In H. Haider & M. Prinzhorn (eds.) *Verb Second Phenomena in Germanic Languages.* Dordrecht: Foris 169–194.

Thráinsson, H. (1993) "On the Structure of Infinitival Complement". *Harvard Working Papers in Linguistics* 3: 181–211.

Thráinsson, H. (1994) "Comments on the Paper by Vikner". In D. Lightfoot & N. Hornstein (eds.) *Verb Movement.* Cambridge: Cambridge University Press 149–162.

Travis, L. (1984) Parameters and Effects of Word Order Variation. Unpublished Ph. D. thesis, MIT.

Travis, L. (1988) "The Syntax of Adverbs". *McGill Working Papers in Linguistics* Special Issue on Comparative Germanic Syntax 280–310.

Trosterud, T. (1989) "The Null Subject Parameter and the New Mainlands Scandinavian Word Order: A Possible Counterexample from a Norwegian Dialect". *Papers from the 11th Scandinavian Conference of Linguistics* 87–100.

Trosterud, T. (1992) *Binding Relations in two Finnmark Finnish Dialects. A Comparative Syntactic Study.* University of Trondheim Working Papers in Linguistics 12.

Vainikka, A. and Y. Levy (1995) Empty Subjects in Finnish and Hebrew. Unpublished ms., University of Pennsylvania and The Hebrew University.

Valian, V. and Z. Eisenberg (1995) "The Development of Syntactic Subjects in Portuguese-Speaking Children". Unpublished Ms., Hunter College.

Verrips, M. and J. Weissenborn (1992) "Routes to Verb Placement in Early German and French: The Independence of Finiteness and Agreement". In Meisel (ed.) 283–331.

Vikner, S. (1988) *Modals in Danish and Event Expressions.* Working Papers in Scandinavian Syntax 39.

Vikner, S. (1991) Verb Movement and the Licensing of NP-Positions in the Germanic Languages. Unpublished Ph. D. thesis, University of Geneva.

Vikner, S. (1994) "Finite Verb Movement in Scandinavian Embedded Clauses". In D. Lightfoot & N. Hornstein (eds.) *Verb Movement.* Cambridge: Cambridge University Press 117–147.

Vikner, S. (1995a) *Verb Movement and Expletive Subjects in the Germanic Languages.* New York: Oxford University Press.

Vikner, S. (1995b) "V°–to–I° Movement and Inflection for Person in all Tenses". *Working Papers in Scandinavian Syntax* 55: 1-27.

Warner, A. (1983) review article of Lightfoot 1979. *Journal of Linguistics* 19: 187–209.

Warner, A.. (1990) "Reworking the History of English Auxiliaries". In S. Adamson, V. Law, N. Vincent and S. Wright (eds.) *Papers from the 5th International Conference on English Historical Linguistics.* Amsterdam: Benjamins 537–558.

Weerman, Fred (1989) *The V2 Conspiracy.* Dordrecht: Foris.

Wessen, E. (1970) *Schwedische Sprachgeschichte.* Berlin: de Gruyter.

Wilder, C. and D. Cavar (1994) "Word Order Variation, Verb Movement, and Economy Principles". *Studia Linguistica* 48: 46–86.

Wyld, H. (1927) *A Short History of English.* London: Murray.

Zwart, J.-W. (1991) "Clitics in Dutch: Evidence for the Position of Infl". *Groninger Arbeiten zur Germanistischen Linguistik* 33: 71–92.

Zwart, J.-W. (1994) "On Holmberg's Generalization". In A. de Boer, H. de Hoop & H. de Swart (eds.) *Language and Cognition 4. Yearbook 1994 of the Research Group for Theoretical and Experimental Linguistics of the University of Groningen.* Groningen: Department of Linguistics, University of Groningen 229–242.

Zwart, J.-W. (1997) *Morphosyntax of Verb Movement. A Minimalist Approach to the Syntax of Dutch.* Dordrecht: Kluwer.

Subject Index

Afrikaans 262
adverbs 39, 42–43, 87, 158, 201
  scope of 47–52
Åfarli, T 137
affix hopping 132, 161
Akmajian, A. 161, 194
Allan, W. 189
A-movement 271–272
Anderson, S. 85, 134
Arabic 146
aspectual *come* and *go* 162
asymmetric c-command 37
auxiliaries 14, 19, 42, 55, 66, 86, 119,
  178–198, 226
Avrutin, S. 151

Baker, M. 24, 27, 59
Bailyn, J. 150
bare phrase structure 135, 245, 267
Barnes, B. 219
Barnes, M. 68, 142, 154
barrier 24–25, 59, 61, 64–65, 95
Bavarian 252
Beard, R. 114–115, 134
Belletti, A. 206–209, 212, 267
Benedicto, E. 150, 219–220
Benmamoun, E. 94–95, 97–98, 101,
  145–146
Berber 146
Besten, H. den 20

Bianchi, V. 5–6, 222, 224, 230
Bobaljik, J. 8, 63, 89, 123, 125, 127,
  137–138, 151, 200, 244, 261–266,
  271–273
Bolinger, D. 53
Borer, H. 3, 149, 239
Bouchard, P. 129
Brandi, L. 219
Brannigan, P. 43, 47, 55, 86
bridge verbs 14–17, 19–21, 83

Cardinaletti, A. 69
case 20–21, 43, 100–106, 147, 162,
  189–190, 251–253, 259–260
Cavar, D. 154
centering theory 254–257, 271
Chinese 229
Chomsky, N. 2–4, 8, 25, 36, 59, 86,
  88–89, 123–124, 132–133,
  135–136, 147, 161, 181, 202, 245,
  267, 271
clitics 4–6, 79, 85, 145, 154, 198, 202,
  207, 214, 218–221, 223, 234–242,
  269
Collins, C. 43, 47, 55, 86
complementizer agreement 252–253
complex inversion 24
contraction 194–195
control verbs 78–79, 190, 203, 211
Cordin, P. 219

core language 168, 202
CP recursion 21, 71–72, 75, 78, 89, 176
Czech 115

Danish 12–13, 15–17, 58, 117, 120, 142,
　　177–179, 182, 198, 262
　Early Modern 197
　Old 120, 171, 173
degree phrases 89
Denison, D. 189
Deprez, V. 24
Diesing, M. 63, 69, 81, 84, 271
Diesing effects 271
do-support 145–147, 161–166, 168, 183,
　　196, 200–201, 203
double base hypothesis 144, 202
d-structure 139–140
Duarte, M. 247, 249
Dutch 12–20, 29–30, 36, 39, 72, 82–83,
　　201–202, 252, 262

economy of derivation 124, 133, 267
economy of projection 8, 243–246
Eisenberg, Z. 247
Ellegård, A. 157
Emiliani, M. 239
Emonds, J. 42
empty category principle (ECP) 24,
　　58–66, 95, 132
English 3, 7, 9, 14, 19–20, 28, 42–56,
　　82, 87, 90, 96–97, 101, 108, 110,
　　113, 120, 144–148, 151, 158,
　　162–164, 178–184, 188, 194, 196,
　　200–201, 203, 210, 224, 243–246,
　　254, 261–262, 267–269, 271,
　　275–276
　African American 181–182
　(Standard) American 196, 203
　British 196, 203

Early Modern 113–114, 117, 120,
　　123, 157, 168, 187, 193, 202
Hiberno 181–182
Middle 112–114, 117, 120–121,
　　144–145, 156, 158, 163–164, 168,
　　171, 184–187, 189–193, 196, 200,
　　203
Old 144, 169–171, 184, 186,
　　189–193, 196, 198–200, 203
event operator 102–104
exceptional case marking (ECM) 78, 80
existentials 250, 270
expletive subjects 8, 77, 137, 261–266,
　　271
extend target condition 132
extraposition 32–35, 54, 85–86, 210, 224
　PP- 43, 47, 50, 87

Falk, C. 109, 112, 148, 173, 175,
　　202–203
Faroese 9, 12–17, 67–69, 82–83, 89,
　　106, 108–113, 117, 120, 123, 125,
　　131–135, 140–144, 154, 178–179,
　　182–182, 202–203, 246–247, 262,
　　269–270
Farrell, P. 230
features, strong and weak 139–141
Figueiredo Silva, M. 5–6, 222, 224–226,
　　230
Finnish 116, 130, 142, 170, 230
focus 49
French 80, 95–97, 101, 128, 145–147,
　　213–221, 225, 234–235, 237–242,
　　268
　Canadian 218
　Early Middle 220–221
　North African 218
　Old 260
Frisian 89, 252, 262

Galves, C. 210, 222, 224, 230, 234
Geilfuß, J. 92
German 3, 7, 13–15, 17–20, 29–36,
    39–42, 82–83, 92, 128, 148, 153,
    201–203, 252, 262, 270, 275–276
Gleason, H. 161
Green, L. 181–182
Grewendorf, G. 29
Grimshaw, J. 201
Grosz, B. 254–255

Haider, H. 32, 85
Hale, K. 151
Haugen, E. 110, 112, 154, 172–173
head movement constraint 22–23, 25,
    28, 94, 238, 241
heavy NP shift 54, 87
Hebrew 116, 148–151, 230
    Biblical 149
Henry, A. 181–182
Heny, F. 161
Höhle, T. 30–32
Holmberg, A. 20–21, 56–57, 85, 87, 90,
    113, 147, 149, 259
Holmberg's generalization 87–88, 262
Hornstein, N. 71, 79, 84
Huang, C.-T.J. 229
Hungarian 115
Hyams, N. 162, 251–252

Iatridou, S. 21, 268
Icelandic 1, 9, 12–21, 39, 57, 69–84,
    89–92, 97–99, 101–102, 105–106,
    110, 113–114, 117, 120, 122–123,
    132–133, 135–137, 140–141, 147,
    154, 201–202, 220, 246–247,
    250–251, 261–264, 270–272
impersonal passives 250, 270
infinitival markers 78–80, 114, 147, 188,
    190, 194, 211, 217, 220, 268–269

intonation 50–51
islands
    complex NP 228
    sentential subjects 228
    topic- 91
    wh- 91
Italian 4–6, 24, 80, 115, 206–213, 215,
    220, 222–225, 227, 234–235,
    237–242, 254, 258–259, 267–270
    Northern 219
    Salentino 239

Jackendoff, R. 48
Jaeggli, O. 162, 219, 244, 251–252
Japanese 243, 245–246
Jellinek, E. 63
Jensen, J. 139
Johnson, K. 24, 44, 47,55, 79
Jónsson, J. 71, 90, 158
Jonas, D. 63, 272–273
Joshi, A. 255

Kayne, R. 36–39, 53–54, 84–86, 90,
    113, 148, 181–183, 235–237
Keiser, G. 219
Kok, A. de 221
Kosmeijer, W. 70, 84–85
Krenn, E. 154
Kroch, A. 21, 144, 157, 159, 202

Laka, I. 145, 162
language acquisition 168
    of Dutch 202
    of English 125–127, 194
    of Faroese 153
    of French 125–127
    of German 151–153
    of Italian 239
Larsson, C. 173
Lasnik, H. 181, 183, 200, 203

Lasnik's Filter 132–133, 137, 153,
    161–162, 200
left dislocation 218–219, 223–224
Lexicon 4, 132–133, 139–140
Lieber, R. 132
Lightfoot, D. 189, 203
linear correspondence axiom 36–37,
    85–86
Lockwood, W. 147, 154
logical form (LF) 139–140
    deletion 21

Maling, J. 158
Manzini, R. 25, 88–89
McKee, C. 239
Mendes, L. 222
Meisel, J. 219
Middle Scots 119, 169–170
Miskitu 121–122, 129
Mitchell, E. 119
modals 66, 78–80, 144, 158, 178,
    180–182, 184, 186–190, 193–194,
    196–197, 200, 203, 211

narrative inversion 82
Neeleman, A. 85
negation 39, 63, 87, 94–95, 99–100, 158
negative polarity items 207, 211, 220,
    222–224
Norwegian 12–13, 15–18, 67, 83, 117,
    120, 177–179, 182, 262
    Hallingdalen 117–118, 120
    Middle 173
    Old 120, 171, 197
null objects 227–233, 268
null subjects
    quasi argumental 270
    see generally pro-drop and topic drop

object agreement 6

object shift 8, 44, 54, 57–58, 61–63, 66,
    75–76, 87–89, 137, 261–266, 271
Old Norse 169–170
O'Neil, W. 169
operator 229–231
optimality theory 201
Orešnik, J. 110
Ottósson, K. 71, 84
Ouhalla, J. 94–95, 97–101, 145–146

paradigm 7
particle constructions 53
periphery 168, 202
Pesetsky, D. 43, 47–48, 51, 55
phonetic form (PF) 134, 139–140
Pierce, A. 127
Pintzuck, S. 144, 190–191, 202
Plank, F. 189
Platzack, C. 20–21, 56–57, 70, 72, 113,
    147, 149, 173–174, 202, 259
Pollock 42, 79, 94, 106, 108, 181, 194,
    203, 215
Portuguese 148
    Brazilian 4–6, 148, 210, 221–234,
        240–242, 247–249, 268–269
    European 221–234, 240, 242, 247,
        268–269
preterit-present verbs 144–145, 154, 186,
    191
Prince, E. 254–258, 271
procrastinate 136
pro-drop 8, 116, 121, 129, 141, 148,
    151, 230, 242–261, 269–271

quantifier floating 45, 49, 53, 150, 212,
    215, 222, 224–227
quotative inversion 87

Radford, A. 194, 196
raising verbs 78–80, 190, 203

Raposo, E. 229
relativized minimality 72
Reuland, E. 85
right dislocation 208
Rizzi, L. 72, 85, 129, 219, 243, 251
Roberge, Y. 218–219
Roberts, I. 69, 109, 111, 148, 158,
    188–189, 203, 220, 260, 269
Rögnvaldsson, E. 70, 84
Rouveret, A. 22, 269
Russian 150–151

Sabel. J. 85
Safir, K. 244
Sandqvist, C. 154
Sankoff, G. 218
Santorini, B. 20, 70, 89, 144, 202
Schäufele, S. 167, 202
schwa-deletion 148
scrambling 84, 262
Seip, D. 173
Shawn, N. 196
shortest move 25–28, 58–66, 72–73, 81,
    88, 95, 271–273
Sigurðsson 82
small clauses 53–54
Spanish 149, 230, 243–244, 246
    Puerto Rican 219
Speas, M. 8, 243–244, 247, 249–250
spell-out rules 134
Spencer, A. 7
Sportiche, D. 45, 212
s-structure 139–140
Stechow, A. von 36, 84
Steele, S. 194
Sternefeld, W. 36, 84
Stong-Jensen, M. 139
structure preservation 57, 89, 236
stylistic fronting 90, 158–159, 173,
    175–176, 202

subjacency 91
Swedish 1, 12–13, 15–16, 18, 56, 58,
    76, 78, 81, 98–99, 102, 104, 108,
    113, 117–120, 123, 142, 147,
    173–179, 182–183, 203, 250–251,
    261–262, 264, 272
Älvdalen 118, 120
Early Modern 172–173, 197
Kronoby 118–120, 149, 170
Old 171–172, 197–198, 202

Taraldsen, T. 84
tense operator [+F] 20–22
Thrainsson, H. 70, 79, 84, 91
topicalization 11, 14–16, 19, 58, 72, 74,
    77, 80, 90–92, 152, 208, 223–225
VP 32, 34
topic drop 246, 253–254, 258–260,
    269–271
Travis, L. 22, 36, 84, 92, 94
Trosterud, T. 101–105
Turkish 115

Vainikka 153
Valian, V. 247
verb prefixes
    (in-) separable 30–32, 40–41, 44
verb (projection) raising 86, 92, 191
verb second (V2) 11, 14–17, 19–21, 28,
    30, 36, 67–72, 75, 77, 80, 83, 85,
    89, 147, 151–153, 190, 198, 200,
    251–253, 259–260, 270, 275
Vikner, S. 56, 68, 70, 83, 85, 122,
    125–127, 142, 151, 170, 270
vowel reduction 148
vowel truncation 110, 112

Walsh-Dickey, M. 151
Warner, A. 189
Wasow, T. 194

Weinstein, S. 254–255
Wessen, E. 172
West Flemish 252
West Futuna 121
Wexler, K. 239
Wilder, C. 154

Yiddish 9, 12–20, 39, 80–84, 92, 97–98, 108, 110, 113, 117, 120, 122–123, 130–131, 144, 148, 186, 201, 203, 231, 246, 252–262, 271
Yuma

Zwart, J.-W. 36, 84, 87, 89

In the series LINGUISTIK AKTUELL/LINGUISTICS TODAY (LA) the following titles have been published thus far, or are scheduled for publication:

1. KLAPPENBACH, Ruth (1911-1977): *Studien zur Modernen Deutschen Lexikographie. Auswahl aus den Lexikographischen Arbeiten von Ruth Klappenbach, erweitert um drei Beiträge von Helene Malige-Klappenbach.* 1980.

2. EHLICH, Konrad & Jochen REHBEIN: *Augenkommunikation. Methodenreflexion und Beispielanalyse.* 1982.

3. ABRAHAM, Werner (ed.): *On the Formal Syntax of the Westgermania. Papers from the 3rd Groningen Grammar Talks (3e Groninger Grammatikgespräche), Groningen, January 1981.* 1983.

4. ABRAHAM, Werner & Sjaak De MEIJ (eds): *Topic, Focus and Configurationality. Papers from the 6th Groningen Grammar Talks, Groningen, 1984.* 1986.

5. GREWENDORF, Günther and Wolfgang STERNEFELD (eds): *Scrambling and Barriers.* 1990.

6. BHATT, Christa, Elisabeth LÖBEL and Claudia SCHMIDT (eds): *Syntactic Phrase Structure Phenomena in Noun Phrases and Sentences.* 1989.

7. ÅFARLI, Tor A.: *The Syntax of Norwegian Passive Constructions.* 1992.

8. FANSELOW, Gisbert (ed.): *The Parametrization of Universal Grammar.* 1993.

9. GELDEREN, Elly van: *The Rise of Functional Categories.* 1993.

10. CINQUE, Guglielmo and Guiliana GIUSTI (eds): *Advances in Roumanian Linguistics.* 1995.

11. LUTZ, Uli and Jürgen PAFEL (eds): *On Extraction and Extraposition in German.* 1995.

12. ABRAHAM, W., S. EPSTEIN, H. THRÁINSSON and C.J.W. ZWART (eds): *Minimal Ideas. Linguistic studies in the minimalist framework.* 1996.

13. ALEXIADOU Artemis and T. Alan HALL (eds): *Studies on Universal Grammar and Typological Variation.* 1997.

14. ANAGNOSTOPOULOU, Elena, Henk VAN RIEMSDIJK and Frans ZWARTS (eds): *Materials on Left Dislocation.* 1997.

15. ROHRBACHER, Bernhard Wolfgang: *Morphology-Driven Syntax. A theory of V to I raising and pro-drop.* 1999.

16. LIU, FENG-HSI: *Scope and Specificity.* 1997.

17. BEERMAN, Dorothee, David LEBLANC and Henk van RIEMSDIJK (eds): *Rightward Movement.* 1997.

18. ALEXIADOU, Artemis: *Adverb Placement. A case study in antisymmetric syntax.* 1997.

19. JOSEFSSON, Gunlög: *Minimal Words in a Minimal Syntax. Word formation in Swedish.* 1998.

20. LAENZLINGER, Christopher: *Comparative Studies in Word Order Variation. Adverbs, pronouns, and clause structure in Romance and Germanic.* 1998.

21. KLEIN, Henny: *Adverbs of Degree in Dutch and Related Languages.* 1998.

22. ALEXIADOU, Artemis and Chris WILDER (eds): *Possessors, Predicates and Movement in the Determiner Phrase.* 1998.

23. GIANNAKIDOU, Anastasia: *Polarity Sensitivity as (Non)Veridical Dependency.* 1998.

24. REBUSCHI, Georges and Laurice TULLER (eds): *The Grammar of Focus.* n.y.p.

25. FELSER, Claudia: *Verbal Complement Clauses. A minimalist study of direct perception constructions.* 1999.

26. ACKEMA, Peter: *Issues in Morphosyntax.* 1999.
27. RŮŽIČKA, Rudolf: *Control in Grammar and Pragmatics. A cross-linguistic study.* n.y.p.